Film After Jung

Popular film as a medium of communication, expression and storytelling has proved one of the most durable and fascinating cultural forms to emerge during the twentieth century, and has long been the object of debate, discussion and interpretation. *Film After Jung* provides the reader with an overview of the history of film theory and delves into analytical psychology to consider the reaction that popular film can evoke through emotional and empathetic engagement with its audience. This book includes:

- an introduction to film scholarship
- discussions of key Jungian concepts
- post-Jungian film studies beyond film.

It also considers the potential for post-Jungian contributions to film studies, and the ways in which these can help to enrich the lives of those undergoing clinical analysis.

Film After Jung encourages students of film and psychology to explore the insights and experiences of everyday life that film has to offer by applying post-Jungian concepts to film, image construction, narrative, and issues in cultural theory. It will enhance the film student's knowledge of film engagement as well as introducing the Jungian analyst to previously unexplored traditions in film theory.

Greg Singh is Senior Lecturer in Media Studies at Buckinghamshire New University.

Film After Jung

Post-Jungian approaches to film theory

Greg Singh

Routledge
Taylor & Francis Group

LONDON AND NEW YORK

First published 2009
by Routledge
27 Church Road, Hove, East Sussex BN3 2FA

Simultaneously published in the USA and Canada
by Routledge
270 Madison Avenue, New York, NY 10016

Routledge is an imprint of the Taylor & Francis Group, an Informa business

Typeset in Times by Garfield Morgan, Swansea, West Glamorgan
Printed and bound in Great Britain by TJ International Ltd, Padstow,
Cornwall
Paperback cover design by Lisa Dynan

This publication has been produced with paper manufactured to strict
environmental standards and with pulp derived from sustainable forests.

British Library Cataloguing in Publication Data
A catalogue record for this book is available from the British Library

Library of Congress Cataloging-in-Publication Data
Singh, Gregory Matthew, 1976–
    Film after Jung : post-Jungian approaches to film theory / Greg Singh. – 1st
ed.
        p. cm.
    Includes bibliographical references and index.
    ISBN 978-0-415-43089-0 (hardback) – ISBN 978-0-415-43090-6 (pbk.) 1.
Jungian psychology. 2. Motion pictures–Psychological aspects. I. Title.
    BF173.J85S56 2009
    791.4301'9–dc22
                                                    2008054317
ISBN: 978-0-415-43089-0 (hbk)
ISBN: 978-0-415-43090-6 (pbk)

Contents

Foreword

Film After Jung takes the theorizing of film to another level. Not because it makes intelligent use of concepts derived from post-Jungian psychology – a number of writers, albeit a minority in film-writing, are picking up on this approach these days – but because it does not expect us to take anything for granted. From the start Greg Singh takes us through his arguments for validating not only Jungian theory (which often needs re-explaining), but also film theory, which many think can be taken for granted. It cannot, and this book reminds us by making demands of concepts in film theory and Jungian psychology made necessary by the juxtapositions and syntheses in this highly original approach.

By his own admission, Singh is 'not a Jungian' but he *is* a film scholar – part of a growing number who theorize on the arts who find post-Jungian approaches exciting and meaningful. He is interested in 'the power film has to *move* people' and finds the Jungian tradition a better vehicle than the cognitive tradition, especially for exploring questions around emotion and empathy in the experience of film. As he writes, 'the act of viewing film engages our subjectivity (and sense of subjectivity) . . . It is a sensuous and affective act, connecting . . . the intimacy of perception-expression and our experience of it . . . Connectedness seems to pervade the experience of film, and it is this curiosity that also pervades the Jungian and post-Jungian concerns with normative subjectivity' (p. 177).

One of the book's key themes is the exploration of *meaningfulness* – not only what film narratives and images *mean*, but the human, all too human, experience of finding films meaningful. 'Meaningfulness and popular film go together, as films resonate with the real world and our experience of it' (p. 176).

Yet none of these claims and arguments are made casually. We start with a thorough survey of scientific and philosophical considerations around film theorizing and Jungian psychology. Particularly important is the emphasis on phenomenology – Jung's own position when it came to his psychology – using Merleau-Ponty and Sobchack as texts to orient by.

This is followed by the first of many new approaches when post-Jungian political thinking is brought together with post-Jungian image-thinking in the example of the trailer for *The Pursuit of Happyness* (Muccino, US, 2006). Singh's synthesis articulates the familiar semiotic–symbolic approach with an important analysis of the institutional and ideological aspects of film and its production – something he never loses sight of throughout the book.

Another emphasis is on *affect* and how the *image* – the product *and* the experience of the audiovisual – is always an *embodied image*. 'This crucial awareness of the importance of the body as a site of both reception and feeling, of process and emotion, in fully articulating the experience of actually watching a film, indicates another affinity between film studies and analytical psychology' (p. 120).

I am impressed with the way *Film After Jung* manages to break down and critique and yet find new value in concepts such as synchronicity and the archetype – a Jungian idea all too casually understood when applied outside the boundaries of analytical psychology itself. Singh re-links the archetype not only with its possibilities for helping us understand how images are meaningful, but also in the struggle between ideas of narrative (from the film side) and myth (from the Jungians). Examples from popular films like *Star Wars* and *The Matrix* here supersede the often clichéd use of these found in other texts.

The writing keeps a political focus, again, when discussing racial motifs – running neither towards a racial cinema nor away into a Jungian mythology that might ignore it. Instead it brings up the issue of race as a prime example of double-consciousness and hence a modern psychological condition in general. This post-Jungian approach takes the issue of race *beyond* the subjective experience of the ethnically 'other' subject. Referring to the work of the African-American activist W. E. B. Du Bois, Singh asserts, 'Jung's questions are being answered from another perspective, focusing on a specific problem in order to engage a more general problem of consciousness' (p. 156).

Film After Jung revisits classic concerns in film theory such as the *gaze*, gender and difference. The writing moves effortlessly between the ideas of Lacan and Jung on the same psychological trajectory showing us how film studies can bring attention to the coterminous quality of psychological views that are frequently de-linked through the politics of competing 'schools' of clinical rivalry and academic bigotry. By showing how different voices may be talking about the same thing, this book demonstrates the additional value to be discovered in the engagement of academic, cultural and arts studies with psychological theorizing.

A scan of the chapter headings will show you how very few stones are left unturned. Even Jung's religious emphasis – always a question mark for contemporary readers, especially in film studies – is tackled through a reading of the numinosity of some films. 'Indeed, the very experience of cinema itself supports a powerful argument suggesting that the essentially religious experiences Jung returns to time and again in his classical formulae are still very much a part of everyday engagement with our stories and myths' (p. 165). Post-Jungians like myself have pointed out how purchasing your seat in the cinema (and enthusiastic retail consumption in general) has an aura of religiosity and ritual previously reserved for the church and temple. Like all good theorists of analytical psychology and film, Singh reminds us of how social conditions are vital to the manifestation of any archetypal potential before it is known as an Image.

You will find this book indispensable . . . probably because everyone else will be quoting it at you! Not only does Greg Singh share his comprehensive grasp of theorists from both sides like Grodal, Mulvey and Sobchack on film and Izod, Fredericksen, Hauke and Tacey of the post-Jungians, but he makes more of each of them through his intertextual discoveries which take Jungian film theorizing to a brand new level.

More than a valuable resource for both Jungian theorists and film theorists, *Film After Jung* offers a stimulating critique. It not only adds to both fields, but creates an original one of its own.

Christopher Hauke
London, January 2009

Christopher Hauke is Senior Lecturer in Psychoanalytic Studies at Goldsmiths, University of London and an IAAP Jungian analyst in private practice. He is author of *Jung and the Postmodern: The Interpretation of Realities* and *Human Being Human: Culture and the Soul*, and co-editor of *Jung and Film: Post-Jungian Takes on the Moving Image* and the forthcoming *Jung and Film II. Further Takes on the Moving Image*. His next book will be *The Ideas of C. G. Jung: A Critical Introduction*.

Acknowledgements

There are far too many people who have been an influence on my writing to name in a list here but I attempt it, nonetheless, in the hope that some of these extraordinary characters will glance through these pages and recognize themselves in at least some shape or form. I would like to thank my lecturers, colleagues, students and friends at Buckinghamshire Chilterns University College (now Bucks New University): in particular, my undergraduate supervisor, Alison Tedman and my partner in funk, Martin Patrick – both have had a particular and lasting influence on this project. I should also mention Caroline Bainbridge in this group and Andy Butler for first bringing up the subject of Jung in a seminar on the unconscious all those years ago. A thank you goes to all my tutors at Birkbeck, especially Mike Allen, Ian Christie, Laura Mulvey, Lucia Nagib and Rachel Moore for various reasons. Thank you to Jonathan Bignell, my supervisor at the University of Reading, for having such patience in dealing with my rather unorthodox decision of writing a publication and a thesis at the same time.

Special thanks go to my publisher, Kate Hawes, whose belief in and enthusiasm for the project from our first initial discussion has been invaluable. Thanks also to Jane Harris at Routledge, for her advice on all sorts of technical matters. In addition, Susan Rowland's invitation to speak at the IAJS *Psyche and Imagination* conference led directly to the proposal for this project, and initiated many fruitful discussions with, among others, Chris Hauke and the Young Jungians.

A very special thank you goes to Susan Alexander and Greg Tuck for their kind support and ongoing generosity, and to Mark Bould and Kathrina Glitre for putting me up (and putting up with me). I should also give a special mention to my cousin, Tony Buchanan, who got me interested in film and film culture in the first place – thanks Tone, I still have nightmares about Chocolate-Chip Charlie and *The Stuff*, but I wouldn't have it any other way.

GS

Introduction

'The Image and the Material'

> Film theory is in crisis. This frequently made assertion can be seen as a reflection of a general concern about the status and value of theory and theorising.
>
> Catherine Constable, *Thinking in Images*

Had I originally structured this introduction as an overview of the literature available in the field concerning Jungian film theory, it would have been, to quote John Cleese in *Monty Python's The Meaning of Life*, 'waffer thin'. During the course of writing, I discovered fresh, frequent reminders that this is precisely the reason why this book needed to be written in the first place. Such literature on Jungian film theory does not exist in any substantial form, except in a piecemeal fashion where the critical and analytical discussions within existing work tend to have recourse to film theory to establish arguments within the historical field of discussion. In other words, much Jungian film scholarship attempts to address film scholars and students using familiar vocabulary and terminology specific to the discipline, without necessarily and substantially developing a Jungian film theory. Currently available literature is therefore rather minimal and tends to serve only to support the main drive of Jungian film criticism and analysis without actually addressing the problems and assumptions inherent in film theory itself.

The discrepancy involved in the absence of material and engagement with the problematics of film theory is a rather complex one that I elaborate in the opening chapter. However, the reasons for this discrepancy are, I feel, fairly simple and largely involve the cultural shifts in both film studies and Jungian studies, especially in the UK at this time. These shifts are intrinsically political in character, and I shall return to them during the course of this book.

As I discuss at length in Chapter 1, there are, broadly speaking, three typologies or 'perspective statements', that are addressed by film studies generally. These might be loosely termed historical, theoretical, and critical.

Don Fredericksen, one of the leading proponents of Jungian content analysis in film, has stated that Jungians do not normally differentiate between the three. In addition to this, Jungian film scholarship is almost wholly concentrated in criticism due to its affinity with, and emphasis on, analysis. This may be seen as a rudimentary flaw in many specific approaches to film brought to bear by Jungian film scholars. As I discuss, one of the ways in which Jungian thought differs from Freudian psychoanalysis is based largely on Jung's own shift from a content-led analysis to one of form after his split with Freud. This is an emphasis that was, for example, taken up by Hillman and archetypal psychology more forcefully. Therefore, it follows that it would make sense to emphasize a form-led approach within Jungian film scholarship, concentrating on aspects of the history and theory of film form that lend themselves to post-Jungian thought, rather than a content-led criticism of specific films. Content-led approaches sometimes tend to lead up the path of interpretation – a path that has as its main obstacle the big question of *meaning* that I address in Part II of this book. Not the preserve of Jungian film scholars, this quest for meaning has a long history in film theory, as we shall see in Chapter 2, extending back to the beginnings of cinema itself.

Of course, many commentators seem to word the split between Freud and Jung in terms of prodigal-son metaphors, a 'schism' or some other pseudo-religious term. This is a telling vocabulary to use, as Freud was known to have considered Jung his natural successor as the figurehead of modern psychology, and much classical Jungian terminology relies on religious and quasi-religious ideas such as spiritual quest narratives. This is significant, because the lasting influence of Freudian (and Lacanian) thought on film theory, based within political wrangling in 1970s debates on the nature of film, betrays a kind of theological devotion to the search for the 'next big thing' in psychoanalytical film analysis. I am not saying that the 'next big thing' in this field is Jungian film studies, because that would lead into the same trap that 'the Freudians' seem to have fallen into. After all, when the 'cine-subject' has been fully mapped out, there remains only the lack and anxiety associated with such subjectivity, and the theoretical withdrawals from real-world material effects that follow. The recent revisiting by some film scholars from historical materialist backgrounds of the relationship between Marxist approaches to cinema subjectivity and the cine-subject of psychoanalytic film studies (e.g. Bould, 2002; Homer, 2005) is vitally important here. The attempts to reconcile the need for a theorization of subjectivity in historical materialist analysis with the need for a discussion of socio-historical factors in psychoanalytic film theories address another 'theological' schism, this time within film theory itself. This will be discussed in more detail in Chapter 3 of this book in relation to the theoretical writing found in *Screen* during the mid-1970s, and the Althusserian appropriation of Lacanian subject formation.

We may say with a degree of certainty that the 'next big thing' in film studies is not Jung-influenced, because Jungian film studies has yet to address fully the vital interstices between the three typologies or 'statements' within film studies outlined above. What this approach has been missing, in my view, is that it leaves no room to acknowledge the clear relationship of these 'statements' with each other and impact on each other, nor their mutual development in real-world effects. In short, Jungian film analysis largely ignores the relationship between the three 'statements' of history, theory and criticism in the academic study of film as a whole. Although there have been recent attempts to address this problem to an extent through textual analysis, what is lacking in current literature is a historical, theoretical and critical approach to the films themselves, their audiences, and the socio-political context in which films are produced and consumed. Although this is not a specific aim of this book, it is hoped that my approach will provide a starting point from which further inquiry may be made, as the structure of the book loosely follows these dimensions in turn. Such an approach, starting from here, will also begin to lay the groundwork with regard to the notion of film form, from a theoretical perspective, and to suggest an entry point to the potential of Jungian approaches to form in particular.

So, what are the 'key texts' available in Jungian film studies? Such questions raise the problem that there is a canon of literature that one must familiarize oneself with to fully engage with the notion of a proper Jungian-based film analysis in the first place. This, to my mind, is something of a fallacy, as it feeds into the myth of some elite group of film scholars whose exclusive right to be proponents of the sub-discipline goes unquestioned. I do not wish to labour the point, but this is really just a myth that many academics will be loosely familiar with in any number of disciplines. However, in reference to comments I make in Chapter 1, I find that Don Fredericksen's statement on the pertinence of Jungian analysis for film scholarship is a fairly worrying one. Fredericksen stated in his International Association for Jungian Studies (IAJS) seminar on Jung and Film at *Psyche and Imagination* that the affinity between film and analytical psychology is such that it is a wonder that there are not more Jungian analysts 'dabbling' in film scholarship, and that there are 'only, maybe, five people doing this' (Fredericksen, 2006). This is, of course incorrect. Many students of Jungian studies and affiliated subject areas based in various universities in the UK, for example, are embarking on some serious considerations of the place of film within British culture, and its relationship to the psychic lives of individuals in the UK today. This was evident by the large numbers of young academics, research students and clinicians present at the same conference. This is particularly encouraging, and is symptomatic of a much larger global movement within the sub-discipline that suggests that its leaders are, in contrast to many academic disciplines, much younger and more open to rigorous study than Fredericksen seems to allow.

If my intentions here appear confrontational, they need not be read as such. We are effectively at a crucial moment in film studies in the UK, when many of the key thinkers (at one time, key 'young thinkers') of the apparatus and 'Screen theory' movement of the 1970s are approaching retirement. Their lasting influence is testament to the groundbreaking perspectives that have been developed during the past three decades and more. The scholars who immediately followed these pioneers are, by and large, from slightly different traditions more closely associated with the shift towards cultural studies and technical skills education. For the emergent post-Jungian film scholarship, however, the case is slightly different. The contemporary movement is, in effect, led by cutting-edge 'young research', building on the rare and valuable work set out by a handful of film scholars and clinicians (including Fredericksen himself) who have, at one time or another, tackled Jung's psychology as a tool for film analysis. Therefore, this introduction is dedicated, in the best modernist tradition, to both the influence of those on whose work I build and the 'young Jungians' whose work will influence the generations to follow.

It is difficult, now, to imagine that this book actually started life as the topic for my undergraduate dissertation at Buckinghamshire Chilterns. Written as a critical discussion of the use of archetypes in film, but also a negotiation of the theoretical implications of Jungian themes such as synchronicity, individuation, the autonomous complex and myth, the dissertation already had one eye on the uses of analytical psychology for film theory itself. Not surprisingly, perhaps, this project was particularly 'leftfield' in that we had not studied Jungian psychology on the film degree programme, with the exception of a single seminar discussion of the films of Dario Argento. My dissertation supervisor, Alison Tedman, specialized in myth and fairytale narratives in film – topics that, thankfully, located the little amount of literature on Jungian film scholarship available at the time. Not long after I completed 'In Search of Meaning' (the dissertation's precocious and slightly misleading title), I embarked on my MA at Birkbeck. There, the emphasis of study shifted away from theoretical concerns, and was more firmly geared towards the historical and material culture associated with film production and consumption. This emphasis influenced my thinking away from Jungian ideas and, to an extent, from theory itself, although I was keen to play to my strengths as a theorist and I shall always be grateful to the staff at Birkbeck who were very generous in their support of my particular interests. Indeed, their knowledge of such theoretical and historical treatment of film was astounding and has its own part to play in the production of this book.

It was there that, in my independent study, I had first encountered the work of Chris Hauke, Luke Hockley, Don Fredericksen and John Izod, and discovered the wealth of material and ongoing tradition associated with the study of film from a post-Jungian perspective. This was to prove both invigorating and frustrating, as although some of my early work engaged mythology and the psychology of modernity in contemporary film practice, my other research areas had long since moved away from Jung and psychoanalysis: I had been bitten by the remediation bug. My general outlook on film at the time was shaped by my fascination with historical materialist accounts of commodification, technology and narrative (by Jameson, Sobchack and Eagleton in particular) applied to remediated film franchises such as videogame and comic book adaptations, and film trilogies.

It was not until I had started teaching and doing the rounds at various conferences that my interest in Jungian thought was rekindled. Quite by chance, I met the Jungian scholar Susan Rowland at a conference on 'The Metropolis' at Greenwich University and, aware of her post-Jungian approach to textuality and literature, I mentioned that there was an almost complete absence of this kind of theorization in the arena of film studies. Susan invited me to submit a paper proposal on this subject to the IAJS, which was convening a special conference at Greenwich in 2006 called *Psyche and Imagination*. I did so and I am still very grateful to Susan for her encouragement and correspondence (it led directly to the idea for writing this book, in that Routledge was one of the conference sponsors) and an account of the proceedings of that particular event is embedded in Chapter 1. The curious thing about this book is that it is not just a mix or synthesis of Jungian ideas with film theory. It is largely made up of discussion of particularly pressing themes in the history of theorizing about film, which are of most relevance to Jungian scholars and practitioners. It is not intended to be an exhaustive account of the history of film theory, covering every topic. It is designed to illuminate the interstices between Jungian studies and film studies, with a special emphasis on theory that has been lacking until now.

Many of the ideas that move towards specifically Jungian-led film theory are, in fact, not particularly Jungian at all on the surface. The resonance of this notion will no doubt not be lost on psychologists and analysts who encounter these ideas. For example, my commitment to a political integration and engagement with modes of film practice, production and consumption (a historical materialist-inflected position) is something that is outlined in the analytical strategies I use throughout the book. I consider that many of the reading strategies and objects of analysis posed by post-Jungian thinkers tend to coincide with the same need for critical inquiry into certain notions that have tended to go unquestioned in classical depth psychology. I will not go into detailed explanation here, but Chris Hauke's excellent *Jung and the Postmodern* (2000) is an example of much-needed critical inquiry, renegotiating the traditional engagement between depth psychology in general and the specific concerns of cultural studies. In many ways, Hauke's book is a precursor or signpost to this one, as it negotiates some of the perceived 'truths' that inhabit the everyday, and that lead to the prejudices that cloud our ability to engage with our cultural (and indeed, internal or psychic) lives. Prejudices such as the valuation of scientific objectivity over experiential reality and subjectivity in modern life, or functionality (demonstrable, practical use) over theory (ideas). These, for me, are specifically crucial political dimensions of cultural study to which I return intermittently. For now, it is worth flagging up the last dichotomy as an example of false economy: the dubious 'value' of theory.

As noted in the above epigraph, Catherine Constable writes that 'theory is in crisis'. It is, and film theory in particular has been under attack from all kinds of directions for some time now – especially from within film studies itself. Constable (2005, p. 1) writes that the attitude towards theory and its inevitable failure has led to the suggestion of some drastic solutions:

> One such solution has been the suggestion that all theory should be abandoned because it is overly complex and ultimately unproductive . . . I would argue that complexity is not an indication of lack of efficacy and the claim that all theory should be simple if it is to be useful is itself a problematic assumption.

I agree. In Chapters 3 and 4 in particular, I outline a case that this is ultimately the materialization of a political shift within the cultural sphere that has been ongoing for the past 30 years or so. It is a political shift that, even now, is changing the face of film culture in the UK. For example, the post-Blair cultural policies that have begun to introduce PPP (public–private partnership) to all spheres of public spending have extended to the radical restructuring of the British Film Institute along market-led and 'public-facing' lines.[1] The reactionary stance towards theoretical approaches to the study and understanding of film, as witnessed in the current move towards 'vocational' degrees in HE institutions in the UK as more practical and useful, appropriates a utilitarian model embodied by neoliberal notions of productivity. Perhaps this is why theory has not been, until now, a principal concern of post-Jungian film study. Whatever the reason, the absence of material on the subject has prompted a number of questions as to how one might go about integrating such fields into a coherent solution that satisfactorily addresses the twin concerns of film theory and analytical psychology. The answer is not so simple: Engaging film using Jungian models and paradigms has inevitably led, in many examples, to an interpretative reduction; no matter how often Jungians might insist on the term 'amplification', it is still hermeneutic and problematically (for film theorists) an interpretative gesture. This is why at times I appropriate the contemporary notion of film phenomenology, and in particular, existential phenomenology. It seems to me that this particular approach not only is productive in itself, but shares a number of themes and concerns with post-Jungian thought. Once again, ostensibly following the signpost that Hauke sets up in his exhaustive comparative analysis of post-Jungianism and postmodernism, I am similarly addressing post-Jungian thought in relation to existential phenomenology, and their contextual application to film theory. As a psychology that I feel addresses above all the interstices of affect, experience and narrative, post-Jungian thought fundamentally relates to phenomenology's concerns with embodiment, appearance and experience. In short, both of these approaches are valuable in rethinking aspects of subjectivity and cinema that have been largely abandoned in the past two decades: They provide the fundamental theoretical link between the Image and the Material.

Part I

Film theory: A critical historiography

Chapter 1

Film matters, but how, and why?

I am not a Jungian. I realize that this is quite a controversial statement to make at the beginning of a book that, in its subject matter, tackles the possibility of a post-Jungian approach to film theory. I would like to qualify this statement by invoking a number of points that are relevant to the subject matter of this book, one of which has special importance: namely, the study of film through a properly materialist analytical psychology. Firstly, however, it is worth bearing in mind the approach taken by Marie-Louise von Franz, one of Carl Jung's immediate and most important followers, to the subject of 'Jungianism'. In Chuck Swartz's (1998: 107) memoriam to von Franz in *Harvest*, he states that:

> She always advised that it would be wrong to become a 'Jungian'. If you do that, you miss the whole point of his psychology, which was to become the one unique individual you are meant to be.

Thus, Von Franz both identified and condemned the theological strand perceived to be inherent in much Jungian-inflected thinking considered from outside its practice, and also helped to reveal an inner teleological narrative that classical Jungian thinkers seem to have embraced whole-heartedly. These are issues that I hope to address intermittently throughout this book, as they underpin many of the presumptions about analytical psychology as well as the presuppositions that may be said to exist in psychological thinking in general.

This is not the *raison d'être* of this book – it is, however, one of a number of key concerns for thinking about the usefulness of analytical psychology in film scholarship. That said, we may now take a fuller account of my opening statement, 'I am not a Jungian'. I am, first and foremost, a film scholar. I am interested in film and the reaction that film invokes through emotional and empathic engagement from, and with, audiences. I am interested in the power film has to *move* people. I am interested in how film, as a medium of communication, expression and storytelling has proved one of the most durable and fascinating cultural forms to emerge during the

20th century. It occurs to me that all these concerns find common ground in analytical psychology in one form or another. Throughout my studies, I have found a certain warmth and compassion in the Jungian tradition that is centred around questions of emotion and empathy: There seems to be an inherent lack of warmth in the cognitive tradition, for example, despite its direct and tenacious engagement with questions of emotion. I am moved by the infamous synchronistic tale of Monsieur Fortgibu and the plum pudding every bit as much as I have been moved by *The Bicycle Thieves* (*Ladri di biciclette*, De Sica, It, 1948). The means by which our patterns of communication and collective thinking are informed by the cultural practices of storytelling have been illuminated by Jungian thought. Analytical psychology provides for us fascinating models of typology and meaningfulness that are consistently being rethought, elaborated and shared in sophisticated debate across many scholarly disciplines.

As a result of the durability of film as a popular medium (in particular, the ubiquitous narrative form of the feature film), I would argue that it has become crucial for the film academic to consider the evolution of film as a media form in particular, within the context of a substantial growth of associated media practices during the past 30 years or so. So-called 'home cinema' technologies, for example, are beginning to transform the way that many people watch films. Broadband Internet developments have enabled the remote sharing of movies. Increasingly, it seems to matter less whether films come in the form of mainstream Hollywood fare projected in a theatre, pirated DVDs found on file-sharing platforms, or the latest antics of kids in a skate park captured on a video phone and uploaded onto YouTube. Whatever the format, these developments in exhibition practice have led to DIY cultures of production and consumption that, less than a decade ago, were nothing more than a technophile's dream. What matters more, it seems, is the form the *engagement* with film takes, particularly within popular youth culture; it matters less that films are restricted to the narrow definition of projected film viewed in theatres.

This has necessitated that film scholars think about the impact of technologies and forms of cinema, film, video, and so on, as interrelated phenomena, intimately connected with the practices and attitudes of both mass audiences and individuals. The need to 'capture' the audience's imagination has provided the impetus for the development of these technologies, and their popularity in everyday life. Whether one articulates that need as economic in character or something rather more noble and expressive, it is a reality that we must deal with as film scholars. The counterpart to this reality is, of course, the impact that these technologies and consumption patterns have on audiences, and John Izod's recent work (2006) approaches this question from a specifically audience-oriented post-Jungian position. In theoretical terms, however, the consumption of film as either a public or a private experience is, I would argue, primarily one of pleasure. Emotional responses and personal idiosyncratic notions of the films themselves are most often articulated in the most basic of terms, but in ways with which most of us are very familiar. As Gibbs and Pye suggest in the introduction to their recent book *Style and Meaning* (2005), when we leave a movie theatre with a group of friends, we tend to recall events that happened in the film in a highly narrativized way. This is partly due to the proliferation of narrative film, partly due to the way that film is talked and written about in both academic and popular film reviews, and most importantly perhaps, partly due to the way that we most readily 'make sense' of the world of the film. That is, we make the story a figural centre-piece, with a beginning, middle and an end, in which characters act and interact in a specific setting. Part of the power and pleasure comes from the story's retelling, and of course this includes the playful telling of the tale through the real-world filter of production knowledge, the star system, and how we felt while watching the film. This adds to the 'making sense' of the film and gives it, and the experience of watching it, meaning.

The sense of 'making sense', that most comforting experience of resolutions and play with non-resolution when telling and retelling stories, is an important part of the negotiation of everyday life. It is also an important part of Jungian high-concepts such as the individuation process. However, one might argue that this process is an articulation of metanarrative, a summation of the way individuals make sense of their world and their place within it, filtered through architectonics of both signification and emotion. It need not be the subject of totalizing abstractions such as stone archetypes (see von Franz, 'The Process of Individuation', 1964) or monomyths (see Joseph Campbell, *The Hero With a Thousand Faces*, 1993). Here, we may concern ourselves, for the moment, with the tension involved in the play of resolution and non-resolution in the act of telling itself. As Frank Kermode famously stated, 'the sense of an ending', established at the conclusion of tensions and pleasures afforded teller and told alike in the story-telling process, may come about only in the same figural structure as the ambiguous experience of being 'in the middest' (2000: 4). That is, the resolution is contingent on the journey towards the resolution itself. One may argue that, in retelling the story, one re-experiences the journey itself as much as the resolution, hence the commonplace saying that 'the journey is as important as the destination'. There is, following Paul Ricoeur in his three-volume *Time and Narrative*, a mimesis involved in the construction and deconstruction of texts (even, one might say, at an unconscious level), upon which we might map out enunciative and emotional cues that the audience chooses (or not) to follow. Why this is a vital element of pleasurable spectatorship is as obvious to the casual filmgoer as it is to the clinician. It is also a key question in the negotiation of audiences in film studies, but it should be noted that it is given different emphasis and importance depending on the particular approach that the film student takes.

This is one of the key problems that this book aims to tackle in Part I: an evaluation of the various approaches to screen studies in film scholarship through a post-Jungian lens. It seems to me that, in addressing the pleasures and displeasures afforded the spectator in textual negotiation, the context of production and consumption of film is always a given historical and material question. This is a question to which we need to add that the embodied experience of watching film is felt to be a highly subjective (and classical Jungians might say of attending the cinema theatre, numinous) experience. This complex of embodied and material relations between production and consumption, text and context, film and viewer, reveals a dialectical tension that is too often overlooked in Jungian film analysis. Far from being an element of analysis alien to Jungian psychology, this dialectical tension is not only a good fit here, but lies comfortably with Jung's play with the concepts of 'inner' and 'outer' worlds. This is the grounding of subject matter that I tackle in some depth in my discussion of identification in this book but also has its antecedents in Hugo Münsterberg's early formalist approach to film, discussed in Chapter 3. This is why I have chosen to position my considera-tion of post-Jungian film criticism within the critical forum of phenom-enological and historical materialist approaches to cultural production. Essential to advocating an approach that uses the fantastical magnitude of such a notion as the collective unconscious as one of its central tenets, a robust post-Jungian account of film and its popular consumption needs to be grounded in the historical circumstance, social ontology and embodied experience of film and its forms.

A note on methodology

Methodologically speaking, this book is not interested in pursuing empirical research, at least in its quantitative form. Empirical research in the most general sense tends to give credence to the notion of empiricism as a scientific method with more validity than other methods: other methods which, while 'observing' real effects of cinema in real bodies, rely on abstractions that are frequently derided as unscientific, and therefore unusable. Of course, empirical approaches should not be the concern of a book motivated by the notion that post-Jungian ideas are useful for the negotiation of film form at the theoretical level. As Nitzan Ben-Shaul has recently noted, 'Differing from film history, film criticism or filmmaking . . . film theory strives to offer general ideas on the nature of film and models for film analysis, presumably applicable to every film irrespective of its specific context of production' (2007: 1). While I would not necessarily support this presumption, Ben-Shaul is making a very important distinction here, and one that I will address specifically in relation to recent post-Jungian film scholarship momentarily. However, this generalized approach to film theory – an approach that quite rightly invokes film theory as a potentially enriching resource for historians, critics and filmmakers – nevertheless invites a separation between the various disciplinary strands within film studies. This invitation is, to my mind, an extension of the tension between theory and empiricism within the humanities in general and always–already negates the necessity to bear in mind the historical and material conditions within which, a film is made. Inevitably, these shape the production choices that filmmakers have to make (which may be grounded in both theory *and* practice).

The main problem that I see empirical research as presenting to the film scholar is related to the very notion of its usefulness. Quantitative research may provide us with hard data and qualitative research may provide very detailed accounts of everyday engagements with film, but this kind of audience research cannot by itself explain, or indeed even describe with any meaningful outcome, the phenomenon of film spectatorship. The inter-viewed subject may recall the feeling of experiences in great detail, but the experience of those feelings, actually *feeling about film* is, in my opinion, almost impossible to articulate in verbal terms (although this is, as Gibbs and Pye (2005) point out, the very thing that we frequently attempt to do). Feelings are not necessarily linguistic in nature and it follows that their articulation in language could only ever be partial. Therefore, a theoretical refit is in order.

I shall phrase this refit in a central question: Film matters, but how, and why? Such an important question, one would have thought, is absolutely crucial to an academic discipline that, as one of its central conceits, attempts to unravel the importance of the medium of film within (especially) Western cultures, through analysis of texts, institutions, and audiences. Indeed, the attempts at formulating methods of critical discussion of the production of meaning have formed the basis of a canonical body of work throughout the history of the discipline. However, to quote Victor Perkins, 'Must we say what they mean?' (1990: 1). To put it another way, can we *ever* say for certain what films mean? Can we say, for example, why Forrest Gump 'just kept on running' with any certainty? We may have a good idea as to why Forrest feels this urge to run: He wants to escape, to meditate and to long for a return to the unobtainable; hearth, home and his beloved Jenny. In that last sentence, I have already placed emphasis on certain verbs that are not explicit in the film text at all. These verbs articulate a meaning that is not necessarily a part of the film's narrative project. I have inferred these based on presuppositions of a personal experience of modernity which, if I am not careful, might lead to generalizations of meaning in the text. It is this reductive kind of interpretation that John Hollwitz (2001) is critical of in his evaluation of straightforward applications of analytical constructs to literary processes. Jung himself and many psychoanalytic critics are guilty of this direct appropriation of assumptions drawn straight from clinical practice and used for critical purposes. Hollowitz cites three criticisms of this, which I elaborate as follows:

1   It is a reductive method. Films may be argued to be *like* dreams, but they are *not* dreams; they are films, and cannot be analysed in the same fashion. In fact, I would argue that narrative films are only like dreams insofar as their assemblage is prototypical of the way that people often recount dreams in a narrative way. We do not necessarily dream like narrative films, but we certainly tell stories verbally in a similar fashion, often evoking imagery in order to elaborate our tales.
2   So what? For example, Obi Wan Kenobi is like the Wise Old Man archetype. Perhaps, but so what if he is? What are we to do with this information?
3   This method is inconsistent with empirical psychological fact. Often using Jungian typology (a system that Jung hardly utilized after the 1920s), criticism along these lines, itself based on outdated models, will inevitably be outdated in its own right.

The meaning I give to the film will inevitably be based on what I think of the film, the characters and the plot, and where I was/what I was doing/what my life was like in general when I watched the film. It may even be contingent on the number of times that I have watched the film. It is this problematic of presupposition that binds the film scholar to the question of meaning, and this, more than anything perhaps, is the central problematic of film form, particularly as a storytelling medium. More recent Jungian film criticism, as we shall see, has taken account of context as an important determining principle, and the reasoning behind much post-Jungian thinking, particularly as a theoretical paradigm, centres on a regeneration of analytical constructs within production and reception contexts. More often in Jungian approaches, we are seeing interaction between different levels of consumption and interpretation as key to understanding the films themselves as cultural products.

Notes on materiality

In establishing a post-Jungian position on film, the Jungian film scholar encounters a number of problems in terms of conflict with persuasive arguments already prevalent in the field. Classical Jungian psychology is often treated with utter suspicion by historical materialists, as a collection of superstitious and irrelevant meditations on the modern 'mind'. It is a model that is based on fantasy and overwhelmingly bourgeois concerns rather than historical class struggle within cultural and social production contexts. However, a brief scan of the literature in the discussion of Jungian approaches to materiality suggests that the relationship between psychological processes and their material counterparts is rather more complex. As Roger Brooke has pointed out, 'If one recalls Jung's analysis of the body's carbon as "simply carbon", it seems possible that Jung some-times thought of the self as a kind of entity, or linked to material continuity through space' (1991: 99).

What we often think of as 'our selves' is linked to the body as a possible carrier of that 'self', and sometimes more specifically linked to the head/brain/mind as a centre of self. But here, we see that even Jung, who was a fundamental Cartesian/Kantian, thought of this 'self thinking' as an articu-lation of the continuity of world and body. This is a fundamental point, as the Cartesian dualism of mind and body infiltrates and underpins the assumption of the difference between self and other, and the meanings that are wrought through that split. If there is a seed of existential doubt in Jung's frame of thought here, it is necessarily sown onto other fields of clinical investigation such as experience and interpretation. As Edwina Taborsky (1998: 16) suggests, with this Cartesian distinction between the sensual and the conceptual:

> The individual loses two means of codification of energy – a simpli-fication that is reductionist rather than scientific. The selection of a unileveled direct frame of interaction between the sensual and the conceptual means that the transformative codal generalities of a third codal action, that of a meditative level, are lost. The rejection of both the sensual and conceptual codifications as ongoing codal *actions*, their transformation into *static* forms whose codal identity was a priori fixed, and the actual existential separation of these two nodal sites into two self-existent realities, meant that only one codal phase was avail-able to the individual – the conceptual . . . and its task was simple mnemonic 'perception' of that external and eternal truth.

By 'energy', Taborsky here refers to an abstraction: that which seeks as its *raison d'être* its own growth and proliferation within the natural world. Its concern is potential, and its outcome is action. Even within the highly theoretical arena of codification, one needs to articulate the *relation* between the thinking body and the worldly body (its *mediation*) as intent towards sensation in every sense of the word, whether conceptual or perceptual. For, in this way, we may both feel and emote. Thus, inner and outer worlds, traditionally exclusive and interactive, should more properly be accorded active, dialectic roles as mutually contingent and supportive sites of the other's mediation, in order for meaning to matter more properly. Brooke (1991: 128) situates this mediative ambiguity in a comparative analysis of Jung's position with that of the French existentialist phenomenologist, Maurice Merleau-Ponty:

> Both Jung and Merleau-Ponty render the terms conscious and uncon-scious ambiguous, and regard the unconscious as a latent, unreflective

intentionality . . . Merleau-Ponty, more clearly than Jung, situates the complexities of the lived body in the historical, perceptual, linguistic, and interpersonal matrices that are meant by the term existence. Jung, more clearly than Merleau-Ponty, reveals the bodies imaginal matrices which inspire structure, limit, and transform existence in all its dimensions (historical, perceptual, and so on).

I explore the complex relationship between these two traditionally opposed positions during the course of this book. What we have in the Jung and Merleau-Ponty articulations of the body and the imaginary is a clear continuity in terms of our experience of self and world – importantly, not a binary but a dialectical dehiscence (a bursting forth) of what it is to be in the world. In their very different takes on existence, Jung and Merleau-Ponty are ultimately discussing the same thing. One problem here, however, is that they are using different vocabulary most of the time, and this gives the appearance of fundamentally oppositional world-views. This is related to a second problem, a problem that confounds matters: Jung's discussions of the experience of self and world are most often framed within his model of inner and outer worlds – the spiritual (or pneumatic) and the material (or hylic) – based upon Hellenistic syncretism. This is important because philosophically speaking Jung sought to bring this split to balance through the unity of the psyche in the psychic realm of existence, therefore fully accommodating the potential for psychic growth within the spiritual and material realms. The problem, however, reveals itself in the seemingly contradictory (and often confusing) language that he used throughout his writings on the subject. For example, in 1936 he stated that:

> Somewhere the psyche is living body, and the living body is animated matter; somehow and somewhere there is an undiscoverable unity of psyche and body which would need investigating psychically as well as physically; in other words, this unity must be dependent on the body as it is on the psyche so far as the investigator is concerned.
>
> (Jung, 1998: 134–135)

Later in his career, he spoke more directly of this 'unity':

> We now know that a factor exists which mediates between the apparent incommensurability of body and psyche, giving matter a kind of 'materiality', by means of which the one can work with the other . . . both views, the materialistic as well as the spiritualistic, are metaphysical prejudices. It accords better with experience to suppose that living matter has a psychic aspect, and the psyche a physical aspect.
>
> (Jung, 1998: 333)

What this amounts to might be described as the *appearance* of a dialectics of the psyche, although Jung himself would not be likely to describe it in this way. His position ultimately reveals is that the unity of psyche and body of which Jung writes can never be properly dialectical. This is because he never really committed to their relational properties, reducing them to mere aspects reflected in one another. The mediative ambiguity that exists in the thinking body and the worldly body which I have discussed above is itself reduced to that of some sort of third element; a mediating 'factor'. This reduction is Kantian in flavour, confirming the realms of the experience of existence that Kant formulated in his *Critiques*; realms split off from each other.

The psychoanalyst Wolfgang Giegrich has written several articles on and around this subject, the most notable of which is his essay 'Jung's Betrayal of his Truth', addressing Jung's wholesale adoption of Kant's empiricism, and simultaneous rejection of Hegel. Although I do not wish to dwell on this, it is important to consider Giegrich's work as crucial for the subject matter in this book. It enables us to rethink Jung's notion of the inner/outer interplay – the implications that this has for the notion of filmic spaces (those occupied by audiences, critics, and filmmakers) are central to the articulation of analytical psychology within film studies. Giegrich suggests that the position taken by Jung on the case of 'Kant versus Hegel' had far-reaching consequences for his conception of psychology as a whole. To briefly restate Giegrich's argument here:

> What Kant did was to state that the object, the transcendent, the thing-in-itself is absolutely inaccessible so that you have to once and for all confine yourself to the empirical world, to the finite, to what Kant termed the appearance . . . He [Jung] adopted, as his own unshakeable theoretical foundation for psychology, the restriction to the Kantian phenomenal and Kant's closing the door on the *noumenon*. This is why he time and again proudly insisted on his being 'an empiricist first and foremost'.
>
> (Giegrich, 1998: 49–50, emphasis in original)

What is necessary here is that the implications for analytical psychology are manifold, and entail the elision of the unity of which Jung often spoke, as lying beyond human categories of time and space, and beyond the separation of physical and mental as categories of human potential. This seemingly contradictory stance is in fact nothing more than a philosophical roundabout, within which Jung seems to have caught himself by not fully addressing the dialectical potential of Hegelian thinking and dismissing his thought through what Giegrich describes as defamation of Hegel himself. This not only reflects a problematic facet of the term 'empiricism', but also reveals the problematic core of Jung's conception of space and time – an essential categorisation within film scholarship, of the experience of the film itself. This is why I devote an entire chapter to Jung's notion of synchronicity: It is one of his most fascinating and under-theorized ideas. What might have occurred had Jung been a Hegelian, rather than a Kantian, is of significant importance to the usefulness of Jung's psychology at the level of theory – one of those fascinating 'what if?' questions of history. The discussion of the minutiae of Kant's position will necessarily have to wait for future work in this area, as will the implications for Hegelian thought on the central conceits of analytical psychology. The last word on this matter I give to Jung himself (1998: 331), who wrote:

> The place or the medium of realization is neither mind nor matter, but the intermediate realm of subtle reality which can adequately be expressed only by the symbol.

This confirms the Kantian position of appearance, here articulated by Jung within the realms of signification, symbolism and language – that aspect of object-relations from which we find the split between subjectivity and objectification within space-time, and the fundamental approach to difference that characterizes much psychological theory today. But there are other aspects of object-relations that are absolutely crucial to our understanding of the way we engage phenomenally with the world in which we find ourselves, and I shall return to these momentarily, and throughout the course of this book.

Filmic space and analytical psychology

Space, in all its productions, its manifestations as a location within which bodies exist, interact, repel and attract, is fundamentally connected to the way we relate to ourselves and to our own bodies. This self-perception and perception of/within the world is a fascinating object of analysis when taken within the context of film consumption. As with so many of the clichéd descriptions of what film is and does, it (film and our relation to it) is often regarded as similar to observing the world, observing our selves. The proliferation of metaphors describing the experience of film form as a 'window on the world', a 'mirror reflecting the world', a 'magical looking-glass', 'dream machine' and so on, testifies to this. Again, one might say that presupposition forms an important part of the analytical process, especially regarding the representation of ourselves and the world we live in, on film. The Jungian analyst reading this chapter will no doubt be aware of certain structures (archetypes) that drive us, or at least provide impetus, motivation and imperative, for us to think and act in certain ways. That is, thought and action are given a meaning based on recurrent structures that form the very fabric of our social being. This helps us to make sense of ourselves as collective and individual beings within a contemporary existence that often demands that we put aside such consideration in favour of rather empty gestures towards the acquisition of material wealth, or the pursuit of pleasures more akin to *schadenfreude* than collective action. The raft of 'reality' TV shows currently on our screens, as well as sadistic TV and film depicting self-harm, masochism and psychotic practical jokes such as *Jackass* (MTV, 2000–2) and *Dirty Sanchez* (MTV, 2002–), show a grotesque side to popular culture and humour that is foolhardy and desperate, yet somehow oddly reflective and honest. As with the Freudian joke, these last types of media texts sublimate an undercurrent of tragedy in the expression of laughter, a vein mined so effectively by Ricky Gervais and Stephen Merchant in the pseudo-documentary sitcom style of *The Office* (BBC, 1999–2004).

These political and existential questions of social being and collectivity concretize the relation that consumers have with cultural products such as film, and are therefore crucial in their importance as determining/ determined factors. Although I do not intend to tackle these questions directly, their implications impact on the very notion of emotional engagement. They inevitably provide the momentum for much film scholarship in general, articulating the need to re-engage film and our relation to it as a political and embodied relation. That is, the importance of film as a medium is underscored by its ability as a form to reconnect audiences to such questions – no matter that this reconnection may last only as long as the film's running time. I am not saying here that this is what film does (in all probability, this is what it often does *not* do). However, this does not negate film's ability to emote and to invoke feelings that are very real, very palpable.

So, in short, we might say that this is why film matters. It does not necessarily have to mean anything. It does, however, have the potential for meanings and feelings, and inevitably will mean some things to some people – and this is what matters to spectators. The 'fanish' anticipation of the spectacle offered by the next *Harry Potter* (2001–) movie, or the narrative intrigue of the next series of *Battlestar Galactica* (Sky One, 2003–), for example, suggests that the motivation for the audience to experience these texts derives, in part, from this. Much of this book is concerned with a discussion of this potential, because the potential of film is aligned with value-based notions of the functionality of film. An important point to make here is that, whereas I do discuss films that have not found a mass audience (and, in many cases, were perhaps never intended for such an audience), I am mostly concerned with the potential of mainstream texts. Many of these are Hollywood films that have, as their bottom line, one purpose – to make profit. As harsh a reality as this may be, it does not negate the power of these films to affect their audience through visual, auditory and narrative spectacles. *United 93* (Greengrass, USA/UK/Fr, 2006) is an exemplar of this kind of filmmaking. A contemporary drama-documentary, utilizing documentary aesthetics and research protocols employed in film-journalism to inject a sense of the real in the film's narrative, this film is nevertheless driven by a number of factors that have more in common with action blockbusters than with documentary films: the preoccupation with popular choice of subject matter, for example (the terrorist attacks of 9/11), or the mythologizing of individual tenacity in the face of adversity related to what Izod (2006: 11) has identified as plot culture and the reliance on formal realism in popular filmic story-telling. These themes (both structurally and discursively) are familiar, and therefore are appealing to an audience naturalized to the realist conventions facilitated by such a plot-driven film culture. Whether intentionally or not, the experience of the spectator who watches conversely *The Return of the King* (Peter Jackson, 2003) is partly the result of its budget, its (simulational) spectacle, and the very real pleasures that these factors provide. This is not an oppositional tendency in popular cinema to that argued by formalist theories, but is a complementary one (much the same structurally and discursively, in fact), implicated in the film's formal makeup. As Pat Berry (2001: 71–72) notes in her article, 'Image in motion':

> Art binds chaotic impressions into form. Once bound, the impressions can then become pleasurable. Perhaps film emerged when it did because it was just the therapy people needed to bind into manageable form the chaos of modern overstimulation.

So, it seems that *form* itself can be pleasurable, and this makes sense in the context of studying films and their audiences. There is much pleasure to be found in the familiarity of filmic convention – knowledge of how the film was put together, for example, or its play on genre.

I have found myself returning to the notion of pleasure frequently during the course of my research, and these kinds of self-aware pleasures in particular. I feel that these pleasures based on signification systems that in Don Fredericksen's words would constitute 'dead symbols' do not go anywhere once identified as such. In fact, their effect is magnified to an extent by the very realization of their brevity and disposability. This is a notable eventuality of the observation that Chris Hauke makes in his book *Jung and the Postmodern*, whereby symbolism and semiosis become mutually constitutive and infinitely reversible in postmodernity. Hence, the morbid fascination with which we behold the CGI spectacle of a floating, working *SS Titanic* is nonetheless real for its identifiably simulated origin, and is as pleasurable as any closure offered by the clichéd boy-meets-girl narrative found in *Titanic* (Cameron, US, 1997) as a narrative film.

At the IAJS annual conference *Psyche and Imagination*, in July 2006, Don Fredericksen stated with a modicum of obviousness in his address to the seminar that Jungian psychology and analysis are all about the study of images. By this, he explained that the pertinence of Jungian analysis for film scholarship was obvious and that the natural affinity for the interpretation of images was such that it is a wonder that there are not more Jungian analysts 'dabbling' in film scholarship. Although I have deep reservations concerning the second implication in his statements (to which I shall return), I find myself having to agree with Fredericksen in that both analytical psychology and film studies have as their central concern the study of images. However, the reason for the reluctance to take up Jungian approaches by film scholars is partly to do with the innate problems associated with Jung's reputation as an opportunist (and anti-Semite – unfounded or not, the reputation still works as a deterrent). It is also connected to what Renos Papadopoulos described at the same IAJS conference as the mutual suspicion of analysts and academics.

This last is a phenomenon that I would say prejudices my own view of the use of Jung in film scholarship. Film studies is sometimes seen as a 'soft' discipline, sometimes even some sort of academic hobbyhorse indulged by English departments the world over. It is, of course, nothing of the sort. As the reader will discover over the course of Part I of this book, film studies has had a long and tortuous history as an academic discipline. Although embryonic as a discipline in comparison to some of its more established antecedents (for example, literary studies, sociology, art history), it has undergone massive transformations during the past three decades, to become one of the most interdisciplinary, dynamic and engaging areas of humanities study that currently exists. Although traditionally a dilettante in terms of its acceptance of interdisciplinary influence (in fact, one might say that film studies has traditionally relied on this for its very dynamism), there exists a corpus of scholarship that mobilizes both position and vocabulary. This corpus would (and perhaps should) resist 'dabbling', as film studies is not a 'wide open field' or 'open territory', as Fredericksen would have it. Jungian psychology can make an important contribution to film theory, and film theory can make a difference to analysis: After all, both fields are concerned with 'the study of images'. However, similar to the example of Jung and Merleau-Ponty on materiality, the languages spoken by film studies and analytical psychology are very different, and at times are contradictory – a further reflection of mutual suspicion, mobilizing the different prejudices associated with each tradition. After all, arts and sciences often do not make happy bedfellows.

This is borne out in a typical statement made by Hollwitz (2001: 85) in his essay on *Field of Dreams* (Robinson, US, 1989). He states in no uncertain terms that:

> It is intellectually dishonest and psychologically irresponsible to create film criticism from a patchwork of critical constructs known or strongly suspected to be scientifically untenable.

From a sociological perspective this kind of statement is highly suspect: Has Hollwitz read Thomas S. Kuhn? From a film studies perspective also, this is somewhat nonsensical as it negates wholesale virtually all film theory that has not developed from a specifically (empirical) scientific approach. Hollwitz's statement is as much a commentary on value and usefulness, that is, economy, as on academic procedure. This echoes his third statement about the appropriation of analytical constructs for use in criticism, noted previously. The notion of 'empirical psychological fact' is, arguably, a largely theoretical matter, as it draws from the opposite assumption that its measurability is commensurate with functionality and usefulness. Coming full circle in this model of thought, this approach presupposes an economy yet again taken directly from Kant. On the subject of the legitimacy of thought systems, Kant (1974: 6) identifies, in his *Critique of Pure Reason*, a tendency through which metaphysics:

> Is the only science which admits of completion – and with little labour, if it is united, in a short time; so that nothing will be left to future generations except the task of illustrating and applying it *didactically*. For this science is nothing more than the *inventory* of all that is given us by *pure reason*, systematically arranged.
>
> (emphasis in original)

Thus, Kant is suggesting, after much distillation, a valuation placed on the division of natural science (the empirical, the measured and the considered), over and above mathematics (the abstract, the critical and the ideal). Although one might not suggest that Kant was a true idealist (as many of his detractors accused), one may nevertheless see this valuation as a system of legitimacy to which film theory (often situated wholly and erroneously in opposition to film criticism and film practice) is submitted. This system has its continuation through the contemporary tendency to quantify in all spheres of public life, from education, 'human resources' and government performance through to the consumption of leisure goods such as films and media.

This book will both identify and critically discuss the literature currently available to the film student regarding applications of analytical psychology to film, with a view to re-establishing the value of film theory as a 'perspective statement' in Jungian film scholarship. More generally, an overview of the traditions of theoretical perspectives in the academic discipline of film studies will be offered, with specific attention to the position of analytical psychology in relation to film theory. This in no way implies that this study claims to be a value-free, *wertfreiheit* negotiation of dominant themes within Jungian film analysis, but rather seeks to engage varying notions of academic value and its place in film historiographies. In effect, I will give the analyst and film student a broad historiography of film theory, introducing the more relevant currents for post-Jungian film scholarship. Rather inevitably, this will involve a discussion of 'Screen theory', a collective term for specific positions debated by film scholars writing in the film journal *Screen* during the early–mid 1970s. Of particular relevance in this, the introduction of psychoanalysis as a dominant paradigm in film theory in response to the need to account for the subject in film spectatorship will be considered. A brief overview of alternative psychologies in film theory, such as cognitive approaches, will be included as a partial response to problems arising from the psychoanalytic intervention, as well as aspects of film phenomenology that have more recently been explored. In other words, this book will locate post-Jungian approaches within the context of the theoretical traditions of the film studies discipline, and offer a critique of the place of Jungian film studies within this history, and an application of Jung's psychological theory to film.

Chapter 2

Film as film; film as art; film as authored artefact

> The critic's experience is not essentially grounded in or guaranteed by the essence of the film itself. The critic is not at the heart of the matter. The critic is someone who persists in learning to see the film differently and is able to specify the mechanisms which make this possible.
>
> Peter Wollen, 'The auteur theory'

Under the entry on 'Theory' in her book *Key Concepts in Cinema Studies*, Susan Hayward states that the genesis of film theory was probably in France, at least as long ago as the early 1910s. For instance, in 1911, Ricciotto Canudo published a manifesto in France entitled 'The Birth of a Sixth Art', in which he established two distinct lines of critical debate within the appreciation of film that we may broadly define as realism and formalism. As conceptual and analytical frameworks for the establishment of cinema as an art form similar to other visual arts predating its inception, these debates preoccupied film critics well into the 1930s, often following similar logic to the formalist/realist debates on photography in the late nineteenth century. Traces of realist and formalist criticism may be seen implicitly, such as in debates on cinematic spectacle, or in the influence of structuralism, for example. Equally, they may be discerned explicitly in critical discussion of these very categories in, for instance, the work of Bazin in the 1940s and 1950s, or Victor Perkins' perspective on 'film as film' in the 1970s. Either way, the thrust to establish cinema as an art form in its own right came early in the medium's history and was to dominate early approaches to its criticism.

Film theory and criticism have long since matured to the point where justification of the serious academic study of film is no longer necessary. However, outside the discipline of film studies there is still a suspicion levelled at the practice of film analysis. The characteristic apologetic tone that some post-Jungian film scholars still feel the need to take results in a cheapening of film scholarship itself. This cheapening effect is rather alien to those of us brought up with the discipline: The study of popular cultural production is a long-established given. However, what is commonly regarded as 'art form', along with the capacity to render an impression of the world or to express inner conflict or emotion, tends to ignore some of the more obvious problems associated with the identification, classi-fication and interpretation of 'art'. In short, the very notion of art itself goes unquestioned, and with it, an unproblematic association of cultural production attributable to artist, author, visionary, critic, dramaturg, etc. The purpose of this book is not to examine the notion of film-as-art in detail, as this would take up a volume in its own right. However, the notion has been the subject of serious debate, and therefore must feature to an extent in any overview of the history of film theory. For example, Nicolas Tredell argues that Canudo found in the embryonic cinema a 'superb conciliation of Rhythms of Space (the Plastic Arts) and the Rhythms of Time (Music and Poetry)' (2002: 16). Nonetheless, cinema itself:

> is not yet an art, because it lacks the freedom of choice peculiar to plastic *interpretation*, conditioned as it is to being the *copy* of a subject, the condition that prevents photography from becoming an art . . . [yet, Canudo] has the highest hopes for the development of film as an art. As a plastic art in motion it will effect a revival of theatre and bring about a new sense of human community.
>
> (Tredell, 2002: 18–19, emphasis in original)

There are, of course, many reasons why this issue is of particular import-ance to Jungian and post-Jungian academics. The central position afforded expression and interpretation in both clinical and critical practice appeals to the idea that something of our psychic lives reveals itself in/through the production and consumption of cultural artefacts. This does raise the question, however, of how such theoretical assumptions and clinical appro-priations of the centrality of the producing/consuming subject fit in with the vicissitudes of film theory.

Of course, the short answer to that question is that there is no short answer. Chapter 3 will be devoted to the issue of cine-subjectivity, appro-priations of psychoanalytic constructs within film theory, and the historical debates regarding cinematic apparatus. For now, the questions of author-ship and artistry emphasized in many approaches espoused by Jungian film scholars suggest that a discussion of the very notion of film as an art form, and the filmmaker as an author, is urgently needed. But how should one proceed with such an overview of these issues in the history of film theory? How might one choose what is relevant or irrelevant for the clinician and film student alike? Where might one start in history, even? As stated above, Hayward suggests a starting point in France, around 1910. For Perkins in *Film as Film*, important criticisms of film appear in the US also around this time. He opens his book with the quote about movies being 'galloping tintypes [that] no one can expect . . . to develop into anything which could, by the wildest stretch of the imagination, be called art' (DeMille, cited in Perkins, 1991: 9). An equally propagandist statement about film comes from Vachel Lindsay in 1915, where motion picture art is 'great high art' (Lindsay, cited in Perkins, 1991: 9). This is further complicated by the debates surrounding formalism and realism in film first brought to light by Canudo's manifesto. Formalist approaches and realist approaches have in common the idea that cinema should be judged in a similar fashion to photography, based as it is on the mechanical reproduction of the world and the ways we see it. Anthony Easthope suggests that classical film theory, whether formalist or realist, rests on the assumption that 'cinema, based as it is in photography, must be judged as in part a mechanical reproduction, whether feeble or convincing' (1993: 5). Where they differ, as we shall see during the course of this chapter, is that whereas formalists such as Rudolph Arnheim thought of the artistic possibilities of film as more than a mere reproduction of life, realists such as Andre Bazin tended to think of film's realistic reproductive capabilities.

In many ways, this polarization echoes a certain tendency film historians have had of splitting the very earliest films into two camps: respectively *trucage* films such as those produced by Georges Méliès, and actuality films such as those produced by the Lumiéres brothers. The former are often thought of as presentational in character, extending though the imagination the potential of what the medium is capable of, performing tricks and providing spectacle for the audience. The latter are thought of more often for their representational scope, for 'realistic' or simulational reproduction capabilities, and the depiction of minutiae and 'everydayness'. This has been the discussion of many debates involving the material status of contemporary film in relation to both spectacle and spectatorship (see in particular Metz, 1977; Gunning, 2004; and Pierson, 1999, 2002). I will be devoting further attention to these debates in Part II of this book, but for now it is worth pointing out the difficulties inherent in separating formalist and realist perspectives so sharply.

Firstly, one might easily identify the 'presentational' aspects of the early actuality films, as Tom Gunning has pointed out. The reproductive capabilities of the medium itself are foregrounded as an attractive showcase through its ability to be 'realistic' and therefore provide a specific kind of spectacle for its audience. This is very much evident in recent Hollywood cinema and special effects – the 'wow factor' is often provided by the film's ability to simulate photo-realism or to reproduce historical epochs to the last detail, for example. This might be described as dialectical in the Hegelian sense, as it draws out the relationship between real/simulation and fantastic/spectacular as a tension in constant struggle, expressed in a notion of the 'spectacle of the real'. It is interesting to point out Siegfried Kracauer's (1999: 173) later thoughts on the dialectical nature of actuality and trucage films in early cinema, published in *Theory of Film: The Redemption of Physical Reality* in 1960:

> If film grows out of photography, the realistic and formative tendencies must be operative in it also . . . Their prototypes were Lumiere, a strict realist, and Melies, who gave free reign to his artistic imagination. The films they made embody, so to speak, thesis and antithesis in a Hegelian sense.
>
> (1999: 173)

Well, yes, in a sense they did, but as ever, the nature of dialectics is not a constant flow of binary material structurally opposed, but is made up of a consistent tension between elements in conflict. This is the drive behind historical movements in the social, political and aesthetic realms for historical materialists. It comes as quite a surprise, then, that Kracauer misses the opportunity to rethink film (*both* actuality and trucage film) as a dialectical beast in his discussion. True, it does seem in retrospect that Lumiere 'realized that story telling was none of his business; [because] it involved problems with which he apparently did not care to cope' (1999: 174). However, the object of Kracauer's analysis, an early Lumiere actuality short called *Teasing the Gardener* (*L'Arroseur arose*, 1895) does have its presentational (imaginative, spectacular) as well as representational (realistic, simulational) elements. It was a reproduction of reality in that it depicted everyday life, but told its story through a strictly narrative thread, complete with funny climax. The static camera shoots a gardener watering his flowers. Unknown to him, a boy stands on the hose, halting the flow of water. The gardener peers into the end of the hose to investigate the cause of the blockage. The boy steps off the hose, releasing the flow of water, which hits the gardener square in the face. He sees the boy laughing and, realizing what has happened, chases him down and spanks him. The presentational aspect stems from a rather innocuous fact: The boy has run out of the frame, and so the gardener has to drag him back, in front of the static camera, to give him his punishment. Thus, denouement itself embodies the potentiality of this particular film; its story-telling capacity, rather than the recording and revealing of physical reality, as Kracauer seems to emphasize in his discussion. The narrative is resolved before the end of the take.

The tension highlighted within this dialectic of simulation and spectacle in cinema tends to come to the fore through a second difficulty. Very early film theory often had to justify itself through the idea that film is not a reproductive medium at all. In this way, film theory could be classed as a theory of comparable seriousness to the painting, writing and musical styles dominant at the time (i.e. 1910s, post-Impressionism). Within the first decade of film theories, then, three issues emerge. These may be loosely grouped as follows: film as art; film as authored artefact; and film as a reproductive medium. But how should one properly determine a chronology along which currents of film theory might be mapped? There are, perhaps, three strands that may be identified throughout the history of orthodox film theory, which roughly correspond to the issues of art, author and medium, and which may be alluded to in order to account for the difficulties of chronicling the history of film theory. They are by no means exhaustive, nor determinist in the strictest sense, but follow a rough chronology that occasionally reveals their mutual relationships.

The first of these strands is the attempt to theorize the world of the film itself – film as 'text', and film as a medium. The second is the attempt to theorize the socio-economic context of the film, including its impact on the act of filmmaking. The third is the attempt to theorize the intersubjective relation between film and audience. Each strand impacts on the others in surprisingly complex ways. In addition, although each strand may be related to other aspects of the cultural sphere that lie outside the scope of this study, all three underpin the orthodox theories associated with film as art, as realistic medium and as authored artefact.

Formalism, realism and cinematic art

As mentioned above, Canudo's concern in engaging film largely centred on establishing film as an art comparable to theatre, bringing about 'a new sense of human community'. However, Canudo's qualification of film as an art form comparable with theatre – a development of theatre – is a relationship that Hugo Münsterberg would later de-emphasize. Münsterberg stated that 'photoplays' (his term for moving pictures):

> are not and ought never to be imitations of the theatre. They can never give the esthetic values of the theatre; but no more can the theatre give the esthetic values of the photoplay.
>
> (Münsterberg, cited in Tredell, 2002: 20)

Münsterberg sought to draw parallels between the techniques that are possible in film and the subjective operations of the human mind, rather than as a mimetic form of theatre. In doing so, he attempted to establish the distinctiveness of film, and its unified perception within the field of psychology:

> The photoplay, incomparable in this respect with the drama, gave us a view of dramatic events which was completely shaped by inner movements of the mind . . . The events are seen in continuous movement; and yet the pictures break up the movement into a rapid succession of instantaneous impressions.
>
> (Münsterberg, 1999: 401)

As we shall see in Chapter 3, this approach has much in common with later developments in cognitive film theories, but is also arguably related in essence with the gestaltist psychological paradigm, very little of which has been included in film theory. It is related because of its emphasis on the shifting attention between parts and the whole as objects of inquiry – a useful notion that will be explored in the context of inter-objectivity later in this book. To reiterate a point from earlier, it is a question of the film theorist having to define film not as reproductive, but as the medium through which the imagination is somehow captured in a mimesis of the 'inner movements of the mind', or 'inner forms' reflected by and through 'outer forms'. There are, of course, a number of problems with generalizing in this way, including the recognition of documentary film, for example, as a specific type of filmmaking that revolves around discourses of capturing reality. It is also a matter of unproblematically engaging the notion of filmmaker as an artist, for, as Perkins (1991: 16–17) points out when addressing the formalists (most notably Arnheim and Paul Rotha):

> What mattered was the way it was *rendered* in paint and marble, or on film. The resulting dislocations can be seen in the theorists' inability to find the recorded action a place in the critical scheme or to allow it any artistic status. The object in front of the camera was simply reality. The important concern was with the way in which the act or process of cinematography could be shown to impose a pattern on that reality.
>
> (emphasis in original)

In other words, for a film to be good, to truly reflect the medium's capabilities, it had to *add* something to the recorded event. This required theorists to think both of film as a pure form (just as is painting) and of intention behind that form (ultimately, an authorial intention). Before this notion became orthodox, however, the formalist/realist appropriation of the relation of film to reality needed to address intentionality as a medium-specific imposition upon the event recorded. The most productive discussions centred on what might be considered the most discernible of these impositions – editing – and more specifically, by the early Soviet montage theorists (notably Kuleshov, Pudovkin and Eisenstein). What is interesting to note here is that, through their attention to the importance of editing in forming intention (and thus meaning) in film production and consumption, the Soviet montage theorists addressed 'film' (the medium) and 'movies' (what we see as spectators, on the screen) at the same time. This relationship was seen as crucial: the articulation of one in/through the other. Pudovkin, in *Film Technique and Film Acting*, developed a theory of 'relational editing', suggesting that through adopting a building-block approach to editing, the filmmaker may create sensations for the spectator. These were, for Pudovkin, contrast (editing a scene or sequence together depicting contrasting representations), parallelism (e.g. cross-cutting), symbolism (juxtaposing one image next to another in a symbolic gesture), or simultaneity (the simultaneous rapid development of two intercut actions). Pudovkin's account of editing constituted nothing less than a creative language of the cinema: 'Editing is the language of the film director. Just as in living speech, so, one may say, in editing: there is a word – the piece of exposed film, the image; a phrase – the combination of these pieces' (1958: 24).

For our purposes, the need to rethink this misconception is absolutely imperative if we are to begin to explore a material rather than linguistic notion of the film text. For Perkins, even if we were to accept this parallel between language and film, the non-verbal aspect of communication available in the silent film, and the emotional impact of a single close-up or jump-cut for the spectator can express so much more than a single word: 'Even in edited film, the object (noun) cannot be disassociated from what it does (verb) or how it looks (adjective). The more complex the content of a shot, the less relevant the verbal parallels become' (1991: 21). The development of 'film language' then, as a conceptual framework is a highly contentious one, and this is a theme that we shall return to in the discussion of the appropriation of structural linguistic models in Chapter 3. For now, it would be more productive to consider the response of Sergei Eisenstein towards Pudovkin's 'building block' approach to editing, and the constitution of film language.

Kuleshov regarded montage as producing meaning by describing it, adding individual shots to one another. In common with Pudovkin, this interpretation of montage was, for Eisenstein, 'the means of *unrolling* an idea through single shots' (1999: 28, emphasis in original). By contrast, through the course of several essays (most notably in his 1929 essay 'Dramaturgy of Film Form'), Eisenstein formulated a manifesto that engaged the role of the film director in a more political, interventionist sense. He predated Arnheim with the idea that film could be considered an authored imposition on the real world, effecting real change. Emphasizing, as Kuleshov and Pudovkin had before him, that editing was central to creativity, he developed a consciously political film theory in which dialectical objects and our encounter with them produce dialectical modes of thought. In effect, this was film theory in keeping with early Soviet policy on dialectical materialism – a dialectical philosophy and understanding of the world. For Eisenstein, such dialectical projections of dialectical objects would constitute a dialectical form of art. In defining dialectical philosophy, objects and art, Eisenstein wrote that 'the basis of this philosophy is the *dynamic* conception of objects: being as a constant evolution from the interaction between two contradictory opposites' (1999: 25, enphasis in original). Therefore, his goal was nothing less than the construction of a dialectical mode of filmmaking that reflected the dialectical struggle of history; produced a new, dialectical art form; and engaged spectators in dialectical modes of thought (and therefore) action. It was, in other words, a revolutionary film theory for revolutionary means, reflecting the early Soviet context within which, Eisenstein worked. For him, film was an art form, and like all art, was 'always conflict.' In his view montage was 'not an idea composed of successive shots stuck together but an idea that DERIVES from the collision between two shots that are independent of one another' (1999: 28). Successive theorists writing in Europe did not pursue this dialectical line of thinking (although certain leftist thinkers on film were familiar with Hegel and dialectics, such as Béla Balázs and Kracauer). This is hardly surprising, considering the ideological positions in the West, brought about by the Cold War in the post-war period, but this is a real oversight in retrospect, as Eisenstein's writings on film took account of the formal qualities of film as well as its real political and psychological effects. As Tredell (2002: 44) states:

No director of his stature has been so prolific in theorising about film; and his writings on cinema are fascinating not only because of their vigour and inventiveness but also because they show his ideas about film developing in response to his own work as a director, to the films of other directors, and to the turbulent political and social situation of the Soviet Union from 1917.

It is because of this commitment to so many different aspects of the critical appreciation and practice of film that this book will return to the work of Eisenstein in later chapters. That his legacy was not championed explicitly by the so-called realist critics is clear in the way in which Kracauer later adopted many of the premises of Andre Bazin's approach, effectively reiterating the much earlier assumption that cinematography is an extension of photography. Indeed, Bazin went so far as to formulate an 'ontology of the photograph'. As Perkins (1991: 28–29) comments:

Bazin argued that a film aesthetic must, at least, take account of the nature and function of photography . . . The cinema, which extended the power of the camera through time, derived its nature from that of photography and its aesthetic appeal came from the same source; the revelation of reality.

Bazin suggested that aesthetically satisfying films were films that reflected the director-as-investigator rather than director-as-creator. For Kracauer similarly, in *Theory of Film*, photography and its extension (film) have a marked affinity for recording the physical world, and an ability to 'penetrate' the world before our eyes. The category of 'art' and its concomitant value system – the privileging of the artist's vision of the world, rather than the world itself – tended to undermine the medium's ability to reproduce reality. In the realist view, then, editing was viewed as the most intrusive element of the filmmaking process and was therefore suspect as the essential source of film art. As Perkins comments, 'it sacrificed the natural relationship between an object and its context in order to construct an arbitrary relationship between shots' (1991: 32). What the realist perspective attempted was to expose this arbitrary relationship, but it also took the view that Soviet montage theory privileged a hierarchical meaning-structure that tended to ignore the ambiguity inherent in reality itself, thereby foreclosing on the multiplicity of meaning potential. Montage theory was therefore also propagandist in the rather subtle sense of disregarding viewer-response as at least partly autonomous, although it should be said that Eisenstein's theory certainly embraced ideas of class-specificity and intra-class differentiation in audience-response.

For Perkins also, the Soviet montage theorists' view of film remained unproductive, for it tended to emphasize the creation of movies, rather than the perception of them: 'In order to arrive at a more accurate and inclusive definition of film as it exists for the spectator, [theory] will need to concentrate not on the viewfinder and the cutting bench but on the screen' (1991: 27). However, Perkins wrote this within the context of the immediate aftermath of the collapse of the structuralist movement, some 40 years after Eisenstein wrote 'Dramaturgy of Film Form'. It was only then that Perkins' anticipation of emphasis on viewing context in mainstream film theory could have found a ready audience: After the classical formalist/realist debate, the idea of authorship in film took hold through, among others, Bazin's criticism, and the creative aspects of film remained the main concerns of film theorists until the advent of Apparatus Theory in the 1970s. It is to this post-classical concern with creativity and authorship that we now turn.

Film authorship

John Caughie, writing for the journal *Screen Education* in 1975/76, sought to draw a plan for teaching approaches to film, and aimed to identify authorship as only one among many approaches to cinematic meaning. His essay 'Teaching through Authorship' (1975) explored the confrontation of authorial freedom with genre criticism, as well as the antinomy of what he identified as the main strands of thinking within film criticism at the time. These he outlined as structural auteurism (common motifs in films), and humanistic/evaluative auteurism (attributed commonalities to a warm authorial body). Exploring the role of human agency in relation to less individualized determinants of meaning-making, especially institutional and commercial contexts of filmmaking, Caughie identified the contradiction between structural analysis and evaluative criticism. These antinomies and contradictory forces were brought to bear on the process of film criticism itself. It is worth exploring these in depth for those unfamiliar with the vicissitudes of approaches to authorship in film, as they are key to understanding the historiographies that currently exist on the appreciation of film in the post-war period. It will also be useful to lay down some groundwork in terms of thinking through both structural and humanistic approaches to the subject. This will become invaluable to the discussion of the ways in which Jungian themes such as the autonomous complex, the symbol and active imagination may be employed in theorizing film, in Part II of this book.

Although a familiar term in both academic and popular film appreciation, the 'auteur' as a person (an author who intends his/her work to mean something) and as a construct (an ideal, projected personality, working with the text to produce meaning) is a far from simple concept. As Helen Stoddart puts it, auteur criticism 'mainly carried out impressionistic readings under veiled agendas' (1995: 44). Therefore it should come as no surprise to the film student that there are a number of reasons why we should think beyond both person and personality, to the very institutions that insist these categories are legitimate. True, the 'author' of a film (an epithet usually attributed to the director) will have a creative input in the way the film will be shot/cast/performed, and therefore something of an artistic interpretation of the world will be reflected in the way the film plays. However, as we have already seen, the categories of 'art' are a minefield of antiquated, value-laden presuppositions. So how, then, do we get to the point in the history of film theory whereby it has become a given in popular discourses on film that films are 'authored' by a director, when the categories of 'art' have long since been dismantled? It would be appropriate to start answering this question with some definitions of relevant terms.

Caughie states that auteur 'theory' has posed as a theory since the 1950s without clear theoretical definition. He goes through three criticisms of the approach, emphasizing its positive and negative impact on ways of seeing film in general. Firstly, he establishes the differences between auteur theory/ auteurism and authorship: 'Auteurism' is the critical practice specifically addressing *la politique des auteur* and auteur theory, whereas authorship is a more neutral term presumably applicable to cultural productivity in a more general sense. For Lapsley and Westlake, auteurism is 'the belief that cinema was an art of personal expression, and that its great directors were as much to be esteemed as the authors of their work as any writer' (1988: 105). If the director as the identifiable author of the work is given status of artist, this means that film falls into the canon of high art. This then leads to the notion of camera to director as brush is to painter. This is, very simply, a replaying of the formalist/realist debate present in film theory since its inception. It is a cyclical argument that started with Canudo, and has stayed within various strains of film criticism (including Jungian film scholarship) to this day.

In the post-war period, however, the cycle took on a very particular course, starting in France, 1948 with Alexandre Astruc's highly influential essay, 'The Birth of a New Avant-Garde: Le Camera-Stylo', first published by the Communist-sponsored journal *Ecran Français*. As the title suggests, Astruc made the comparison between camera and pen, suggesting an artistry and authorship attributable to the process of directing film: 'Cinema is quite simply becoming a means of expression. Just as all other arts before it, and in particular painting and the novel' (Astruc, 1968: 17). Astruc thus builds on the romantic view of authorship, of the kind that we have already seen in early theorists such as Arnheim. Astruc expressed a need to elevate film to the status of high art and a means of individual creative expression, thus justifying its place in the canon of art. Critics of film should thus be afforded the status enjoyed by critics of art. This impulse of justification still exists today in popular auteurism, to the extent that, for example, Jonathan Ross can declare himself a 'film critic' without a sense of irony and, in an albeit kitschy way, talk seriously about very inane fare.

Much subsequent Francophone film criticism, typified by the work written during the 1950s in the journal *Cahiers du cinema*, was underpinned by three assumptions by Astruc, as follows.

1   Cinema has obtained an artistic and cultural equivalence to literature and other forms.
2   It is constituted through a unique (filmic) language.
3   It is not a mere mass art form to appease popular pleasures: Its status as a high art equivalent with its own unique language allows for the director to work with material to express himself personally, creatively and artistically.

Francois Truffaut, in his seminal 1954 essay, 'A certain tendency of the French cinema', consolidated this evaluative spirit of auteurism by dismissing the popularly valued literary adaptations, and the kinds of film that we might now classify as 'heritage films' prevalent in French cinema at the time. Provocatively calling this kind of film 'cinema du papa', Truffaut and the other *Cahiers* critics sought to emphasize that the American imports flooding the post-war market, as well as less popular expressionistic and neo-realist films in Europe, were every bit as worthy of serious consideration as 'serious' literary films. Therefore, as Stoddart points out, 'Though popular cinema is produced precisely to attract as wide an audience as possible, *Cahiers* critics appear to fly in the face of this imperative in their selection of auteurs who were great artists despite their being popular' (1995: 41).

The Truffaut article may be seen as something of a departure, from which the *Cahiers* group galvanized around a loosely based doctrine. Although the writers (including other future filmmakers Jean-Luc Godard, Jacques Rivette and Claude Chabrol) were diverse in their political and critical perspectives, they were, in editor Jacques Doniol-Valcroze's opinion, 'all in solidarity, something bound us together. From then on, it was known that we were for Renoir, Rossellini, Hitchcock, Cocteau, Bresson . . . and against X, Y and Z' (cited in Hillier, 1985: 4). This evaluative list of good versus bad film artists tended, as Lapsley and Westlake have noted, 'to be those whose films reflected the critics' own ideology' (1988: 106).

So, from the outset of the auteurist tradition of film criticism, a hierarchy was established that, while importantly acknowledging the cultural impact (and thus worthiness of serious critical consideration) of commercial cinema, nevertheless did not engage with production contexts nor the status of 'artistry'. Rather, what it tended to celebrate was the aesthetic impact of social commentary of various movements such as British social realism or Italian neo-realism and, perhaps more significantly, the artistic productivity of popular American cinema according to the critics' own predilections. However, as Andre Bazin (Valcroze's co-editor on *Cahiers* at the time) noted, cinema, and especially American cinema, was 'an art which was both popular and industrial' (cited in Stoddart, 1995: 41), something that the auteurist critics often disengaged from their criticism.

This relates to the second aspect of auteurism in Caughie's sights: the centrality of the director in auteur criticism as a creative source, to which he was extremely unsympathetic. The director should, for Caughie, be considered only as one of the *potential* sources of meaning-making. After all, applied to American cinema, auteurism implied that the auteur was a director who could work creatively within the constraints of the Hollywood production system, so that even highly commercial 'B' pictures could be deemed 'art'. This happened in marked contrast to the mode of production of prestige pictures, which tended to be straight adaptations of pre-existing literary material: the abovementioned 'cinema du papa'. As Lapsley and Westlake note of commercial filmmaking: 'Given that they often had to contend with a variety of scriptwriters, studios, actors and genres, the only possible source of this unity was the director himself'. However, 'because any system of rules brings with it the possibility of transgression, genre [for example] can be seen as providing a field for variation and elaboration of meaning' (1988: 107).

Thirdly for Caughie, auteurist critics such as Bazin, and (as we shall see) Sarris and Wollen had been willing to justify the auteur approach on positive empirical results without sufficiently theorizing it. This had, in Caughie's view, led to 'blockages' that auteurism erected within film criticism, based on a classification system of evaluative judgements rather than reflecting on those very classification systems themselves. An evaluative distinction had been established between stylists and auteurs, based on personalities and artistic tendencies of the directors themselves, and their virtuosity with the language of film itself: the mise-en-scène. The early auteurist critics placed the consideration of film outside of conditions of production, and intentionality was placed above the concerns of industrial and popular bases of production. However, the *'politique des auteur'* should perhaps best be regarded as a transitional or galvanizing stage. Without such a stage and focus, film might not have been given the same level of consideration, nor resources and effort given over to the development of film studies itself at such a crucial time in the development of the post-war popular cultural landscape.

Not for the first time, but given fresh emphasis from young blood through the relatively youthful and unknown *Cahiers* group, film was given same critical consideration as high art – a fact that Peter Wollen reflected upon in his own reworking of the auteurist approach some years later. 'The politique des auteurs,' he wrote, 'sprang from the conviction that the American cinema was worth studying in depth, that masterpieces were made not only by a small upper crust of directors . . . but by a whole range of authors' (1999: 519). Film was granted the artistic status of any cultural product stemming from an identifiable creative source/author, and the auteur was identifiably responsible for his own creation and created out of his own personality. In sharp contrast to a *metteur-en-scene* – a stylist who merely translates given material onto the screen – the auteur injects his world-view into the material.

Arguably, two developments were achieved as a result of the *politique*. The cinematic qualities of the films themselves provided the focus of analysis (rather than socio-economic factors, as in mass culture theory), and promoted research into the work of directors previously dismissed, such as Sirk, Fuller and Hawks. Also, by applying romantic assumptions of authorship to a mass cultural form, auteurism arguably opened up film criticism to a range of theoretical paradigms through exposing the contradiction of such romanticized, totalizing tendencies in cultural criticism thus far. It would take the intervention of structuralism in auteurist criticism to sound the death-knell of auteur theory as a self-sustaining critical system. Ironically, however, this would help to expose some of the systemic contradictions within structuralism itself, as well as the tendency to 'justify' critical theory through scientific method.

The ideas of the *Cahiers* group were brought to the attention of Anglophone film criticism largely through the work of American film critic Andrew Sarris, and in particular through his essay 'Notes on the Auteur Theory in 1962' first published in the journal *Film Culture*. Crucial to Sarris' overall reading strategy was the distribution of named directors in a hierarchical positioning. Sarris differed from the *Cahiers* critics in that, in formalizing the rather loose arrangement of the *politique des auteur* into a 'theory', Sarris explicitly solidified the criteria on which critical judgements may be made into a 'pantheon', even though he admitted that his particular pantheon would change with time. Nevertheless, this formalization of such ideas into a 'theory' resulted from the very informality of the original

Cahiers policy. This policy centred on the rediscovery of US cinema in the post-war period through an influx of American imports (Vichy France, needless to say, did not import US product) tied to interests of the French intelligentsia in the cinema as an art form. Sarris' goal was, for Helen Stoddart, 'a refusal of the separation between artists and their work. Interpretation, under these conditions, constituted a search for a "meaningful coherence" between the two' (1995: 42). Like the *Cahiers* critics, however, the emphasis still lay in the cinematic qualities of the films themselves, which provided the focus of analysis. In Sarris' (1999: 516) own words:

> By the *auteur* theory, if the director has no technical competence, no elementary flair for the cinema, he is automatically cast out from the pantheon of directors . . . what constitutes directorial talent is more difficult to define abstractly.

In saying this, Sarris is denying any extra-cinematic forces from impeding the primacy of the director as a central producer of meaning, as well as the criteria by which we should judge the film a success or failure. He goes on to say that 'the second premise of the *auteur* theory, is the distinguishable personality of the director as a criterion of value' (1999: 516). This, in conjunction with the directorial exertion of control over the materials at his disposal, allowed conditions to take hold in the director's work to produce an 'interior meaning'. This is, for Sarris, what makes an *auteur* – the ability to express this, as well as its discernible presence for the critic. So much so, in fact that it constituted 'The third and ultimate premise of the *auteur* theory', concerned with 'interior meaning, the ultimate glory of the cinema as an art. Interior meaning is extrapolated from the tension between a director's personality and his material' (1999: 516).

In establishing these premises, Sarris was able to establish a hierarchy (largely, though not exclusively, US-biased, it should be noted) based on evaluative criteria extrapolated from the *Cahiers* critics. The 'policy of authors' was not necessarily intended to be formalized as a theory initially, but in Sarris' interpretation and application it became just that. His approach, then, merely reflected a commonplace misconception of the director as creative source of meaning, but, as British critic Ian Cameron said at the time, 'Hollywood films are not so much custom-built as manufactured . . . Only by happy accident can anything good escape from this industrial complex' (1981: 52). It should be noted that this does not by any means shift the emphasis to a sustained criticism of Hollywood's political economy in Anglophone auteurist criticism. Cameron maintains that the director is the 'most likely' element in the production process to shape and determine the final form of the film. Therefore, auteurism becomes the appreciation of personal vision in the face of adverse industrial conditions. As an interesting afterthought, this establishes the general characteristics of discrepancy between the approaches taken by many critics writing in Britain for *Movie* and the position taken up by Sarris in *Film Culture*. For the *Movie* critics, American directors were disadvantaged by their position within industrial conventions, but for Sarris these conditions *enabled* the artistry of American directors – his first premise of auteur theory was a 'criterion of value' based on such artistry.

Auteurism signalled a retreat from wider concrete social issues – a kind of political withdrawal into a hermeneutics of itself. However, attention to *mise-en-scène* highlighted the need for analysis to return to cinematic specificity, echoing tendencies in earlier realist approaches, as well as theories of form most notably embodied in Soviet montage theory. Some of the more influential studies of this type owe their approach to other analytical conditions. For example, Bordwell's approach owes more to Russian and Czech formalism than to the Western auteurist tradition. Despite this move, however, and to combat criticisms of auteurist analysis, the auteurist critics turned to Levi-Straussian structuralism in order to bolster the centrality of the director via discernible motifs. Interestingly, in the specifically British tradition of film criticism most notably present in *Movie* in the 1960s, critics who were to become huge names in Anglophone film theory such as Robin Wood, Victor Perkins and Geoffrey Nowell-Smith were to an extent pre-empting this move. As Lapsley and Westlake note, these critics were 'very different in their attention to textuality from anything that had preceded them and would not be surpassed for seriousness in relation to their objects of study until the shot-by-shot semiotic analyses of the post-1968 structuralists' (1988: 107).

The most influential exponent of auteur-structuralism was Peter Wollen, whose work is worth looking at in some detail before levelling criticisms against the paradigm in general. As Patrick Phillips (1996: 124) notes:

> A structure is a combination of elements, this combination governed either explicitly or implicitly by 'rules' which can be identified as a result of study. The elements available for inclusion in a particular structure are united by convention or common sense.

'Auteur-structuralism' then, might be said to be the critical appreciation of the structure of meanings throughout an agreed body of work of a single director, and of the relationships running throughout in a coherent way. For Geoffrey Nowell-Smith (cited in Wollen, 1999: 521), this suggests that:

> The purpose of criticism thus becomes to uncover behind the superficial contrasts of subject and treatment a hard core of basic and often recondite motifs. The pattern formed by these motifs . . . is what gives an author's work its particular structure, both defining it internally and distinguishing one body of work from another.

Once the 'core of meanings' is established, based on the identification of such 'basic and recondite motifs', it may be used as an interpretative device to understand single works by the director. However,

> The notion behind criteria is that they are timeless and universal . . . Almost all current theories of evaluation depend on identifying the work first and then confronting it with criteria. The work is then criticised for falling short on one score or another. It is blemished in some way. Evidently, if we reject the idea of an exhaustive interpretation, we have to reject this kind of evaluation. Instead, we should concentrate on the *productivity* of the work.
>
> (Wollen, 1999: 534)

Wollen's analysis reveals a systemic series of binary oppositions in a given director's films. In particular, for example, the films of Howard Hawks revealed especially strong binary motifs throughout his body of work: whether action-adventure or screwball comedy. It is possible to trace a discernible and ostensible auteurist tendency in Wollen's work. Given the variety and range within Hawks' oeuvre, his work proved the perfect foil to Wollen's critical perspective.

Following Levi-Strauss, Wollen engages the protagonist of the story as well as the worlds in which he operates, in order to tease out the structural antinomies at work in the film text. It is the dynamism of the antinomic tension, rather than the consistency of style and type, that creates the strength within Hawks' films as a corpus of work. This allows the critic to tease out the unconscious meaning of/within the films themselves: Identifying 'Howard Hawks' as a structural identity rather than Hawks as a person imposing his personality on the text, Wollen thus formed a critique of biographical relevance upon meaning-making. He wrote (1999: 532) that:

> It is important to detach the *auteur* theory from any suspicion that it simply represents a 'cult of personality' or apotheosis of the director. To my mind, the *auteur* theory actually represents a radical break with the idea of an 'art' cinema, not the transplant of traditional ideas about 'art' into Hollywood. The 'art' cinema is rooted in the idea of creativity and the film as the expression of an individual vision. What the *auteur* theory argues is that any film, certainly any Hollywood film, is a network of different statements.

For Wollen, then, the critical emphasis has shifted from having the script act as a catalyst to the director's creative imagination towards the director as an unconscious catalyst to the materials he works with. Therefore,

> The structure is associated with a single director, an individual, not because he has played a role of artist, expressing himself or his own vision in the film, but because it is through the force of his preoccupations that an unconscious, unintended meaning can be decoded in the film.
>
> (Wollen, 1999: 532)

The unconscious here is more firmly associated with Levi-Straussian binary oppositions within a collective unconscious rather than the Freudian topology, and has obvious resonance with Jungian forms of collectivity. This difference system, dealing with tensions between antinomies, was the universal binary organizing principle behind this species of structuralist thinking. Having said this, it is entirely conceivable that, as Wollen was writing in 1969/72, he was invoking the contemporary trend of applying a form of Lacanian unconscious to his critical engagement with authorship. As we shall see in Chapter 3, the Lacanian version drew from the same semiological and linguistic tradition that inspired Levi-Strauss, in turn influencing the Althusserian-inflected film criticism prevalent in Britain at this time. However, Wollen (1999: 526) also drew from Vladimir Propp's *Morphology of the Folktale*, itself a key influence in much of Levi-Strauss' work:

> Propp showed how a whole cycle of Russian fairy-tales could be analysed into variations of a very limited set of basic motifs . . . The protagonists of fairy-tales or myths, as Levi-Strauss has pointed out, can be dissolved into bundles of different elements, pairs of opposites.

The use of Propp in film theory and criticism will form part of the basis for discussion in Chapter 7, and so I will not enter into it here in detail. However, what is important to note is that these bundles of elements and oppositional pairs underpinned the antinomies that operate with such imperative in the abovementioned Levi-Straussian 'deep structure' or unconscious. Again, as with the *politique des auteur*, this synthesis of the auteurist tradition and Levi-Strauss could be read as a transitional phase, through which film theory was able to start to draw, much more productively, from paradigms that before were not compatible with auteurism. As Lapsley and Westlake (1988: 111) state:

> The postscript to the second edition of *Signs and Meaning* may be read more productively not as a resolution of the problem of synthesising auteurism and structuralism, but as a transitional text from a pre-structuralist concept of the author as creator of meaning to a post-structuralist concept of the author as a construct of the reader.

Therefore, for Wollen in his rethink of auteur-structuralism, the 'director' and his/her intentionality are indeterminate, and this indeterminacy takes precedence in the reading process. Therefore the reader takes primacy in meaning production in the later auteur-structuralism by constructing the meaning, the author, and authorial intentionality. This was an idea that would come to dominate the thinking on film authorship. Auteur-structuralism exposed the relationship between meaning production in cultural texts and its place in the social and political realms. In the process, the three romantic premises on which auteur criticism was built – namely, individuality, presence, and intention of an author – were revealed as problematic, and a source of much of the criticism that followed. Brian Henderson, in his essay 'Critique of Cine-Structuralism', noted that: 'The fusion of auteurism and structuralism . . . effectively rules out other modes of study . . . constituting itself as a discourse which does not ask funda-mental and foundational questions, above all, about itself' (1981: 176). Auteur-structuralism was ultimately attacked from several quarters for a number of reasons, among which, as we shall see, were the radicalization of film criticism post-1968, the intervention of historical materialist analysis and the critique of systems of power in discourse theory.

Post-auteur theories

For the historical materialist, the reasons for the simple and somewhat virulent appropriation of the concept of auteur by audiences, critics and the film studios themselves could simply be accounted for by considering films and filmmakers (and the marketing tools used to sell them) as commodities. To put it simply, the film business thrives on branding and the desire for the familiar as well as the novel. As Patrick Phillips (1996: 150) states:

> The director in modern Hollywood can function much like a star in offering an *insurance value* to the industry, and a *trademark value* to an audience. Increasingly films are bought and sold on the basis of a director's name, which takes on the function of a sign.
>
> (emphasis in original)

In a more general sense, however, historical materialism has, as its object of analysis, the relations of production as historically manifested within the material conditions of capital. Within film theory, broadly speaking, this is most often constituted by the relations of commodity-identity and is articulated by two critical focal points:

1   film-as-commodity
2   production of meaning in film and its ideological/political project.

In both of these points of focus, the 'author' loses its central role as source of meaning, since the director works within prescribed conventions of filmmaking and within institutionalized conditions of film production. Although certainly radicalized in the post-1968 political atmosphere and by the influence of Marxist thinking in the spheres of arts and education in Europe and North America in general, this species of hostility towards the notion of authorship was nothing new. Andre Bazin, during the time he was editor of *Cahiers du cinema*, wrote that many of the young critics on the journal ignored the 'historical combination of circumstances and technical background' by which directorial talent is allowed to flourish or fade (1968: 142). However, the events of May 1968 reverberated within the spheres of cultural production and criticism to the point where such romanticized notions of traditional auteurism became untenable, and a radical political stance became necessary to eradicate it once and for all.

Criticism exploring the status of film-as-commodity and the ideological implications of mass production came from theorists such as Siegfried Kracauer and Walter Benjamin in the 1920s and 1930s. Its radicalization therefore predates 1968 by quite some time, as the critical theory of the Frankfurt School and its associates engaged with the production context of popular media throughout the inter-war period. However, the events of 1968 galvanized cultural criticism around a political critique of humanist notions such as authority and authenticity. It is within this context that I shall consider the historical materialist wave of criticism that followed in the early 1970s in film theory. For brevity, I shall limit the discussion of the two focal points (commodity and ideology) outlined above to two examples, within the context of auteur theory.

The first example originally stems from the immediate aftermath of the events of 1968, and concerns the radicalization of the *Cahiers du cinema* group. In their essay 'John Ford's *Young Mr. Lincoln*', the editors of the journal put forward the argument that the analysis of film necessarily entails 'the films, within the ideology, and their different relations to it' (Camolli and Narboni, 1999: 758). This radically shifted the emphasis of criticism of Ford's film from John Ford (or, indeed, 'John Ford' as a structure) as central to meaning-making, to John Ford the director working within the industrial and commercial mode of film production. It is explicitly stated in this essay that commercial filmmaking therefore exists as an extension of the capitalist mode of production, and would therefore reflect (and construct) capitalist ideological concerns for its survival and growth. The focal point of the article is the notion of authorial intention, and the discussion of this crucial question starts to bridge the historical materialist concern with economic determination and post-structuralist concerns with the productivity of discourse.

As Roland Barthes put it, 'It is the language that speaks, not the author' (1977: 143). Therefore, to follow the materialist logic of the late-1960s

Cahiers editors, if the language is late capitalism, then the 'speech act' of the film itself is a rendering of its ideology, and a reproduction of its precepts, rather than an intended act of artistry-for-itself. Therefore, extending beyond Wollen's approach, meaning was necessarily an effect of the facilitation of unintended or unconscious authorial structure within a specific ideological and value-laden system. In short, meaning does not originate in the mind of the author, but emerges through the act of reading. As the *Cahiers* editors wrote: 'An artistic product cannot be linked to its socio-historical context according to a linear, expressive, direct causality' since any such relationship is 'complex, mediated and decentred' (Camolli and Narboni, 1999 (1972): 7). This became the focus of much British attention on the question of authorship, with significant interventions in *Screen* from John Caughie, Ed Buscombe and Stephen Heath in particular. For Heath the very notion of authorship effaced the ability to think beyond its presuppositions, to appreciate film from a more political stance. As Lapsley and Westlake point out: 'Only if this conception of an imaginary unity and punctual source of meaning were discarded could there be any materialist theory of the subject, the possibility of which, argued Heath in 1973, had been indicated by Althusser's reworking of Marxism' (1988: 124). It suggested, in Barthes words, the 'death of the author' and a refusal of hypostasis, or final causality in the form of an 'author', which had far-reaching implications for auteurism as a critical approach.

There were, however, many problems with the appropriation of Althusserian Marxism in rethinking the question of authorship; indeed, far too many to address here. However, critics themselves attempted to address these problems, while still endeavouring to push the historical materialist paradigm forward. A key intervention here was made by John Ellis in his 1975 article, 'Made in Ealing'. An overview of industrial relationships between Ealing Studios and the filmmakers who worked there in the post-war period, Ellis' piece emphasized the dialectical, fluctuating tension between studio and filmmaker, and the relationship between structure and agency. This new focus on agency was important, as it enabled the critic to think about material filmmaking decisions based on specific economic, technological and ideological considerations; not stuck in the abstract problematic of meaning-making. Each decision, based on these considerations, led to effects in the subsequent structure of future decision-making within the production process, thus enabling certain modes of filmmaking while simultaneously foreclosing on others. A useful approach, the model of structure and agency proposed by Ellis is not an over-determined structuralist or artisanal model, and is firmly ensconced within socio-economic, political and above all (immediate) material concerns. Therefore, it would be fair to say that a variant of his proposal may be appropriated for critical approaches to any studio system, including Hollywood.

This is in contravention of Bordwell, Staiger and Thompson, and the position they put forward in their book *The Classical Hollywood Cinema*. They imagine that 'Hollywood films constitute a fairly coherent aesthetic tradition which sustains individual creation' (cited in Lapsley and Westlake, 1988: 115). However, it may be argued that this particular approach reveals more about Bordwell *et al.*'s particular political stance than the directors, creative choices and production contexts (a theme to which I shall return in later chapters). It does not fully account, for example, for the fairly coherent political tradition in Hollywood, which *implies* individual creativity discursively rather than *employing* it specifically. The very logic of author as artist, so comprehensively attacked by the radicalized auteur critics of the late 1960s/early 1970s as romanticized idealism, is implied here as a standard, ironically contrary to the development of the auteurist critical tradition. Whereas Ellis' argument implied a species of Althusserian relative autonomy within the cultural production process, Bordwell *et al.* refused a politicized statement of position. Perhaps a precursor of things to come from these authors (as well as Bordwell and Thompson's sometime coauthor, Noël Carroll), the apolitical or anti-political position taken up by Bordwell *et al.* may be read through a filter of local determinism and particular historicity.

Various critics attempted to remove their argument from such limitations: Roland Barthes' notion of 'death of the author' was an influential example, a significant contribution to thinking past notions of authorship. However, in his formulation, spectatorship is not as autonomous as the phrase 'death of the author' might first suggest. Although it is arguably empowering for the audience from an experiential point of view, the audience is no more emancipated from its position of subjection. This is arguably due to two constraints: hegemony and language.

Hegemony relies on the pleasurable consumption of film. This may take the shape of recognition of convention, for example, as in being a 'fan' of the Western. Otherwise, it might be the familiarity of a star's presence such as that of John Wayne or Keanu Reeves, or overt intertextual references such as *Big Brother* (Ch4, 2000–present)'s invocation of Orwell's dystopian nightmare. In all cases, hegemony relies on consensus and consent – especially shared cultural meanings and resonance. However, even a fan-base or a specific audience relies on conventional means of 'reading' films. For example, most popular filmmaking is widely considered to function as entertainment. This is a conventional reading of, say, *Road Trip* (Todd Phillips, US, 2000), but this film also functions to 'say something' about the course of young heterosexual love, supposedly meaningful to us all. Equally, for many people, *March of the Penguins* (*La Marche de l'empereur*, Jacquet, Fr, 2005) is a documentary film, showing footage of real penguins, being observed without the filmmaker's intervention. However, the presence of Oscar-winning actor Morgan Freeman as the narrator of the English-language release tends to play to the sensibilities of an audience familiar with his star persona. What occurs thereafter is a narrativization (as well as anthropomorphization) of the penguins, their personalities, and their 'road trip', which tends to do our thinking for us. The 'language' of convention, genre, iconography, and narrative form therefore all play their part in influencing the meaning-making process.

Of course the audience's capacity for distinctions is also arguably compromised through a branding process, a commodity-identification. Therefore, it follows that, in the aftermath of auteur-structuralism, an institutional convention was established, whereby we see that the emphasis of making sense of film shifts to an author as constructed through the act of reading and audience desire. There is almost, then, a return to romanticized notions of author and artist in the sense that the person of the director could now be located (by an audience) within the institutional, socio-cultural context of film production, much in the same way that Ellis conceived of the director. Production constraints necessitate certain production choices during the project, in turn affecting both the shape of the finished product and, structurally, available choices in the future. This availability anticipates box-office return, as well as funding for future projects, and is a key element of Hollywood film to this day.

Barthes' work did acknowledge that films are *made for* audiences, and from (/for?) their point of view, the text is constituted. He called for the reader to be regarded as 'without history, biography, psychology; he is simply that someone who holds together in a single field all the traces by which the written text is constituted' (1977: 148). French historian Michele Foucault takes a philosophical move away from the theme of originating subject, by acknowledging Barthes' 'death of the author'. But Foucault extends this by emphasizing the institution of authorship over the empirical author as the defining component. The corpus of texts attributable to an author is thus discursively constructed around the author's name, which exists within concrete relations of power, functioning as a means of classification and regulating associated texts as differentiating from other groups of texts. This author-function with different institutional contexts of meaning-production is not a consistent variable. For example, advertising copy and art direction tend to be anonymous, whereas film directing is a fully authored institution.

It is, however, historically variable. For example, literature (and the novel in particular) is now fully dependent on the institution of authorship (as in 'best-selling author') but was not always so. The same could be said for film authorship: It clearly developed as a means of branding for both the industry and the audience, offering, as previously mentioned, 'an *insurance value* to the industry, and a *trademark value* to an audience'. However, the purpose for crediting a first-time director is ambiguous, as the 'trademark' is not yet established. It is almost as if the director-as-auteur is itself being produced. This could be considered as a straightforward commodity-relation between audiences-as-consumers and the products they consume (including director-as-commodity), giving the film a value beyond its mere function as entertainment. In other words, it engages the notion of art as a cultural value, much in the same way that many early film theorists attempted to justify the serious appreciation of film.

Foucault took the view that although one might question the veracity of authorial presence in the text, as in traditional auteurist approaches, it would be futile to suggest that the institution of authorship does not exist as a historically determined force in Western society. Furthermore, it relates to the notion of taste – why, for example, must anonymity be avoided? The lack of critical popularity of uncredited TV movies and the commonplace rejection of straight-to-video movies does not necessarily emphasize discerning viewing publics or inferior products. It emphasizes the necessity for legitimacy through some sense or appropriation of authorship, as these kinds of film often do not credit the director in the same way as mainstream cinema: 'A Film by . . .' for example. Although Barthes may not have accounted fully for the determining influences on reading subjects as Foucault did later, he nevertheless contributed significantly to negotiating the notion of authorship in terms of textuality and pleasure through cine-subjective reading. In this way, the path was cleared for the incorporation of theories of the subject, which took under consideration the political, linguistic and psychosexual facets of subjectivity in cultural reception: facets that engaged both Althusserian Marxist thinking and Lacanian psychoanalytic theories. It is to an account of these approaches that we shall now turn.

Chapter 3

Film and audience, a 'felt' relation
The politics of cine-subjectivity

For Hillman, conventional notions of fantasy and reality are not opposed, but could swap places. Fantasy is always being embodied; whilst behind what is actual there is always a fantasy image.

John Izod, *Screen, Culture, Psyche*

For psychoanalysis, when we analyse the gaze we are also examining the structures, functions, and operations of ourselves as subjects (both conscious and unconscious beings) within socio-cultural and historical contexts. This is an extraordinary project, an undertaking of sometimes breathtaking proportions.

Patrick Fuery, *New Developments in Film Theory*

As we saw in the last chapter, psychological approaches to the cinema are contemporary even with the earliest attempts to theorize film as aesthetic objects in general. This reflects the modernist preoccupation with production (of art), representation (of the real), and intersubjective relations (sometimes potentially alienating, as in Reisman's 'lonely crowd', sometimes potentially progressive, as in Benedict's 'imagined community') between the two. Of modern art production, it could be said that there is an irreducible relation between artistic endeavour and liberatory emancipation, for, at the same time as modernist scientific discourses sought to reveal something of humanity's place in the universe, this tendency flourished in the arts. However, political expression differs between the two methodological orders of arts and sciences. As Eagleton points out in *The Ideology of the Aesthetic*: 'As far as scientific or sociological questions are concerned, only the expert seems licensed to speak; when it comes to art, each of us can hope to contribute our two ha'pence worth' (1990: 2).

As discussed in the last chapter, the romantic preoccupation with matters of the artist in the production of filmic artefacts was taken to an extreme insofar as it led to the elevation of some filmmakers at the expense of others in a hierarchical canon. Critical consideration of bodies of work in this way was at odds with modernism's emancipatory designs, but was also well in keeping with its scientific order, in that specialisms had developed in fields where previously there were none. As, for Eagleton among many others including Clement Greenberg in *Art and Culture*, this is intimately linked with the rise of new class relations under urbanization and capital, it extends into fields beyond the scope of this book. It is, however, still of great importance and relevance, as we shall see in Chapter 4, as these socio-political relations impact on the experiential realms of embodied spectator-ship in cinema and aesthetics of film. What is immediately relevant is that this preoccupation with artistic endeavour also located the importance of the psyche, or the capacity of human consciousness to articulate and express the experience of being-in-the-world (the experiential, the embodied) through artistic, analytic and other endeavours. The subjective articulation of being-in-the-world is, of course, of prime importance in the notion of the spectator-as-subject. As we have seen, Hugo Münsterberg sought to draw parallels between the techniques that are possible in film and the subjective operations of the human mind. In doing so, he attempted to establish the distinctiveness of film, and its unified perception within the field of psy-chology, and not simply a poor artistic relation of theatre. His approach has much in common with later developments in cognitive film theories as well as gestalt theories because of its emphasis on the shifting attention between parts and the whole as objects of inquiry. The subjective experience formed such an important part of this process partly because of the contradictions of early spectatorship. It was, after all, a mass art form that elicited highly subjective responses – a factor that mirrored shifting attentions, oscillating between objective reality and subjective experience, contributing to meaning-making processes, at least as commonly felt by audiences.

In relation to recent cognitive approaches to cinema, there are a number of ways in which it may be useful to break down common misconceptions of meaning-making as posed by established paradigms in film theory. Nicolas Tredell has discussed this, especially in relation to post-structuralism and deconstruction: paradigms that schematically comprise three, often over-lapping, approaches to meaning – arbitrary, oppressive and erroneous. Arbitrary meaning-making stems from linguistic approaches to signification, where what is signified by a sign (an image, for example) does not necessarily have an innate connection to meaning; it is arbitrarily assigned meaning through cultural norms and shared practices. Oppressive meaning-making stems from the cultural artefact's capacity to carry with it meanings that have ideological value, and therefore contain the process within a limitation of choices of meaning. Such cultural production is perhaps most obvious in the direct propaganda films of totalitarian regimes such as *Triumph of the Will* (Riefenstahl, Ger, 1935) or *Old and New* (Eisenstein, USSR, 1929) but is also insinuated in the criticism of film, highlighting criticism itself as another form of cultural production. For example, the Republican Right in the US

often cites Hollywood as a morass of decadent or leftist ideological representation, whereas leftist thinkers often take Hollywood's inherent conservatism for granted. The apolitical criticism of Bordwell *et al.*, discussed in
Chapter 2, might downplay the oppressive angle in favour of a 'middle-level'
approach, which 'tackles more localized film-based problems without
making such overarching theoretical commitments' (Bordwell, 1996: 3). The
concept of erroneous meaning-making stems from philosophy-oriented
approaches within post-structuralism and deconstruction. This is a process
in which, the spectator forms meaning erroneously through their endorse-
ment by immutable metaphysical essences – a labour that itself is in part a
cultural production of a kind, ultimately producing 'impossible' meanings,
as these essences can never be fixed in experience, even though they are
unchanging.

Cognitive approaches to film audiences and post-Jungian readings

Cognitive approaches to cinema tend to sidestep these traditional concerns
with meaning. Cognitive psychology sees meaning construction as 'the
product of social negotiations between human beings with brains and bodies
who are trying to function effectively in a world of which they are a part'
(Tredell, 2002: 208). Such cognition is not necessarily arbitrary, oppressive
or impossible: It is not a question of accuracy or inaccuracy, of getting
things right or wrong, but of the notion that 'the possibility of inaccuracy
entails the possibility of accuracy' (or indeed, vice versa). This paradigm
attempts to articulate the shifting attention between reality and subjective
experience that has been crucial to both film-going and film theory from
cinema's inception. In fact, attention itself as a cognitive, psychosomatic
process is one of the four mental operations that Münsterberg (1999: 402)
states as key to uncovering the relationship between screen and spectator:

> The photoplay tells us the human story by overcoming the forms of the
> outer world, namely, space, time, and causality, and by adjusting the
> events to the forms of the inner world, namely, attention, memory,
> imagination and emotion.

It is worth emphasizing these 'forms of the inner world' to get a firm idea of
how Münsterberg situates them within his approach. This will reveal
intimate connections with the contemporary cognitive approach. Attention,
for Münsterberg, 'turns to detailed points in the outer world and ignores
everything else: the photoplay is doing exactly this when in close-up a detail
is enlarged and everything else disappears' (1999: 402). To take this to its
logical conclusion, then, one might say that for Münsterberg, cinema is

psychomimetic, and might reveal something of the motivation behind certain camera movements and other techniques in the filmmaking process itself. If one thinks, for example, of the consistent and noticeable use of zoom in the films of Robert Altman, the way that attention on an element of the frame's composition (usually a character) is discernibly encouraged engages its importance in the plot and in the intentions of the filmmaker. The zoom is prurient in that it punctuates the story-world (in the physical, rather than syntactical sense), allowing the intimacy necessary to 'read' characters at certain points. That, in Altman's films, this zoom technique is often accompanied by a dissociated source of sound conflates the role of import-ance and intention as it reveals the forces and formal properties competing for the audience's attention. This not only is cognitive in the sense of being 'thoughtful', but it also emphasizes film's relationship with the mechanical operations involved in the optical apparatus.[1] For Münsterberg, memory also plays a key role in this process of 'thoughtfulness'. It 'breaks into present events by bringing up pictures of the past: the photoplay is doing this by its frequent cutbacks' (1999: 402), thus foregrounding the experience of temporality in the human mind, and the telling of cinematic narrative as a form of art. We shall encounter the disconcerting effect of explicitly toying with memory as a form and as a theme in Chapter 8. Such films navigate conventions of narrative through a leitmotif of memory and emotional investiture. This is how imagination subsequently comes to dominate the filmmaking process for Münsterberg's approach. He states (1999: 405) that:

> The pictorial reflection of the world is not bound by the rigid mech-anism of time. Our mind is here and there, our mind turns to the present and then to the past: the photoplay can equal in its freedom from the bondage of the material world.

It should be mentioned that following this argument, it is through the imagination that we anticipate the future or negate reality through fantasy and representations of the fantastic. Thus, from this very early position in film theory, escapism and speculation as motivational concepts form a principal focus for both criticism and spectatorship. However, as outlined in Chapter 1 and addressed by the epigraphs to this chapter, the lines drawn between imagination and the material, embodied world are sometimes arbitrary, and work from the common presupposition that such divisions are concrete. Clearly, for example, when Fuery writes about the gaze, he is addressing an embodied gaze, one ensconced within social praxis. For Hillman and his followers also, there is a sense of working through images as material phenomena – a break from picture-thinking and preconception, towards an embodied apprehension of the image by human subjects as social beings. This is where Münsterberg's last and most important opera-tion becomes useful as it relates intimately with the other 'forms of the inner world': emotion, 'which fills the spectator's mind [and] can mould the scenes in the photoplay until they appear the embodiment of our feelings' (1999: 402). A very famous and often discussed example of this is the shower scene in Hitchcock's *Psycho* (1960): Although we never actually *see* Marion Crane (Janet Leigh)'s naked body, we *think* that we do through a series of ingenious cuts and imaginative camera positioning. The idea of nakedness tends to add to the shock value of the scene as nakedness often implies vulnerability, and the representation of the quotidian act of cleansing oneself disarms the spectator prior to the inevitable horror that follows. Thus, the anticipation of horror is heightened through imagination on the part of filmmaker (Hitchcock was renowned for the unprecedented editorial control he exerted over his material) and spectator (emotional investment in the main character and our own responses to the material) alike.

Although discussing cinema as a formative artistic medium, Münsterberg's approach immediately adds to the problematic of regarding the formalism/realism debate as inherently schismatic. He addresses questions of reproductive capabilities and yet acknowledges, as a matter of principle, the tendency of the form to produce something other than real life through that reproduction. In many ways, the formalist Rudolph Arnheim (cited in Perkins, 1991: 14) reproduces these sentiments:

> It is not enough to know that one is looking at a reproduction. The interplay of object and depictive medium must be patent in the finished work. The idiosyncrasies of the medium make themselves most felt in the greatest works of art.

The 'fact' of the reproductive capacity of film is considered a given, but the focus on medium-specificity and on the nature of the definition of art is telling here. Arnheim chooses to define art as an evaluative category, structured according to criteria borrowed from art criticism.

Despite this problematic evaluative categorization of art, both Arnheim and Münsterberg should be considered early pioneers of the cognitive approach to film. Their contributions have had far-reaching consequences for film theory, not only in the field of film as a considered art form but also in the field of film psychology. In fact, in recent years a number of theorists have developed cognitive approaches to film along broadly the same lines as Münsterberg. Torben Grodal, for example, showed that 'Feelings and emotions are motivational forces, but they also represent a set of "experience tones" characterizing different holistic body-mind configurations in our experience of everyday life and of visual fiction' (1997: 2). By 'holistic', Grodal is referring to the body, mind and world as an interacting whole. By 'visual fiction', he is alluding to cinema as a simulation of mind–body states, and therefore reveals much in common with Münsterberg's framework of mental operations and inner forms. Where he develops the approach, however, is in the recognition of the need to address realism and formalism as aspects of the same simulational whole. Tredell (2002: 210) explains that, for Grodal:

> Evolutionary development has produced frameworks in the human mind that are the result of human attempts to know the world but also affect the way in which the world is understood . . . Grodal proposes a middle way between realism, which assumes that fiction is an unproblematic representation of (possible) reality, and formalism, which focuses on a visual fiction, or any other text, as an organisation of formal features with no necessary reference to the real world.

As we have seen in the previous chapter, the schismatic view of formalism/realism in film is a false binary system that is overcome through the acknowledgement that one term is articulated in the other, in both production and spectatorship, largely through the interstices of presentation and representation. We do not necessarily need recourse to evolutionary psychology to understand this. However, Grodal's approach does emphasize the dialectic inherent in the formalist/realist orthodoxy: knowledge of the world as shown through reproductive and impressionistic aesthetics. Both are attempts to situate ourselves within the world, and to articulate what is often described as 'the human condition'. More simply, this may be thought of as 'being-in-the-world'. 'Being-in-the-world' is a concept that will be addressed in detail in subsequent chapters, as a fundamentally intersubjective and mediated state of existence, affectively responding to the here and now, while also negotiating the emotional impact of historical and social being. For now, it is useful to turn once again to Eagleton (1990: 18) in his discussion of the relationship between phenomena and aesthetics:

> The body, even before it has come to think, is always a sensibly experiencing organism positioned in its world in a way quite distinct from the placing of an object in a box. Scientific knowledge of an objective reality is always already grounded in this intuitive pregivenness of things to the vulnerably perceptive body, in the primordial physicality of our being-in-the-world.

Grodal, however, does not quite articulate this in terms of a 'creaturely existence' as does Eagleton: His evolutionary frameworks are 'hardwired' and inalterable, unless through a fundamental evolutionary shift in the species. These are distinguished from specific cultural frameworks that alter according to locality, production and reading contexts, and other sociocultural factors.

There are a number of obvious ways in which Grodal's approach has special resonance for students of Jung. The most fundamental of these is worth mentioning here, as it relates to Jungian notions of myth and narrative symbolism. Jung's notion of natural and cultural symbolism denotes a crucial differentiation between the realm of the natural, which should be regarded as an eternally evolving source of images, wholly deriving from embedded forms of the collective unconscious, and that of culture. Jung (1964: 83) states that:

> When the medical psychologist takes an interest in symbols, he is primarily concerned with 'natural' symbols, as distinct from 'cultural' symbols. The former are derived from the unconscious contents of the psyche, and they therefore represent an enormous number of variations on the essential archetypal images . . . The cultural symbols on the other hand, are those that have been used to express 'eternal truths,' and that are still used in many religions.

Culture in this framework tends to be thought of in Jungian psychology as localized, shifting and superficial – it is historically specific. However, the pattern within which these cultural shifts occur may also be regarded as concomitant to shifts within late capital and global in character.[2] We are, after all, living in a world where knowledge has been conceptually super-seded by information, and that information is now a global commodity, being exchanged at unprecedented speeds and levels – obviously a very different world to that envisaged by Jung. These cultural shifts, in the most general sense, therefore tend to be naturalized and internalized through very similar hegemonic processes of consensus and consent discussed briefly in Chapter 2, and tend to (if not negate, then) render symbolic signifying systems redundant in the everyday sense. As Hauke's approach testifies, the reversibility of semiosis and symbolism in postmodernism emphasizes the ambivalence of signification in both positive and negative ways (2000: 191–194). Traces of this reversibility may be read in Fredericksen's seminal Jungian film criticism from the late 1970s.

An excellent example of how this works at the institutional level in film is the recent vehicle for Hollywood star Will Smith, *The Pursuit of Happyness* (Muccino, US, 2006). Here I refer in particular to the trailer for this film, as it condenses precisely the points that I make in relation to the global character of cultural shifts, and the specific address of the spectator-as-subject, into a two-minute trailer. The trailer phenomenon also expresses the brevity of information exchange that can occur in late capital, derived in part from its stringent narrative economy and the way the trailer-of-the-film's narrative is a microcosm of the feature film's narrative. It opens with a montage of an African-American man (Will Smith) playing basketball with his son (played by Smith's real-life son, Jaden). A typically gritty voiceover announces: 'Chris Gardner was doing his best for his family, but his best . . . wasn't enough.' We see Gardner lose his job and his apartment, declaring that he is down to his last $21. He sees a man park his Ferrari on Wall Street and asks him what he did to get the car. The man replies that he is a stockbroker. We hear Smith's voice narrate in character: 'This was my last chance to amount to anything . . . There was no salary, but there was a way to another place.' A sequence follows of Gardner being put through training, and gaining an internship in a stockbroker firm. As well as showing assorted trials and tribulations to be faced, this sequence is accompanied by a non-diegetic song, with various uplifting sentiments such as 'Ooh, child, things are gonna get easier' in the lyrics. It also features a clip from the movie with a board director (a kind of 'wise old man' archetypal caricature) asking Gardner 'You're not gonna give up on us yet, are ya?' The key to the trailer comes about two-thirds through, when Gardner is travelling in a car with a stockbroker suit who is failing to complete a Rubik's cube puzzle. There is a diegetic exchange:

Suit: This thing's impossible.
Gardner: I can do it.
Suit: No you can't. No one can.

Gardner appears to complete the puzzle in three seconds proving, in the common parlance, that he is 'an Ameri*can*, not an Ameri*can't*'. From here the trailer goes into narrative closure overload, as we see Gardner lecture his son in the ways of the world: 'you got a dream, you gotta protect it . . . You want something, you go get it. Period.' Then the end caption reads: 'Inspired by a true story.'

How often have we seen this kind of narrative in popular film? Here we see a number of common themes and motifs that suggest over-determined character types, acting within a variant of the quest narrative. I could go on in this vein, but this reading would constitute a very superficial interpretation. An obvious criticism of this kind of reading would be, 'so what?' So what if it is a quest narrative? It is not enough simply to be content with the reading of such a film as a manifestation of the eternal quest narrative, nor is it adequate to say, for example, that Gardner's son is the eternal youth archetype, guiding Gardner in his choices and motivations. These elements regarded in a classical Jungian framework as archetypal elements and therefore collective in nature are also, in this example, key signifiers of the hegemonic desire for individual success and of fatherhood as a specifically economic productive force, in addition to being reproductive in a biological sense. Furthermore, it also signifies the shifting masculinities common in contemporary representations of African-American men in US cinema. It foregrounds politics of race and gender inherent in a cinema that seems to find a recurrent motif in the essentializing of type. This is a very complex issue, drawing as it does from a number of discourses on race, class, gender and sexuality within an aesthetic framework of positive/ negative binaries.

I shall return to this issue of identity representation and formation in subsequent chapters, but for now it will suffice that some Jungian film scholars, such as David Driver (2006) and Christopher Hauke (2000: 191– 193) in particular, have noted the importance of masculinity in popular film. Men's day-to-day choices and motives are often responses to the ravages of modernity on the importance of masculinity for men in everyday life. For Hauke in particular, this reflects the anxiety over potency and the emasculating tendencies of modernity on the male psyche.

In this example, the mythology of meritocratic pursuit serves as a recurrent theme to engage normative responses to the 'crisis' in masculinity by universalizing the notion through repeated reference to Thomas Jefferson's article in the US Constitution (on the inalienable right to pursue happiness). That in itself is problematic if, according to post-structural cultural studies in general, masculinity is a construction as much subordinate to patriarchy as femininity. It highlights the fixivity that can occur through popular representations of something as innocuous and mundane as a tale about father and son, and the processes of meaning-making that are enabled through such representation. The natural and collective function of such archetypal material is either obscured to the point of meaninglessness or, more importantly, is not a manifestation of the natural at all. It is plausible, therefore, to argue that narratives such as this employ geopolitical aesthetic and narrative patterns through specific mythologies aligned with culturally dominant interests. At the same time, the internalization of such interests breeds a familiarity with the specific kinds of representation that have traditionally been used to tell these 'quest' stories, which enable certain story-telling trends and demobilize others.

Returning to Grodal's cognitive model, his approach in relation to 'hardwired' evolutionary frameworks is problematic in that his use of metaphor is confused. If, for example, Gardner's story is one of universal resonance (father's irrepressible bond with son) but is not archetypal in the classical Jungian sense, it may be alternatively read as metaphor for wider concerns with production anxiety in late capital, as well as concomitant ambiguities in masculinity and race representation. Metaphor works on a representational level, then, and walks the profoundly ambiguous line between the natural and the cultural. For Grodal, however, the corresponding function of metaphor occurs at the cognitive level too. His notion of 'formatting' emphasizes the ease with which the mind may be re-formatted, or rewired. However, when talking of 'innate', hardwired frameworks, he is alluding to a model that has its roots in the nineteenth-century medical models of instinct employed in psychology by (among others) Freud and early Jung. As Tredell (2002: 210) points out:

These ambiguities and shifts in Grodal's use of metaphor raise the question of whether his technical terms function to promote scientific precision or to endow his argument with an aura of quasi-scientific authority.

These accusations may be familiar to many readers who are aware of the criticisms of Jung's own theoretical ambiguities. Jung's somewhat fanciful journeys into Eastern mysticism or Christian theology sometimes lose the interest of clinicians, even though often underpinned by quasi-scientific frames of reference or clinical observation. Whether Jung did this deliberately to give his theories the legitimacy afforded by science or to give the science a more human face is never entirely clear. However, a similar legitimizing process is fairly common in film scholarship. Grodal attempts to legitimize his theoretical frame of reference by using both contemporary terms such as 'formatting' (computer science and business studies) and older notions such as 'innate' (evolutionary psychology, biology and medicine). Whatever the reason, it is an observation of which the Jungian film analyst needs to be aware.

Grodal's approach anticipates the inherent relationship between cinema's capacity for simulation and the human mental capacity to operate within the same perceptive and cognitive frameworks. He states (1997: 278–279) that:

> Narrative simulations of different types and dimensions of reality use the same cognitive and affective mechanisms that we use in our real-life experiences and in our mental representations of them. Higher mental life relies on the ability to execute hypothetical, fictitious imaginations.

Again, there is clear resonance here with Münsterberg's 'inner forms', and film's capacity to mimic these through its various mechanisms and aesthetics. Grodal attempts to overcome the problem of simulation by employing a very useful notion in connection with the attitude that the spectator may (and often does) take in relation to what is on screen and how s/he is addressed. The attitude towards what we are seeing and how we draw meaning from it is determined, in part, by what Grodal terms 'reality-status'. This is an evaluation that enables us to make distinctions as to whether apparent phenomena are reality, fantasy, fiction, dream and so on. This reality-status of apparent phenomena presented to the sensory faculties is filtered through prior knowledge, (reasonable) understanding and emotion, and the evaluations that result 'have cognitive as well as affective representations in consciousness' (Grodal, 1997: 284). If applied to cinema, certain procedures for ascertaining the reality-status of phenomena based on these filters are rendered ambiguous through a variety of techniques peculiar to cinema, including for example, computer-generated special effects. This is one of the reasons why discussion of film returns consistently, to the notion of simulation as well as reality, and is of central importance to Grodal. It is a contributing factor to the overall aesthetic of the film in question, in that the reality-status of the film always carries with it an ambiguity or uncertainty.

It is important to bear in mind, however, that what is inferred in Grodal's model of audience–text is not a direct stimulus–response relation, nor is it a simple 'media effects' model of audience–text relationships. Various psychosomatic dimensions in which mind and body work together (such as perception, cognition, memory and emotion) are activated by the act of watching film. These psychosomatic dimensions are supplemented by what Grodal calls 'enaction': acting in response to situations and to stimuli. Noël Carroll has said of cognitive response to the diegetic reactions of characters under threat within the horror film, for example, that: 'The emotions of the audience are supposed to mirror those of the positive human characters in certain, but not all respects' (Cited in Hills, 2005: 15).

There are a number of problems with this 'identification' model, such as whether one may extend this to all genres and not just the specifics of horror as well as the question of non-representational modes of film. However, there is a sense that once again film is being considered as a kind of psychomimetic form. For Grodal, this 'mirroring' effect is metaphorical, in the sense that the characters on screen are virtual stand-ins for our reactions to the events portrayed. Of course, we do not usually act in a way suggested by the on-screen participants in the real world. It is more likely that we imagine such acts and to an extent our bodies prepare for them through physiological effects. In an early scene in *Casino Royale* (Campbell, US/UK/Int., 2006), for example, James Bond chases a villain hundreds of feet above ground level. The chase is exaggerated through long aerial shots of the two figures clambering along an extended crane arm. Given the impression of height as well as the tense experience of a deadly situation, sensations of excitement, exhilaration, even vertigo are potentially elicited. This is not a universal response, of course, but is a potential one that is channelled into a number of possibilities through various cultural cues, such as expected/unexpected camera movement and positioning, as well as familiarity with character and convention. These are not necessarily the most important elements for Grodal here, who tends to emphasize the associative in relation to a mental process: One phenomenon (e.g. vertigo) is linked to another by visual likeness (a rising aerial shot). However, it is the context of likeness in relation to the normative alignment with cultural interstices that may impact upon specific enaction to a much greater extent than Grodal seems willing to allow. In other words, the conventional and familiar, as well as their opposites (the innovative and unexpected) in relation to viewing habits and context, genre, prior knowledge of the text are all likely to have more of an impact upon enaction than straightforward correspondence between text and cognition. This is relevant for a number of critiques of theories that tend to anthropomorphize the film and the spectator's reaction towards it. But these critiques tend to ignore such institutional conventions, in favour of formal ones. For example, Daniel Frampton (2006: 220) suggests in his book *Filmosophy* that:

> It should be obvious that humans cannot zoom out or in like a camera, and the human experience of vertigo does not exactly 'look' like it looks in cinema. But strangely that does not stop many writers from asserting that film replicates human perception.

Frampton is correct in this, but he makes a similar mistake to Grodal here, from the other end of the spectrum. The emphasis on likeness is, for Frampton, a formal question rather than an institutional or cognitive one, and this is a line of critique to which we shall return. What is interesting in Grodal, however, is that even though he does not specifically emphasize the institutional impact, the 'apparatus', his model allows for just such inter-play of convention and enaction through the notion of subjective experience. For example, the convention of subjective camera positioning (camera assuming point of view of a character) requires a restriction on choices as to where the camera may be placed to render the point of view. This is typically a conventional rendering of the subjective in cinematic terms that, in 'proximity' to the on-screen experience, elicits a corresponding affective response off-screen. I will address such identification processes in detail in subsequent chapters.

While subjectivity is of obvious and crucial importance to psycho-analysis, it is a theme that has featured consistently in this chapter so far in relation to cognitivist approaches, the cinema's simulational capacity, and representational aspects of film. It is worth bearing in mind here that many cognitivist theories and, in particular, Carroll's approach are written in direct response to the use of the psychoanalytic paradigm in film analysis: a paradigm that, as we shall see, was introduced to develop a theory of cine-subjectivity. The impact of psychoanalysis in film studies should not be underestimated. During the 1970s it endured as the dominant paradigm, a dominion lasting well into the 1980s, especially in its post-Lacanian form, and largely through its use as a critical tool in feminist thought. It is also crucial not to underestimate how this necessarily con-ditioned responses to what has been described as its 'grand theorizing' tendencies. Although for Bordwell and Carroll alike psychoanalysis in film studies was not the only such totalizing 'grand theory' to be guilty of formulating universal explanations for global cinematic phenomena, its particular legacy for film theory and the discussion of film's formal aspects is inescapable.

Towards a political notion of subject formation

In a recent intervention in the political journal *Historical Materialism*, Sean Homer (2005) recounts the necessity that arose in post-1968 cultural theory to theorize the subject within cinema, for the political project of the British film journal *Screen*. He outlines a number of problems that occurred with 'Screen theory' and the debates through which many theorists of the early-to-mid-1970s collectively developed a theory of the cinematic apparatus. Chief among these problems was the tendency to be overly abstract, and many of the key theorists placed too much emphasis on the productivity of the text. Eventually, this would lead to criticisms of ahistoricity, as well as accusations of over-reliance on the under-theorized psychoanalytic concepts such as scopophilia and fetishism. In turn, this over-reliance led to insubstantial accounts of sexual difference on which these concepts are at least partly founded, although it should be noted that most of these criticisms have been widely countered in the intervening period (see Homer, 2005: 90–94). As for the recourse to psychoanalytic models of subject formation, Homer (2005: 90) states that:

> Psychoanalysis . . . was introduced into film studies to provide an account of 'visual pleasure' and how spectators identify with the image that was seen to be lacking from previous Marxist and materialist film theory. It was thus part of a wider theoretical framework through which a materialist theory of film could account for both the ideological positioning of cinematic subjects and their affective investment in the image.

For film theory, it seemed that semiotics and psychoanalysis would remedy perceived deficiencies in Marxist accounts of subjectivity by supplying it with a theory of language and of the construction of the subject through Althusser's use of Lacan. For historical materialists following the path of structuralism, a thorough account of film's ideological operation required knowledge of both its status as a signifying system and its affective dimension for the spectator-as-subject. The ideas of Swiss linguist Ferdinand de Saussure provided a material grounding for signification and Lacan provided a linguistic grounding for the subject. In bringing the two together in an Althusserian framework, it was hoped that the cine-subject could be accounted for as a relatively autonomous, historical viewing subject. Therefore, during the course of the mid-1970s, 'Screen theory' developed a notion of the cinematic apparatus that attempted to account for two dialectically related and simultaneous registers of experience:

1   the psychic apparatus, in which subjects are constituted as desiring subjects

2   the institutional apparatus, in which the broader elements of industrial and ideological production find specific cultural purchase as both industrial and psychological organization.

As became apparent, the maintenance of the relationship between the two distinct registers of experience, as well as at the same time maintaining their separation, became necessary to the success of the theoretical cine-subject. This maintenance was, however, not without its problems: In fact, until fairly recently in the work of Homer and Heath (1999), as well as Mulvey (1996) among others, this was regarded by many as a lost cause after the 1970s.

On tentatively formulating the bridge between the production of ideology and the formation of the subject, Lapsley and Westlake (1988: 49) note of the materialist film theorists that:

> There was an attempt to relate the materiality of ideology to that of signification, where ideology was understood not as a system of ideas but as a practice of representation producing 'the subject as the place where a specific meaning is realised'.
>
> (citation from Coward and Ellis, 1975)

In his history of cinema and psychoanalysis, Stephen Heath recounts the *Screen* journal's project thus: '*Screen*'s point was an appropriation of psychoanalysis politically, insofar as it could be made conjuncturally useful, and notably as regards identifying and describing mechanisms of subject inscription for ideology' (1999: 33–34). This was an important development of the approach to ideology espoused in the work of, for example, *Cahiers du cinema*, including that of Camolli and Narboni, whose work, as we have seen, combined a political critique of authorship with the cultural radicalism of Spring 1968. Hence, following in the same vein, in perhaps the most influential essay in the history of film theory, 'Visual Pleasure and Narrative Cinema', Laura Mulvey in 1973 writes that:

> It is helpful to understand what the cinema has been, how its magic has worked in the past, while attempting a theory and a practice which will challenge this cinema of the past. Psychoanalytic theory is thus appropriate here as a political weapon, demonstrating the way the unconscious of patriarchal society has structured film form.
>
> (Mulvey, 1999: 833)

During the early 1970s then, psychoanalysis appeared as a critical tool and a political weapon – as an approach that could be jerry-rigged to establish a materialist notion of subject formation. With this weapon in hand, the political project of the writers in *Screen* attended to the notion of cine-subjectivity, at first with confidence. Ultimately, this would lead to a shift of emphasis from text-based analysis to one based on reception by the end of the 1970s. However, this shift occurred over a period of evolution in two phases that overlapped considerably, concerned as they were with the key idea of subjectivity, and in particular the autonomy of the subject. These two phases were, broadly speaking: Althusserian (primarily engaging Althusser's notion of interpellation) and Lacanian (primarily engaging what Heath termed Lacan's 'dialectic of the subject' (1975/1976: 50)).

These two approaches were interlocked in the question of how subjectivity is both formed and experienced through the act of spectatorship, and came to dominate debates in film theory, particularly in the pages of *Screen*. Most notably, the work of Heath, Colin McCabe and Paul Willemen sought to work through the ideological implications of spectatorship, while at the same time analysing these effects through a psychology of the cine-subject. In order to engage fully with the notion of cine-subjectivity and to note its origins, it may be useful to retrace some of the more important accounts of subject formation in psychoanalysis. The following (brief) account notes the Freudian and Lacanian traditions – of particular importance to *Screen*'s theorists – and the notion of construction in cultural theory more generally. Many readers will already be familiar with these accounts, but I include them here as themes often taught within the film studies discipline for those who are not acquainted.

Subjectivity is essentially a humanist notion stretching back to Descartes, of individuality as a centre of control from which meaning emanates. Subjectivity in modernity de-centres this individuality by engaging a sense of constructed identity – the individual as effect rather than cause, constituted within discourses of social being. Subjectivity is thus determined and regulated by forces of power within the social formation, while at the same time granted the ability of transformation and hence the ability to undermine the very forces that help constitute it. It is therefore granted a status of agency or autonomy relative to the social formation. Freud in *Beyond the Pleasure Principle* noted that the asociality and anarchy of instinctual drives in infancy give way to drives that adhere to social norms, thus helping the individual to lead a coherent social life in maturity. This coherence is however fundamentally unstable, because the mechanism involved in the repression of instinct is semi-permeable. This is problematic for subject formation, because the repression of material moving from being to meaning is founded on a principle of loss, and the reappearance of such repressed material in consciousness can be traumatic, contravening as it does the very framework keeping it repressed. We are thus, according to Freud, always negotiating subjective experience through the fantasy of recuperating such loss to allay alienation and neuroses. He famously recounts this process in his description of the 'fort/da' game.

The staging of the disappearance and return of objects in this game is a replaying of the crucial event when the infant finally allows the mother to go away without complaining. To overcome the displeasure of mother being out of his control, the infant replays disappearance as a game of mastery. In making the object reappear, he is taking an active role in the activity of disappearance so that the fantasy of mastery over loss is materialized. The child is able to repeat the unpleasant experience in play because a 'yield of pleasure' may be found in the repetition. The source of that yield is directly related to the passage from passivity to activity. In the crucial move from Freud to Lacan, Elizabeth Wright says that for the critics under the influence of structuralism: 'A drive is not just pleasure-seeking, but is caught up in the signifying system, characterized by the subject's first entry into that system' (1998: 107). Signification is thus the system through which subject formation occurs for Lacanians, and is thus of obvious use to those film theorists, such as Heath and Metz, who regarded cinema itself as a signifying system. Lacan termed this crucial time of infancy, the first stirrings of the ego, and of naming 'I' 'the mirror stage'.

For Lacan, up to around the age of six months, the infant's world is preoccupied by the Real – the infant experiences as an amorphous, continuative mass, unable to distinguish between self and other. From about six to 18 months, this experience of being changes, as the infant moves into what Lacan terms the Imaginary. A distinction between self and other is introduced: As the infant looks in the mirror, he is able to differentiate between the 'I' that looks and the 'I' that is seen. However, this distinction is characterized by a (mis)recognition in that the other 'I' appears to have a unity and control of self that the looking 'I' lacks. This appearance is imaginary and yet the infant identifies with that which it does not have. This first differentiation is thus defined by lack. The 'Ideal-I' appears as a gestalt, a constituent, pregnant imago: more firmly in control of motor capacity, at once hauntingly unfamiliar and yet more complete. To overcome this sense of alienation, the infant must enter into the Symbolic – acquiring a self that is both produced in language and subjected to pre-existing social laws. The acquisition of language is crucial to the Lacanian framework as it enables the infant to articulate 'I' within discourse, and to assume a position that provisionally constructs meaning. In addition to this, the acquisition of language also signals the development of the unconscious in the infant, and the repression mechanisms necessary to overcoming the potentially alienating lack experienced in the mirror stage. However, as Easthope and McGowan (2004: 74) comment,

> Lacan argues that the position of the 'I' within language does not simply represent the presence of a subject that pre-exists it, but produces the concept of the subject through processes of differentiation between the 'I' and 'not I' of discourse.

Therefore, the subject is no longer fixed but is located in a fluctuating exchange of presence and absence. One of the difficulties with this is that it presupposes a pre-existing subject, a chief concern for detractors of the Althusser/Lacan model. In addition to this – a somewhat paradoxical situation, having much in common with Althusser's relative autonomy – this fluctuating exchange is also characterized by the identification mechanism in the mirror stage described above. It is an identification that is, in the Lacanian framework, subjected to *lack*, but is experienced within the phantasy of completeness. Lacan refers to 'the transformation that takes place in the subject when he assumes an image – whose predestination to this phase-effect is sufficiently indicated by the use, in analytic theory, of the ancient term *imago*' (2004: 82). Lacan's use of the Jungian term 'imago' is significant here, and I refer the reader to my comments on the imago in Chapter 5.

I use the term 'Image' to focus on the *embodied* relation between seer and seen, seer-as-seen, and seen-as-seer: a move towards an account of emotional and affective resonance in the potentiality of spectatorship. This focus is present even in classical Jungian psychology, where Jung illustrates 'the way in which archetypes appear in practical experience: They are, at the same time, both images and emotions. One can speak of an archetype when these two aspects are simultaneous. When there is merely the image, then there is simply a word-picture of little consequence' (Jung, 1964: 87). The emphasis upon the assumption of image in Lacan is significant, as it reinforces the appropriation of the imaginal in and for embodied experience – seeing and being seen is therefore to be regarded as the crucial element within this relationship of (mis)recognition. The importance of this will become immediate in Chapter 5, which redresses the problem of the cinematic gaze and the embodied look in audience–text relations. In the meantime, I shall note the dramatic nature of (mis)recognition that occurs, and the lack that results from the Lacanian identity – fundamental to the theorization of the cine-subject:

> I am led . . . to regard the function of the mirror-stage as a particular case of the function of the *imago*, which is to establish a relation between the organism and its reality – or, as they say, between the *Innenwelt* and the *Umwelt*.
>
> (Lacan, 2004: 83)

Lacan goes on to suggest of inner and outer worlds that 'to break out of the circle of the *Innenwelt* into the *Umwelt* generates the inexhaustible quadrature of the ego's verifications' (2004: 83). What is interesting about this particular account is that Lacan uses both the term 'circle' and the term 'quadrature'. It suggests that the image of internal selfhood (within and from which the ego and the sense of subjectivity are formed) is characterized by circularity – an *internally* verifying ego-identity which acts as a self-sufficient structuring presence. It is also a four-fold structure of the archetype of Selfhood, which is almost fully unconscious in the Jungian topography, standing as it does for the totality of wholeness, a Self/God image. Being almost fully unconscious because it encompasses the inexpressible totality of the psyche, however, this image is consistently haunting in its absence. Therefore, there is a significant precedent to Lacan's fluctuating exchange of presence and absence in the Jungian topography, in terms of subject formation. Both figurations (circular and quadrangular) were offered by Jung, as well as classical Jungians such as Marie-Louise Von Franz and Aniela Jaffé, and featured in their lengthy discussions on the Self in *Man and His Symbols*. For example, Jaffé states that 'Von Franz has explained the circle (or sphere) as a symbol of the Self. It expresses the totality of the psyche in all its aspects, including the relationship between man and the whole of nature' (1964: 266). Von Franz herself said of the mandala motif: 'Usually quadrangular forms symbolize conscious realization of inner wholeness; the wholeness itself is most often represented in circular forms' (1964: 232).

The modernist theme of the perception of ourselves as coherent individuals is thus a projection of selfhood that Jung and his immediate followers saw as fundamentally superficial and flawed. The poverty inherent in the misrecognition of the whole adult self is at the centre of classical analytical theory's project to engage in the process of individuation, ultimately moving towards a realization of coherence and a healing of the Self as an individuated (and potentially, fully autonomous) subject. Therefore, in the psychoanalytic and analytic theory traditions, there is an equally compelling emphasis on subject formation, crucial to productive functioning of such subjectivity within the social formation. This centres on subjective meaning-making as a normal and habitual activity – pleasurable in its scope, and crucially, of immediate consequence to the materialist notion of cine-subjectivity.

Cine-subjectivity and the problem of relative autonomy

Armed with the Freudian and, in particular, Lacanian accounts of subject formation, two claims developed as the bases for materialist analysis in 'Screen theory'. Mark Jancovich (1995) identifies these as follows.

1   Ideology is less a matter of particular opinions than of the ways in which people perceive themselves to be coherent individuals.
2   Existing cinema is somehow implicated in the maintenance of ideology and needs to be countered.

The first claim corrected the 'vulgar Marxist' assumption of ideological repression, in favour of Marx's original formulation of false consciousness, less interested as it was in the politics of representation than in the ideological ramifications of structuring systems within the capitalist mode of production. The theoretical stress on signification rather than representation (although in practice, many key *Screen* thinkers concentrated on the latter) meant that often widely different films, in an ideological sense, fitted into the same broad categories. This resulted in a homogenization of analyses, and led in turn to accusations of (in Bordwell's terminology) 'grand theorizing'.

The second claim, according to Jancovich, too often led to the consignment of popular film to the ideological and the conservative. For a short period, however, the appropriation of Saussurean linguistics and structuralist analysis proved a very productive methodology: 'Screen theory drew on Saussurean or structural linguistics to argue that language is a system of structures, rules and codes which does not just pre-exist individuals, but actually constitutes them' (Jancovich, 1995: 126). For Saussureans, it is language that gives the definition to the experience of the world that gives objects we encounter, including cultural and communicative objects, meaning. Language, in this framework, not only orders the way that we think, but also crucially produces identities, and hence subjectivity. That is, in Saussurean linguistics, language constitutes the subject. It contributes to one's identity, and to the sense of autonomy of the individual in relation to the outside world, and to external objects. It also contributes to the sense of intersubjectivity – the interaction between autonomous subjects in the material world.

One of the key features of this approach as taken up in film theory was that, just as signs are arbitrarily assigned cultural meaning (they do not simply stand-in for pre-existing objects), so cinema does not simply stand-in for pre-existing reality. It is not simply a simulation machine, and therefore the linguistic approach was an important intervention in the critique of the realist tradition. Institutionally, cinema employs a number of techniques for presenting reality, but these techniques are ordered after expressive ways of encountering the world (classic narrative, for example). These techniques become institutionalized after a time, to the point of becoming conventional, and therefore invisible and naturalized. This is, fundamentally, an Althusserian position, and a crucial frame of reference for a number of related approaches by key thinkers writing in *Screen* during the early 1970s.

The Althusserian approach formed the principal theoretical framework to address what Treddell describes as the approach to meaning as an 'oppressive relation' between audience and text. This comes as no surprise, when we consider the Marxist credentials of Althusser and his followers. For him, the institution of cinema constitutes individuals as subjects: the spectator-subject is, quite literally, addressed by the text, and assigned an identity based on this mode of address, which Althusser called 'interpella-tion'. In accepting the identity assigned, the spectator is fixed in a rela-tionship within the cinematic apparatus, which involves misrecognition: The ideological perspective imposed on the spectator makes the text look like a window on the world, or like reality. Thus, in this model, the spec-tator within the cinematic apparatus is locked into an imaginary relation-ship to the real, and to the conditions of his/her social being. As a structure pre-existing the (viewing) subject, in the Althusserian formulation, the text interpellates the spectator, constituting the spectator as a subject. In short, interpellation is nothing less than the conference of social identity.

So, for Althusserians, the cine-subject is a function of cinema as a signi-fying system and, more broadly speaking, is constituted by language itself, but cine-subjectivity (as with all subjectivity) is most often felt as coherently autonomous. When one is addressed as 'you', one is hailed as the object of a sentence. The individual takes up the position defined for him/her within the social formation, defined by the social structure itself. This is not an inherent or natural definition but, as with all linguistic signs, is arbitrary. The illusory/imaginary nature of the way in which subjects take up these positions, or are interpellated in this way, owes a debt to Lacan and his formation of the subject. Just as the infant's identification with self is based on misrecognition of another 'I', so the individual's acceptance of position is based on misrecognition of the social formation as a natural order, and of their position as being natural to themselves. Hence the subjective sen-sation of autonomy framed within a relativity that addresses the individual in a certain position. This is not only the case in Lacanian/Althusserian subject formation but may be traced back to Freud, and Marx, according to Homer. By re-appropriating the concept of fetishism, Homer establishes a link between the libidinal economy of the sexualized fetish in Freud and the actual economy of the commodity fetish in Marx. This is useful, as it helps one to understand further the dialectical relation and differential of the two paradigms within the central concept of subjectivity. Homer (2005: 110) states that:

> Sexual and commodity fetishism delineate structures that are constitu-tive of subjectivity, the sexed subject of the unconscious and the subject of praxis for Marxism. These are not the same subject but neither are they so radically separate that there is no mediation between them.

However, the adequacy of the subject as bearer of position needed to be addressed, as well as its relation to notions of *agency*. Marxist philosopher Etienne Balibar (1995) has suggested that the interface between ideology as a theory of the constitution of state power and fetishism as a mechanism of subjection articulates this subjective positioning. In *Capital*, Marx suggests that commodity fetishism displaces the definite social relation between producers. What is experienced instead is a phantasmatic relation between things (producers are themselves reduced to commodities/things). What is important here is that this relation is real to those who experience it. It is, in short, a *felt* relation. So with Marx and commodity fetishism, so too with Freud and psychic reality: The phantom reality is real for the subjects who have to live it. To deal with this felt relation that is phantasmatic-yet-realistic (and not real), Althusser engages the notion of relative autonomy – a notion that was appropriated with gusto at first by Althusserian film theorists, but one that became more troublesome as the period in question progressed.

Even though Althusser states that the economic is the 'last instance' which, under capitalist relations of production, is typical, nevertheless the experience within the social formation of this determination is never quite resolved. It is an internal contradiction for Althusser, which negotiates the problem of economism, but for his detractors becomes a problem of agency. It either collapses into economic determinism or allows for a full autonomy. If it collapses into economic determinism in the last instance, it reopens the possibility of interpretation, but that this interpretation is a hypostatic reduction (towards the mode of production). It is a trap that can so easily mislead the analyst into engaging the limited options of meaning that are produced by such contained readings.

If full autonomy is granted the interpretation, then equally a number of problems occur. In fact, this is a problem that has similarities to James Hillman's archetypal school of analytical psychology. Hillman's approach holds that: 'The individual may identify any image (even the most banal) as being archetypal.' Furthermore, 'Hillman argued that the archetypal analyst must stick as close to the image as possible, helping clients to feel, experience, play with and respond to what their dreams and associations present them with' (Izod, 2006: 23). Evidently, there are some very useful consequences of this client-oriented approach, one of which would be that it frees interpretation from the classical school's reductive form of interpretative analysis. One of the prominent concerns here, equally for Hillman's approach and for the more immediate concern with representational politics, would be that it would render meaning as an endlessly floating surface of signification – an untenable position in which shared meanings ultimately become meaningless. To combat the problem of both containment and free-play in meaning production, what is needed is a theory that accounts for the emotional and affective properties of film spectatorship, as felt by the spectator/spectators. I will return to a more detailed development of this in subsequent chapters.

Our immediate concern in this regard, however, is the notion of the self-sufficiency of consciousness. Characterized by an illusion of autonomy that we may remark has a tenuous but ever-present link to Althusser's formulation of relative autonomy, this self-sufficiency (again, a perceived coherence of individuated subjectivity) establishes the relation between social praxis and the experience of it. Within this relation, there exists an illusory tendency that is played out through ideological reproduction, and that may be traced back at least as far as Marx and his preface to *A Contribution to a Critique of Political Economy*. He famously stated that: 'It is not the consciousness of men that determines their being, but, on the contrary, their social being that determines their consciousness' (2004: 37). However, this structural constitution is felt to be, in existentialist terms, self-constituting.

As Lacan himself stated: 'Existentialism must be judged by the explanations it gives of the subjective impasses that have indeed resulted from it; a freedom that is never more authentic than when it is within the walls of a prison' (2004: 85). Problems with the notion of authenticity aside, this quote is telling, as it reveals in Lacan a tendency to move beyond the strictures of structural thinking and the agency of existentialism, towards a negotiated notion of subjectivity. Not that this is entirely free of structuring impulses – the structure is the form that underpins the experience of subjectivity (the content). However, there is a kind of relative autonomy of the subject present in Lacan. The 'prison' experienced as lack is only ever imaginary anyway, and subsequent slippage from the symbolic results in direct conflict with the imaginary. This arises not from simple semantic (psychic) error, but from the imposition felt by the harassed (social) subject. Again, the problem of relative autonomy arises, this time as both a nurturing and monstrous other, beguiling in its promises, but always just outside the subject's grasp.

This was a problem considered of such importance that it overtook the historical materialist side of the Screen theory's equation (of Althusser/ Lacan) as a point of focus. However, instead of leading to an attempt at a formulation of subjectivity (as Balibar and Homer have suggested) along the lines of praxis, the fashionable abandonment of political commitment in favour of a film theory in localized (somewhat divisive) approaches had the effect of fragmenting the political in favour of the aesthetics of representation. This is not to belittle the crucial interventions made by (for example) cultural theorists, especially in the fields of feminist thought and Black cultural criticism in the late 1970s and 1980s. However, one cannot help but feel a palpable sense of irony, particularly from a post-Jungian point of view. The divisiveness of identity politics at the expense of a collective movement for social justice against ideological oppression merely reflected neo-liberalism's emphasis on individuality and private ownership ushered in by Thatcherism and Reaganomics.

The Lacanian dialectic of the subject

Subjectivity, tied as it is to language in Lacanianism, is always being constituted through language, necessarily *in process*. So, for Stephen Heath:

There is no subject outside of social formation, outside of social processes which include and defined positions of meaning . . . It is not in other words that there is first of all the construction of a subject for social/ideological functions . . . It is that the two processes are one kind of necessary simultaneity.

(cited in Lapsley and Westlake, 1988: 53)

Therefore the subject is as much constituting as constituted within an area of determinations related to language – what Heath termed the 'dialectic of the subject' (1975/76: 50). Meaning and subjectivity come together simultaneously, constituting each other in a dialectical process. Without the dialectic of the subject, political intervention becomes a redundant exercise: As previously suggested, in an either/or aspect of cine-subjectivity the subject is either inescapably determined by the text or able to create endlessly mobile meanings. The dialectic produces an 'and' possibility between the two extremes, and therefore, in formulating a theory of the dialectical subject Heath was attempting to reconcile the internal contradiction of relative autonomy. In addition to this, the dialectical subjectivity proposed sought to move beyond the problem of interpellation. Although films may adopt interpellation as a direct form of address, nevertheless interpellation itself never exceeds a signifying practice, inadequate as an account of film/spectator relations. Signification, as a 'practice' within the social formation, signals film as involving an active production of meaning: It does not merely reflect pre-existing ideology, nor does it have a politics that can only be rendered through explicit political content.

So, coming back to our example of the trailer for *The Pursuit of Happyness*, we might say that there is a specific address of the spectator in terms of the sensibility of meritocratic principles. These are explicitly rendered within the narrative economy. The political content that is explicit in the film is merely that it carries a 'message' – that reflexive, contemporary approach in cinema to social issues that does not necessarily need to push a manifesto in order to be political. Nor, indeed, does it passively reflect the prevailing ideology of meritocracy and equality through explicit representation: These are elements that are iterated, certainly, but they exist within a contained system of overdetermined possibilities. This partially resolves the critique of the second claim of 'Screen theory', namely that existing (popular) cinema is somehow implicated in the maintenance of ideology and needs to be countered, without compromising the traditional leftist position that renders, for example, Hollywood production as inherently reactionary and conservative. It also points to the period immediately following the Lacanian phase of film theory, when the emphasis shifted towards reception, and to regimes of control within discourses of agency. This approach echoes the idea that if film is the work of active productions of meaning – a process or system of operations – it therefore also involves subjectivity, the experience of which also constitutes the viewing subject: an issue that I shall take up more forcefully in terms of phenomenology in following chapters.

Although Heath was confident that Lacanian psychoanalysis could overcome any difficulties engaged in the idea of cine-subjectivity, he was critical of Lacan's occlusion of history. This was a crucial factor, and one that would feature in the intervention of British cultural studies in film scholarship, but ultimately signalled the end of Althusser's influence. The failure to account adequately for relative autonomy, in particular, proved (albeit momentarily) fatal to the historical materialist project in film theory. The difficulty of establishing a historical materialist integration of Althusserian ideology and Saussurean linguistics rested on the exchange between spectator and text: the problem being that the model employed had the effect of removing history from that exchange. In the next chapter, we shall examine the loss of the project of political effectivity in film theory, and explore ways in which we may begin to move towards its recuperation through post-Jungian analysis.

Chapter 4

The film as political

Phenomenology and the material world of the film

> A film is an act of seeing that makes itself seen, an act of hearing that makes itself heard, an act of physical and reflective movement that makes itself reflexively felt and understood. Objectively projected, visibly and audibly expressed before us, the film's activity of seeing, hearing, and moving signifies in a pervasive, primary, and embodied language that precedes and provides the grounds for the secondary significations of a more discrete, systematic, less 'wild' communication.
>
> Vivian Sobchack, *The Address of the Eye*

Sean Homer, in 'Cinema and Fetishism', states (2005: 85) that:

> The critique of *Screen* theory is now well established and, I would argue, is substantively correct. The theory led to an abstraction of the spectator/screen relationship and placed disproportionate emphasis on the productivity of the text, leaving no room for spectator agency.

Hence, we may trace the shift of emphasis from text-based analysis to one based on reception. However, this should not be taken as a cue to abandon theory altogether. Perhaps these theorists of the mid-1970s were guilty of over-abstraction, to the point where Marxist analysis of cine-subjectivity and the problem of relative autonomy became an issue that most regarded as insoluble. The shift firstly towards psychoanalysis and then towards reception and empirical research seemed to abandon the political project of those theorists originally committed to the post-1968 radical cultural movement. This movement provided avenues for the radical critique of popular culture on a much larger scale than previously afforded. But in abandoning the political project, are we not also simply abandoning the idea of the ideological implications of subjectivity (not to mention the crucial political importance of agency) because they are proving too difficult to theorize sufficiently? Perhaps it is an effect of the overburden of the task on Althusserian/Lacanian models to account for political cine-subjectivity.

The biggest problem that the anti-political theorists of the 'Wisconsin School'[1] present is that their 'middle-level' approach is highly reflective of the reactionary climate within which we find ourselves in contemporary Western society. As Andrew Samuels has stated, 'Politics of both a destructive and a creative kind show up in family patterns, gender relations, connections between wealth and (mental) health, control of information and accompanying imagery, and in religious and artistic assumptions' (2001: 5). For Samuels, then, politics is a matter of subjective forms of identification practices, reinforcing (as well as nominally challenging) existing power relations within the social formation, often accompanied by representational equivalencies. This is an important point for a post-Jungian academic to make, because, as noted previously, the political and ideological effects of artistic assumptions are too often neglected in post-Jungian film analysis.

John Izod's plea for a Jungian approach to film that incorporates ideological effects of creative practice (as well as assumptions about the *function* of art and other cultural formations) in film production and consumption partly constitutes the motivation behind this book. Indeed, it is not for purely political reasons that this issue should stay on the agenda of film analysis. Catherine Constable brilliantly summarizes the current state of play from a philosophical as well as a political perspective, noting that the philosophical poverty of certain orthodox approaches to film often has far-reaching political ramifications and vice versa. This is particularly damaging to the project of film theory to make sense of the everyday practice of viewing film. Constable's critique of the work of David Bordwell and Noël Carroll in particular in their book *Post-Theory* outlines the need to re-engage film theory as a useful tool in understanding this cultural practice. For Constable (2005: 2):

> All theories have practical implication, constructing the world and the place of people in it in different ways. The process of abstraction that is part of the theoretical should not be conceived as an obliteration of the everyday but rather as the crystallisation of specific moments that come to count as key exemplars.

It follows that, if theory has such social implications, then it is also intrinsically political. My view is in line with Constable's here, as she foregrounds the importance of the political in Carroll's approach to the study of film. She writes: 'Carroll's anti-political stance arises out of his insistence that film theory should aim to become a model of scientific neutrality' (2005: 2). It is useful to note here that the Wisconsin School's scientific method and argument is *anti-political* and not *apolitical*. This means, quite simply, that the movement to counter political bias is itself a *political move*. What is more, this move away from the problematics of Althusserian subjectivity and criticism may be classed as a move away from the political left. It is worth emphasizing that a move towards the political centre does not constitute political neutrality: It is every bit as loaded with political implications, values and bias as the theory that Carroll *et al.* are supposedly critiquing. However, it is telling that the re-emergence of the charge of a politically neutral scientific model should come along now, when supposedly such 'master narratives' have long since been stripped of the authority they formerly held in Modernity. It also has implications for the inclusion of a post-Jungian criticism, on which the burden of scientific (and therefore political) neutrality lies heavily. This burden is not only cumbersome and, for postmodern critics, troublesome, but it has also served to label analytical psychology with the accusation that it has failed to grasp the political and cultural implications of the postmodern critical turn. This is a subject that is discussed at length by Christopher Hauke, by Raya Jones, and to an extent by Andrew Samuels before them, and so I will not dwell on it here.

The reactionary political climate of contemporary Western society, and the concomitant reappearance of scientific utility and objectivity, is reflected in what Althusser named the 'problematics' of culture: It allows certain questions that may be asked, and enables certain modes of analysis at the expense of alternatives. So, questions such as 'what is this film about?', 'who is in it?', 'what does this or that film mean?' or 'what is the filmmaker trying to say here?' employ hermeneutic frameworks that are naturalized through the notions of (for example) authorship and interpretation. These questions, present in even the most banal plot summary offered in daily tabloid film reviews, proliferate at the expense of what might be more immediate political and ideological analyses in popular film culture. They also contribute to the suspicion of theory and the reaffirmation of empirical, 'hard' data within academia. This is a reflection of the political climate in general, and dictates the appropriate areas of study for academic film studies. In what follows, I shall briefly summarize these developments in film theory, as well as offering more contemporary, politicized alternatives that begin to take account of the loss of a general theory of political effectivity in cinema.

The viewing subject and political effectivity, post-Althusser

By the end of the 1970s, it became apparent that the political and theoretical ambitions of *Screen*'s post-1968 project were unachievable. The relevance of the notion of class for new identity politics and emerging cultural movements within critical discourse seemed tenuous, and to an extent such criticisms were justified. Since the spring of 1968, a wide range of academic fields had opened up to explore the cultural and political consciousness of a generation of politicized cultural practices. Black studies, feminism, subaltern studies, ecology and queer theory were some of the areas that started to emerge during the 1970s, and, although allied through interstices of concerns for cultural relevance and economic privation, socialism was often considered a failed project from these specialized areas of identity politics. This is not the place for exploring such matters, but it is worth noting Terry Eagleton's (1990: 7) address of the situation here, as he identifies many of the potentially divisive theoretical and political practices that took hold in the 1980s:

> There are now, predominantly in the USA but also in many areas of Europe, those whose undoubted radicalism on particular political issues co-exists with an insouciance and ignorance of socialist struggle typical of any middle-class suburbanite; and I do not believe that socialist men and women should acquiesce in this indifference for fear of being thought sectarian or unfashionable.

It was not always so – for example, Angela Davis wrote about her concerns for a politics that integrated the concerns of black women within specific capitalist systems of stratification, and the reflective social cultural praxis that ensued through relevant relations of power, in *Women, Race and Class* (1981). Such studies, although now sometimes seen as old-fashioned, were effective attempts to redress the question of racial and gendered identity within larger social class struggles. But such integration of identity politics within the debate on political effectivity of the cinema tended to reflect the way that the *Screen* theorists had either not taken a full account of identity formation or had (in many cases, often regrettably) ignored such issues altogether. Some cultural commentators, however, such as Manthia Diawara, made significant interventions in the discussion of cinematic spectatorship and racial identity, whereas many feminist theorists appropriated phallogocentric notions of sexual difference in, for example, Freudian psychoanalysis for subversive readings of cinema. More general criticisms against the primacy of political effectivity in cinema as a central object of analysis often took the form of a direct critique of Althusser's model of the apparatus, and may be summarized in three main ways.

1   *Epistemology (the scientificity of Althusser's approach).* The claim that it was a scientific approach above all else did not necessarily contribute veracity to its claims. In fact, such a claim merely reinforces the normative idea that theory may only ever be relevant and productive if grounded within practical issues and scientific problem-solving.
2   *Althusser's rethought base/superstructure model.* Althusser evaded the question of the hierarchy of instances – that social and cultural movements were ultimately determined by the economic relations of production – rather than answering it. This is why, for example, the critics of the Wisconsin School abandoned the idea of relative autonomy

as inherently unstable. In addition, does the political and ideological within the social formation necessarily reflect the economic, or are there other ways in which determination becomes something more akin to a mutually sustaining system? In other words, does the model ultimately collapse into a vulgar economism? In Althusser's model, either this would happen or the autonomy of politics and ideology would lead to a non-correspondence to the instance of economics, in which case, base and superstructure become mutually autonomous.

3   *Ideology.* For all his attempts to break with Marx's idea that ideology is fundamentally related to false consciousness, representation in the Althusserian model was still considered as the misrepresentation of the reality of relations of production in late capitalism. This is a crucial idea, as even a direct representation of ideological struggle in a film's content did not necessarily constitute an exposure of real relations. In other words, Althusserian approaches exposed the nature of representation as illusory (or in Lacanian terms, imaginary), as well as the complicit relation of ideology and the subject, without ever fully accounting for it.

Writing at the end of the 1970s from a neo-Marxist perspective, Paul Hirst, in *On Law and Ideology*, was even more damning of Althusser's notion of interpellation. Lapsley and Westlake (1988: 14) usefully summarize Hirst's argument as follows:

> If ideology functions by constituting individuals as subjects through interpellation, which involves misrecognition, then it can only do so by virtue of there being a pre-existing subject who can misrecognise him or herself. In short, the notion of interpellation assumes what it aims to explain.

This was to prove the most far-reaching criticism of Althusser's approach within the discourse of film theory. Althusser had attempted to eliminate the humanist notion of the autonomy of the subject as an intending, discerning individual, by suggesting that the subject's beliefs, intentions and so on are the effects – not causes – of social practices. In these effects, however, are certain attributes of agency that allow for individual instances of understanding, evaluation and interpretation. But if this is the case, then it follows that there would be wide discrepancies between Althusser's invariably successful ideological state apparatus and the subject's capacity to resist such constitutive processes, as embodied most notably in interpellation. The desires and drives frequently experienced through historical examples and within subjective reactions to filmic representation testify to this very contradiction. For as Hirst goes on to say, 'The subject is formed in the mechanism of ideology through the recognition of an imaginary

Subject which "hails" its recognisor, recognising him as a subject and thereby giving recognition by the subject the effect of subjectivity' (1979: 57). This imaginary relation, of course, presupposes both a subject who lives that relation and the imaginary, which itself presupposes recognition: 'It is both an image (object or recognition) and a spectral reality (it is only itself, it "reflects" nothing but itself)' (1979: 57). Although some addressed these aspects of internal contradiction and struggle, 'those taking up Althusser's conception of ideology within film theory were slow to appreciate these aspects of his work, a failure that resulted in fatal flaws in early attempts to theorise the relation of the spectator to film' (Lapsley and Westlake, 1988: 15). The text itself was not the univocal determination of spectator response, as this response inevitably drew from other forces within the social formation, alongside the misrecognition process informed by the effect of subjectivity.

Although this would obviously make the task of interpretation an impossible one in its prescriptive sense (following to a degree Hillman's archetypal approach, which is for our purposes a progressive move), it nevertheless reopens for the critic the potential field of mutual articulation between content and form. It also begins to negotiate the notion of embodied spectatorship in an aspect that is peripheral to (but recuperates and incorporates, in an experiential sense) the subjective spectatorship of Lacanian cine-subjectivity, and reignites the idea of political effectivity in the act of spectatorship. In other words, Althusser's elimination of humanist notions of an autonomous subject, and its relative positioning within the social formation, may be rethought. If intention is an effect of such social and cultural practices as film consumption, then it follows that the attributes of agency that allow for individual instances of understanding, evaluation and interpretation are nonetheless experienced as real, and that these instances are political in nature. They are affective responses to the fields of experience that the individual (in a biographical sense) is confronted with, and are therefore indicative of subjective viewing practices and interpretations.

Affective response and the material world of the film, post-Jung

Matt Hills, in *The Pleasures of Horror*, identifies 'the need to address audience "affects" (feelings that are not aimed at, or experienced in response to, a readily identifiable object) *as well as* audience "emotions" (broadly, feelings that have a cognitive knowledge component and a discriminable object)' (2005: 13, emphasis in original). This, of course, highlights the problem of appropriating the classical Jungian position on emotion, as his discourse often confusingly used the terms 'emotion', 'affect' and 'feeling' interchangeably. As we shall see later, this is further complicated by the way that these aspects of subjective experience are eminently interchangeable and reversible. However, for the sake of clarity, it should be noted that in the first instance, following Hills, I employ the term 'feelings' to broadly encompass aspects of both affect (subjective feeling that has no fixed object; feeling-without-an-object) and emotion (subjective feeling that intends toward something, an object; feeling-towards-an-object). I shall use the terms 'emotion' and 'affect' specifically in this respect, rather than interchangeably, as they refer to very different ways of feeling within the field of experience. That the term 'feeling' also alludes to physiological responses compounds the issue, but as this is an essay of analytical psychology and film theory, we can put aside such matters.

A useful way of articulating this aspect of emotion as feeling-towards-an object may be found in the work of Noël Carroll, who states that 'Emotions involve not only physical perturbations but beliefs and thoughts, beliefs and thoughts about the properties of objects and situations. Moreover, these beliefs (and thoughts) are not just factual . . . but also evaluative' (cited in Hills, 2005: 14). These beliefs and thoughts *about* objects, situations and their properties are crucial to any conceptualization of subjective potentiality, political cine-subjectivity, and the attitude towards the object of study: film. This is because the evaluative nature of emotion is subject to any number of historical and material effects within the specific social formation. That is, emotion and its subjective experience are fundamentally shaped by (among other things) ideology. This ideological dimension of the cognitive response known as emotion is an 'object' in itself; a political object, charged as it is with the prior knowledge acquired within epistemological systems and the power relations that exist before the text. Ideology should thus be regarded as an object towards which consciousness intends as a discriminating force of agency, but also needs to be considered as an order of reality that impacts on (and provisionally fixes) our experience and knowledge of the world (and, importantly, the world of the film). Film, like ideology, may be engaged as an object towards which the spectator's consciousness intends. However, it may equally be regarded as that which affects the spectator in rather more subtle and unexpected ways, and for which it is not consciously intentional at all, but non-consciously/ unconsciously intending. This affective dimension of film spectatorship is less discriminating and discriminable, and involves a complex political and embodied relation to ideological systems. Subjective experience of film, then, is an effect of affective and emotional response to a textuality that is subtly informed by its materiality (as a multilayered, emotional, discriminable object) and immateriality (as a multilayered, affective *matrix* of determining factors *through* which systems of meaning-production operate). It thus starts to reincorporate and suspend the very structural problem that the Althusserian subject embodied: relative autonomy.

As Marie-Louise Von Franz has said about the discrepancies in this ambiguous aspect of textuality as experienced in everyday life, 'Many people have criticized the Jungian approach for not presenting psychic material systematically. But these critics forget that the material itself is a living experience charged with emotion, by nature irrational and ever-changing' (1964: 167). In clarifying this emotionally charged experience, Fiona Ross (1998) has considered the pattern of similarities between the body and the psyche to the outside world and our representations of it. Through a series of integrations and relations between body, mind and world as a holistic manifestation of the 'material', Ross formulates an analogy of the textile as a humanly created pattern. Pattern reflects the relation between these various elements extending through the physical (body), mental (psyche) and representational (image), standing as it does for the creativity and understanding found in the body and its activities (movements, feelings and associated thought processes). Ross identifies this materiality as an 'inherent pattern' found in human physiology as a recip-rocal correspondence to both the objective outside world and the emotional subjective inner world. It is found in sensation and motor processes, the reciprocal inhibition of muscle groups, the symmetry of the skeletal struc-ture, and in cycles of menstruation, waking and sleep. This reciprocation is an imperative, as it reflects the striking similarities between the patterning of the outer world of matter and the inner world of the psyche, conjoined as they are through, it should be added, the thinking, feeling, emoting and affected body.

While Ross acknowledges the legacy of the Platonic view that sensory knowledge can only be a shadow of the 'real thing', 'yet we have to admit that it is not "real" in the sense that it is not "the thing"' (1998: 245). Hence, the movements in modernist art forms, including movements in film, such as surrealism, away from the representational are regression through phases of differentiation seen in graphic accomplishments (includ-ing, for example, the development of Cartesian perspective). Such image production moves towards a more provocative simulation of Sobchack's 'wild', embodied and enworlded communication that precedes language, as presented in the above epigraph. Sensory knowledge may not be 'the thing-in-itself', but it is an embodied access point to an experience of that thing. It is crucial to the world of object relations but is also crucial to an understanding of the subjective *experience* of such a relationship. Ross (1998: 246) goes on to state that:

> The laws of humanly created pattern are the laws of relationship, not only the relationship between the pattern and the pattern-maker or observer, but between the unconscious and conscious mind and between the given and the fantasised other. They imply movement, rhythm, repetition, condensation and reversal.

While analogy might be considered a particularly weak instance of correspondence, here it takes on the role of a much stronger relation. The
implications that Ross outlines are fundamentally embodied elements of
experience that find their equivalents in both the representational world and
the inner world of emotional and psychic experience. Every bit as relevant
to the embodied, affective and emotional correspondences suggested by
both Münsterberg and Grodal as representative of cinema's simulational
capabilities, Ross' model of the material centres on the reflexivity of inner
and outer forms. The strength of her analogy, and its relevance for our
concerns here, is to be found in the emphasis on the embodied aspects of
movement, rhythm, repetition and reversibility. This will become more
important in relation to affectivity and object relations, as discussed in the
next couple of chapters, but is worth noting here.

The implications of such affective experiences are charged with potential
for thinking through the ways in which audiences produce meaning in the
act of spectatorship. Furthermore, they enable the elaboration of the notion
of text and textuality as material, rather than linguistic, in origin. They
address the emotionally charged *feeling* of meaning production, at the same
time engaging a sense that the film text is not a flat surface of images but a
multilayered, visceral body, whose limits incorporate subjectivity, ideology
and epistemic elements crucial to our understanding of the film.

This filmic body is, in Sobchack's eminently quotable words, 'an act of
physical and reflective movement that makes itself reflexively felt and
understood [. . . signifying] in a pervasive, primary, and embodied language
that precedes and provides the grounds for the secondary significations of a
more discrete, systematic, less "wild" communication' (1992: 3–4). It also
forms a very important aspect of post-Jungian thinking in general, as this
experience of the materiality of textual production and consumption moves
away from the (rather common) psychoanalytic presupposition of the text–
dream analogy, towards a more practicable transcription from textile to
film text. Textile, in this sense, forms the backdrop to engaging the
materiality of the film and the potentiality of affective response in the
spectator. For example, David Miller (cited in Hauke, 2000: 219) has read
into the textile/text:

A notion of weaving, the weave in which the texture of the textile, and
what Paul [Kugler] called the textuality, is in the effect of the whole.
There is no call for a filling in in a way that the rational mind or the
conscious ego can make sense of it. One can feel the texture, or one can
sense the body of the weave, whether it is in a text or a dream. It is
paratactic. It may look to us like it makes a Gestalt as a whole but it
is like a fine tapestry. When you look at it closely, it begins to dissolve.
It is 'gappy' . . . but the body of it, the texture of it, is felt nonetheless.

This simultaneity of wholeness and layering is an extremely useful means of thinking through the filmic body, incorporating as it does the different subjective, objective, embodied and epistemological registers of spectatorship. I shall return to this momentarily, as it not only involves straightforward cognitive processes of prior knowledge and perception, but also a process that phenomenologists call apperception: 'filling in' in a materialist sense. The simultaneity that Miller describes is a key element in the development of a materialist and phenomenological approach to analytical psychology and film. It is to this phenomenology of film and meaning, in the context of political judgement, that we now must turn.

Phenomenology and the field of experience in film theory

For Daniel Frampton, in his book *Filmosophy*, film phenomenology has been brought into film studies largely to help clarify questions of film spectator experience and interpretation. I am not so sure that 'interpretation' is the correct term here: It assumes content analysis is phenomenology's project, whereas the notion of film-being engages the mutual articulation of content and form. Indeed, Frampton's own negotiation of cinematic beings incorporates structures and objects within and for those structures. Film-being is, for Frampton 'A general term for what we understand to be the origin(ator) of the images and sounds we experience' (2006: 27). Other beings are experienced simultaneous to film-being: author beings (personalities, structures, institutions); ghostly beings (of cinematic intention); and narrator beings. We can say of these filmic beings that intention (both conscious and non-conscious/unconscious) seems to be the overarching theme here: The 'ghostly' beings that Frampton names are indicators of the primary signification that Sobchack has described as providing the grounding for secondary signification. I take this secondary signification to mean the constitution of a 'film language' as it is commonly referred to in everyday academic film-speak. The ideas of several apparatus theorists such as Metz and Baudry, to which we shall briefly return in the next chapter, are profoundly influenced by this linguistic turn. I have already relayed an alternative post-Jungian notion of pattern, which helps us redefine the film text as a material, rather than a linguistic, phenomenon. The primary signification, the grounding, the 'ghost' in the machine is cinema's ability to see, hear and move, to express these activities, and to signify these activities bodily for sight, hearing and kinaesthetics (vehicular embodiment, movement) for its audience. Therefore, cinema appears to be a machine that eminently intends towards its audience, for its audience.

But in what ways does narrative cinema particularly achieve this through the medium of film? To answer this question, it would be useful to return briefly to one of film's most remarkable impositions on the experience of its seeing, hearing and movement: the edit. More specifically, Einsentein's theorization on the edit was an early attempt to explain this intentionality in film-being. As already noted in Chapter 2, through their attention to the importance of editing in forming intention (and thus, meaning) in film production and consumption, the Soviet montage theorists addressed 'film' (the medium) and 'movies' (what we see as spectators, on the screen) at the same time. This relationship was crucial: the articulation of one in/through the other. Pudovkin's account of editing, for example, constituted a creative language of the cinema. However, as discussed, the development of 'film language' as a conceptual framework is highly contentious and Eisenstein's response to Pudovkin's 'building block' approach to editing helps us to re-imagine the constitution of film language.

To reiterate, for Eisenstein film could be considered an authored imposition on the real world effecting real change, and editing was central to this filmic imposition. However, he takes this further by emphasizing the relation between filmic phenomena and the audience's engagement with them, when he states that montage film is fundamentally dialectic. This is crucial for Eisenstein, as dialectical objects and our encounter with them produce dialectical modes of thought. For him, such dialectical projections of dialectical objects would constitute a dialectical form of art: montage was 'not an idea composed of successive shots stuck together but an idea that DERIVES from the collision between two shots that are independent of one another' (1999: 28). At a fundamental level, the edit embodies a touch – the edit is film touching itself in a very real sense. The editor has, of course, intervened in this process and brought it about, but this is the bringing together of two different pieces of film on which the contents also fundamentally differ. The edit itself is invisible, and is only perceptible by the presence of the two shots placed together. In relation to the filmed event, this is, in actuality, a highly artificial phenomenon: No matter how closely the two shots match on action, their relation is in fact quite arbitrary in essence, and the edit serves as a bridge in the tension between the clashing shots. Thus, in a material, filmic sense, we have a 'wild' communication, perceptible but invisible, that grounds secondary linguistic (representational) meanings. This makes sense at the most intuitive, affective level. It is, to return to Miller, 'gappy', but involves an apperceptive 'filling in', as well as a holistic reading based on cinematic conventions of continuity editing.

Cinematically (rather than filmically) speaking, this is where the object that we see (the movie) becomes the primary device for making meaning, as the emotional takes over from the affective. In its representational capacity, the movie reverses the role of visibility and perceptibility, and in the edit we engage the two shots either side rather than the edit itself. What makes the film intelligible is its seeing, hearing and moving activity. These are conventions of human activity, easily comprehensible to anyone used to the normative conventions of expressing their own perception. This is, one should add, quite apart from interpretation: another activity that has its own conventions with which filmgoers are usually familiar.

While the cinema can never fully assure a single interpretation, it may assume and assure its own intelligibility. Even the most abstract film may presuppose that it will be understood as signification (even as it can never assume a single interpretation) through the act of spectatorship. It conveys meaning that moves beyond the mere presence of the play of shadow and projected light on a flat surface and therefore immediately assumes the material status of perceptibility and expression at the same time that it acts as a physical medium. In other words, it most often looks like the way we perceive and successfully mimics expression through this perceptive mode of expression. It is, bluntly, a physically present psychomimetic form, similar in principle to Münsterberg's photoplay. For, as Sobchack states, 'To the baby the film is not yet a film, but to the mature viewing subject, the film is always *more* than its material presence and play before it can be seen as anything less' (1992: 6). In other words, it has *meaningfulness*. The edit, emotionally speaking, becomes meaningful through its visible signifiers (the shots, single frames, to either side) but imperceptible because the narrative function of the edit (hence the phrase 'continuity editing') becomes the overriding concern for the viewing experience. Rather confusingly, in film studies this is often referred to as 'invisible editing' – classical Hollywood cinema is a prime example of the way narrative cinema perfected the technique and established the conventions of unobtrusive, continuity ('invisible') editing. Whereas there are difficulties with other cinematic and audiovisual forms (videogames, music video, experimental video art, etc.) in maintaining this 'invisibility', this is not for immediate concern. At the primary, material level, all editing involving celluloid film has a perceptible but invisible grounding: The edit itself is not seen, but is perceived because of its visible results.

Another factor that needs to be considered at the secondary level of representation is to do with what is within the frame, and the frame itself. In a cinema theatre, the limits of the projected image and of the screen delimit the visible elements of the film. However, that is not to say that other elements extra to the frame may not be intuited or apperceived. As Frampton writes on Merleau-Ponty: 'With film we might . . . say that, at any one moment, one scene is present to the film, with off-frame action being absent but intended – we feel it is there' (2006: 40). One might say, then, that there is a virtuality that is always-already a part of the filmic experience, an intuited or apperceived element of the activities of the film that, although not necessarily visible, is nonetheless perceptible. For Frampton, 'Cinema intends and creates at one and the same moment. Film owns the objects it "sees", because the object is already included in the act of seeing' (2006: 40). Therefore, existential phenomenology can help us to negotiate the double nature of experience in cinema: Both the film and filmgoer are engaged in activities of seeing, hearing and moving, experiences that involve the perception of, and expression in, the world.

In a sense then, film should be considered much more than a mere analogy for the eye/optical/psychic apparatus, as theorized by Baudry, Metz, and other apparatus theorists. In a phenomenological sense, film is the eye that sees and is seen. It is also seen by the spectator (a cine-subjective 'I') to be seeing, and embodies 'other seeing' – that is, another subject (other than the film spectator) that sees. More than analogy for human vision, film is an embodiment of subjectivity, an object that is seen to be materializing an existential, embodied perception. Mechanically speaking, it also embodies further subjectivities, as expression of biographical intentionality, for example: real human labour exerted in the production of such filmic vision. As we have seen in previous chapters, this biographical subject is a very superficial level of embodied subjectivity, and is most readily manifested through the notion of authorship, and its marketed phenomena. For Sobchack, following Merleau-Ponty: 'Film is understood to be itself a "subject", an "object-subject" that sees and is seen. For her film is both presentational and representational, both a viewing subject and a visible object for the filmgoer' (Frampton, 2006: 41). Therefore, in Sobchack's phenomenology of film's experience, film is not just a view, but a viewing view, a view from and of subjectivity: The viewing view presents the body-subject of vision. It is about having and expressing perception, about vision and intention, and it sees objects and expresses intention about those objects. The expressive camera facilitates this viewing view, thus making film's intentionality obvious. Frampton suggests that 'Zooms and the like (active cinema), allows [sic] us to see film-intention in action . . . a creative, questioning act, altering the film's relationship to its world.' For directors such as Altman and P. T. Anderson: 'The zoom is a very expressive thought, sometimes searching and finding, sometimes receding and denying, sometimes questioning and inquisitive' (2006: 45). As discussed in Chapter 3, Altman's zoom expresses not only cognition in the sense of being 'thoughtful', but also an emphasis on film's relationship with the mechanical operations involved in, more accurately, human activities of perception and expression.

So, if this intentionality is made obvious, how does it fit in with the notion of spectator-subject as effect? Firstly, filmgoers do not see film-making. It is true that sometimes they see this in effect through the visibility of the filmmaking process: a well-known example of this is Fellini's *8½* (Fr/It, 1963), where some scenes make visible the film set, as well as the process of the take through visible and audible cues. What spectators actually see mostly is film-being. The spectator's experience of this is complicated, however, because of the Western convention of perspective. As Frampton observes, 'For Sobchack, film images plainly, simply, represent a

Renaissance perspective: representing the visible as originating in and organized by an individual, centred subject. The filmgoer thus experiences film as subjective and intentional' (2006: 42). For Frampton, however, film does not present to us a phenomenologically correct experience of human subjectivity. Therefore, what he describes as the anthropomorphic part of Sobchack's thinking is incomplete. Film, for example, cannot show what a character is thinking and seeing and remembering at the same time. Techniques used in classical Hollywood cinema have attempted to represent this (or, more accurately, simulate this in some way). For example, the simultaneous use of voiceover, point of view and dissolve delimits narration, subjectivity and the re-presentation of spatial and temporal signifiers. But the fact remains for Frampton that film does not make human thinking visible to us: 'Seeing film anthropomorphically thus restricts the possible interpretations of film form' (2006: 42) and would only find human-like styles in film form. This is a problematic assertion, however, and is worth addressing in full. Consider once more Frampton's (2006: 220, note 23) account of the zoom:

> A combination of bodily and optical movement is used in vertigo-inducing or world-altering movements (technically, the film moves forward, while the image zooms back outwards, and vice versa). The downward version is used most famously in *Vertigo*, where it is meant to appropriate the human feeling of queasiness or fear. Yet it should be obvious that humans cannot zoom out or in like a camera, and the human experience of vertigo does not exactly "look" like it looks in cinema. But strangely that does not stop many writers from asserting that film replicates human perception.

Well, it certainly does not replicate human perception, but this is not quite what Sobchack implies in her phenomenology. The zoom as described here merely approximates temporal and spatial disorientation, internal movements that may be visualised as 'zooms' or unfocused sensations such as blurred vision, or disproportionate emphasis on one or more objects in the perceptual field, and so on. When we feel horror in the real world, we do not hear high-pitched stringed instruments repeatedly yelping all around us, and yet Bernard Herman's score for *Psycho* approximates an extremity of feeling that helps orient the viewing strategy of a horrific scene. It works to approximate a sense of 'horror' in the setting, characterization, and the world of the film. It does not by and of itself replicate the sound of horror. Such an assertion would be misled.

Furthermore, Frampton does not engage the notion of the *induction* of feeling (as in vertigo, horror or disorientation). The shot described may not replicate human perception, but it does express a double intention as the world drops from focus (but is still visible) while the object in focus sharpens and enlarges within the frame. This doubling of intention forces focus on the affective response induced by viewing such perceptive–expressive activity, and therefore engages the peculiarity of reflection: that strange sensation of the feeling of having a feeling. For example, a trombone shot that dollies or tracks away from its object while simultaneously zooming in is now a common technique in film, TV and advertising. It was developed in some particularly iconic Hollywood filmmaking to locate the character in the frame as a point of focus when the rest of the world fades away from principal concern in that moment. In a particularly famous example from *Jaws* (Spielberg, US, 1975) a trombone shot of Brody (Roy Schneider)'s reaction to the first daylight shark attack signifies sudden realization. However, implied in this signification is a much more fraught affectation of horror, for which there is no definition except through the feeling of having a feeling of horror.

In suggesting that Sobchack has anthropomorphised film in her phenomenology, Frampton has fundamentally misread her. Although the film does not present *to* us this subjectivity, it does present *for* us. It is both presentational *and* representational, after all. For Sobchack, film represents subjectivity as 'other seeing', and is embodied through a 'viewing view'. Thus, it lets us engage with the notion of subjectivity-as-effect, hence renegotiating the idea that cinema embodies political effectivity in a number of ways. As Sobchack later states (2004: 150) in *Carnal Thoughts*:

> Rather than replacing human vision with mechanical vision, the cinema functions mechanically to bring to visibility the reversible structure of human vision: this structure emerges in the lived body as systematically both a subject and an object, both visual (seeing) and visible (seen), and as simultaneously productive of both an activity of seeing (a 'viewing view') and an image of the seen (a 'viewed view').

It is this comment, less about the likeness of human and cinematic vision and more about film's existential becoming, its bringing to visibility the reversible structure of human activities of perception and expression (of seeing, in particular) through mechanical means, that fully reveals the usefulness of film phenomenology. So, the film is subjective, but that the film's actions may only be human-*like* in character suggests an otherness to this subjectivity. There is, in Sobchack's terms, an *intra*subjectivity – that is, although film is always becoming before us, it is of itself and by itself, but is made *inter*subjective for the spectator. This intersubjective relation is the element of spectatorship that is most readily experienced in an embodied sense, for film viewing involves emotion, cognition and affect in its totality through embodied viewing. Cinema is, for Sobchack, an intersubjective sociality of a language of direct embodied experience: 'A language that not only refers to direct experience but also uses direct experience as its mode of reference' (1992: 11). These human processes within the film viewing experience are what matters – whether from the perspective of a deep philosophy of film or from the point of view of a political economy of film popularity. That connection and intersubjectivity are experienced, felt, remembered, marketed, reviewed, criticized, theorized and/or negotiated in a number of different and familiar ways within the public sphere.

Another critique that Frampton offers is related to Sobchack's notion that film has the capacity to function phenomenologically. He states that 'Cinema may *attempt* to function in a phenomenological way (and often it tries, sometimes beautifully) but that does not mean that film becomes phenomenological *per se*' (Frampton, 2006: 47). This statement misunderstands the move towards a phenomenology of film, and here Frampton appropriates a semiotic attitude towards the phenomenology of film. In fact, as a result, he runs counter to Sobchack's methodology. Any representational or technical attempt to show something in a phenomenological way does *not* make the experience of it somehow more phenomenological, any more than the representation of psychoanalytic methods and psychological disorder in *Vertigo* somehow makes the film more psychoanalytical or more conducive to psychoanalytic modes of analysis. The Obi Wan Kenobi/Wise Old Man archetype analogy mentioned in previous chapters is an example of the superficial appropriation of this semiotic attitude – an interpretative gesture that inevitably needs to be framed within a secondary question that asks: 'so what if Obi Wan is like the Wise Old Man archetype?' Phenomenology is merely a means to elaborate and help understand the experiences of subjectivity, meaning-making, and the processes that underpin such experiences. True, some films may lend themselves more easily or productively than others to phenomenology rather than psychoanalytic reduction or Jungian amplification, for example. However, the charge that this would be the whole point of developing a phenomenology of film is a rather superficial one. Although it should be noted that this is something that Frampton does not state specifically, the implication within his discourse on the development of film phenomenology is an ever-present possibility.

Rather, for film theory, the challenges that present themselves stem from questions that emerge through the act of viewing films. As these questions are frequently underpinned by social, historical, political, institutional and economic imperatives, certain approaches may prove more productive than others in certain instances. However, this does not mean that, for example, because Eisenstein's *Old and New* is a Soviet film it would benefit more from a historical materialist reading than would *The Pursuit of Happyness*. There are, of course, many approaches that may be used, even in synthesis or simultaneity. In addition, film enacts its own intention and vision – a phenomenology *of* film would not deny this, and Frampton's overly critical reading of Sobchack implicates his own emphasis on the 'analogue' of human and cinematic vision. As previously stated, this mechanical transposition is a naïve analogy. This is a factor that Sobchack in fact dismisses as the least important phenomenological element of the relationship between seeing and film. It is the intersubjective notion of seeing–seen and viewing–view that is the most productive element. This is the factor that reflects what Merleau-Ponty would describe as a reversibility of expression–perception in the midst of being. It is what Sobchack has described in the context of film viewing, as 'productive of both an activity of seeing (a "viewing view") and an image of the seen (a "viewed view")' (2004: 150).

Resonance between the semiotic and symbolic attitude

For Merleau-Ponty, the experience of the body is fundamentally by means of the way the body shapes experience. The body is not merely an object but the condition through which objects may be apprehended. In other words, it is the condition through which we relate to the world. The world, therefore, is no longer a collection of determinate things but is, for Merleau-Ponty in his essay 'The Experience of the Body in Classical Psychology', instead a 'horizon, latent in all our experience' (2005: 54). He says of the body (2005: 52):

> It is an object, which means that it is standing in front of us, only because it is observable: situated, that is to say, directly under our hand or gaze, indivisibly overthrown and re-integrated with every moment they make. Otherwise it would be true like an idea and not present like a thing.

In other words, one's body defies exploration: it is always presented to oneself from the same angle. And it is this observation that enables us to rethink the power of film to *move* people. Film makes visible, intelligible for us, the interstice of body and world, that part of us as subjects that grounds our activities of perception and expression and which, we are unable to experience other than as bodies first and thinking subjects second. No wonder that, to be able to experience this through the spectatorship process, film is an effective medium of communication: a viewed and viewing view. Its capacity as a signifying system, on the other hand, is for post-Jungian theory a much more complicated affair. Don Fredericksen, in his seminal essay 'Jung/sign/symbol/film' (2001) for example, sets out a discussion of the contrast between the semiotic and the symbol. In what follows, it will be useful for the reader to bear in mind that I have already considered what Fredericksen describes as the semiotic as a secondary signification, incorporating emotional or evaluative viewing of representation. The symbol, however, may be more closely associated with the primary signification, the 'wild' communication of Sobchack's film phenomenology, or affective response as previously discussed.

Firstly, we should consider that Fredericksen's primary aim 'to argue for the meaning in, and the meaningfulness of, filmic situations in which a known entity [the sign] "stands for" a relatively unknown one [the symbol]' (2001: 21) ultimately reveals his interpretative critical stance. Although he is attempting a more thorough, holistic, rich amplification and analysis, it is, for the purposes of this book's polemic, enough that we consider Fredericksen's use of the term 'meaningfulness' as the principal object for theoretical discussion. It is true that he is attempting to keep in play a multiplicity of meanings, but at what cost? The meaningfulness of a film and its activities is the essential engagement for film phenomenology. Even for Jung, whom Fredericksen quotes at length, this would be the case:

> The symbol is alive only so long as it is pregnant with meaning. But once its meaning has been born out of it, once that expression is found that formulates the thing sought, expected or divined even better than the hitherto accepted symbol, then that symbol is dead.
>
> (Jung, cited in Fredericksen, 2001: 18)

In other words, in order for meaningfulness to retain its significance, in order to suspend the sense of what matters about the film, it is necessary to keep the potentiality of the film's primary signification [symbolism] in dialectical play with its secondary signification [semiosis]. This is easier said than done, however, for, as Fredericksen himself writes, 'We must understand that Jung's distinction between sign and symbol ultimately elaborates two distinct modes of apprehending and explaining the psyche and its products – not just two distinct psychologies but two distinct ontologies and philosophies of value' (2001: 19). This, phenomenologically speaking, in itself is troublesome as we may say, truthfully, that any interpretative gesture involves in its process an epistemological leap from one presupposition to a number of possibilities of meaning, without necessarily mobilizing 'distinct ontologies'. The ontology of film viewing, however, mobilizes the intersubjective potentialities of human activity in perception–expression (seeing and seeing–sight, hearing and hearing–hearing, movement and being moved) through film-being.

To reiterate, Sobchack prefers to think of cinema as an intersubjective sociality of a language of direct embodied experience. That is, an intelligible perception–expression. This is 'a language that not only refers to direct experience but also uses direct experience as its mode of reference' (1992: 11). In essence, the film *represents* the direct perceptual experience of the filmmaker by means of modes of direct and reflective perceptual experience, but is also implicated in the activity of *presenting* the direct and reflective experience of perceptual and expressive existence *as* the film. In this way, the film transcends the filmmaker, constituting and locating its own address, its own perceptual and expressive experience of being and becoming. It is therefore not just a location of the result of biographical labour; it also embodies its own ontology, its own being and becoming, not contingent on the filmmaker's presence. Filmic ontology, therefore, defies the very idea of coherent authorship outlined in auteur theory, even as it is formally institutionalized as authored, through production processes and conventional reading practices associated with the pleasurable consumption of film.

This essentially means that, for consciously intended meaning-production (and in particular authored meaning), film is always in the process of becoming, and the activity of spectatorship is always-already implicated in a pre-representational communication. In other words, the spectator is implicated in the potentiality of what Jung called the symbol – a relatively unknown entity for which the filmgoer affectively responds. That is, film's meaningfulness is always in play, resonating between known, unknown, knowable and unknowable. Fredericksen's other element here – value – is far closer to the underlying differentiation at work. He demonstrates the historically loaded emotional object (sign) as being valued very differently to the affective response (symbol), characterized as having an always-already presence, but for which an evaluative judgement is that much more difficult to pinpoint accurately. It is, after all, the difference between affect (subjective feeling that has no fixed object; feeling-without-an-object) and emotion (subjective feeling that intends towards something, an object; feeling-towards-an-object). This is a subject to which I shall dedicate lengthy discussion in the next chapter, in consolidating a material rather than linguistic notion of the Image. For now in this regard, it is worth quoting from Jung, in the same citation as previously used:

> There are undoubtedly products whose symbolic character does not depend merely on the attitude of the observing consciousness, but manifests itself spontaneously in the symbolic effect they would have on the observer. Such products are so constituted that they would lack any kind of meaning were not a symbolic one conceded to them.
>
> (cited in Fredericksen, 2001: 18)

This ceding of meaning is important, as it underlines the basic interpretative problem of Fredericksen's position. However, this is not to say that Fredericksen is unaware of the underlying problems with semiotic interpretation. Part of his essay is dedicated to a discussion of Marxist and Lacanian interpretative film analysis, and how the 'semiotic attitude' of these paradigms within film criticism inevitably inflects a reductive, interpretativist position. Indeed, many of Fredericksen's comments mirror some of the critiques found in this book. However, the problem with his approach is twofold.

Firstly, Fredericksen is saying that signs constitute dead spaces or elements once they have become interpreted through semiotic or other kinds of interpretative analysis. The idea is that some signs do not conform to our interpretation of them, because they are ultimately based on an unknown (and possibly unknowable) element. This is because they are symbols, pregnant with a multiplicity of meaning. The problem occurs in Fredericksen's qualification of his thesis. He states that, 'I do not wish by my remarks to foster the conclusion that semiotic approaches are inherently "wrong" or useless. Only folly would deny that many films, perhaps a majority, are predominantly semiotic in character' (2001: 27). Although he immediately follows this with a proviso that this is a 'crucial cultural question in need of separate attention', the problem lies in the fact that he seems to be making an arbitrary value judgement concerning 'semiotic' and 'symbolic' films. We have already seen that his reading of Jung's distinction between sign and symbol is at least partly based on two distinct 'philosophies of value'. Although he never gets to the bottom of what he really means by this, it is apparent that Fredericksen is employing a hierarchical structure that presupposes a poverty of meaning in semiotic films, and a pregnancy or richness in symbolic ones. This is a perfectly legitimate reasoning by his own argument, but troublesome in the assumption that the majority of films are probably 'predominantly semiotic in character', an assumption that tars mainstream and popular cinema with symbolic poverty. It risks placing many films *en masse* in this bracket before analysis has even begun.

How does one choose the films to analyse? If some are more obviously impoverished that others, would this mean that they are not worth studying? As indicated, Fredericksen actually states that he does not wish to foster this conclusion. Obviously, one cannot possibly perform textual analysis on every single film, but if most films are probably semiotic, then one would inevitably seek the films that would yield the most fruitful symbolic analyses. Although Fredericksen never goes this far in his essay, the implication is clear, and his much later IAJS seminar on film (see introduction) sustained this implication through the statement that art films (those of Maya Deren, for example) are more pregnant with meaning than other, more popular fare. This is a position that was common in film theory in the 1970s. Many of the theorists writing in *Screen*, such as Laura Mulvey, made statements to the effect that classical Hollywood cinema always restricted itself to formal *mise-en-scene* and normative ideological structures such as political conservatism and patriarchal encoding. The addendum that Mulvey does not wish to reject mainstream film moralistically, but 'to highlight the ways in which its formal preoccupations reflect the psychical obsessions of the society which produced it' (1999: 834) seems to be largely overlooked by Fredericksen. My contention is that, although in principle politically correct, this position risks overlooking the potentiality and meaningfulness of popular cinema and valorizes 'art' films as a category. It is a position that Mulvey later revised substantially in light of developments in feminist responses to film, as we shall see in the next chapter, and I address the question of the popular specifically in my case studies in Chapters 7 and 8.

The second problem occurs when Fredericksen comes very close to engaging a pressing issue involving the separation of the two 'attitudes', but elides this in favour of concentrating almost exclusively on his symbolic approach. It is worth quoting in full here, as his logic suggests that the reciprocation of the symbolic and semiotic is crucial to fully engaging the meaningfulness of film:

> The semiotic attitude is ultimately limiting because it denies the existence of the symbolic realm by definition, or denies its existence in practice by attempting to explain symbolic expressions semiotically. Frequently it does both simultaneously, since the two denials implicate one another. The limiting character of the semiotic attitude involves a clear hubris of – and often a fear by – the rational and the conscious mind toward the irrational and the unconscious mind . . . For Jung, *the point is not to identify with either the conscious or the unconscious mind, but to forge and keep a living tie between them.* To this end a symbolic attitude is crucial, because symbols rising from the deep layers of the unconscious are precisely that tie made manifest.
>
> (2001: 28, emphasis in original)

I should reiterate the fact that Fredericksen is using the terms 'symbol' and 'semiotic' specifically here following Jung's terminology. Complementarily, these are elements that I have addressed throughout this chapter in relation to the primary, embodied, 'wild' communication, expressed through film's activities of seeing, hearing and moving, and the secondary signification located in film's representational capacity. These also have resonance, respectively, in the notions of affective response and emotional object. Again, it is worth restating the point made in Chapter 1, that two very different vocabularies are being employed here from different disciplines: analytical psychology and existential phenomenology. However, following Roger Brooke, a common theme is established between the two approaches, whereby although Merleau-Ponty (and Sobchack following him) predominantly emphasizes the primal power of the lived, enworlded body, and Jung emphasizes the primal power of the collective consciousness, they both engage the same problem. Linguistically they may differ, and approach the problem from different premises, but ultimately they are addressing the *tie* that Fredericksen mentions in his writing: 'For Jung, the point is not to identify with either the conscious or the unconscious mind, but to forge and keep a *living tie* between them' (emphasis added).

In this, Roger Brooke (1991: 128) identifies attitudes common to both paradigms towards the unconscious:

Both Jung and Merleau-Ponty render the terms conscious and unconscious ambiguous, and regard the unconscious as a latent, unreflective
intentionality . . . Merleau-Ponty, more clearly than Jung, situates the
complexities of the lived body in the historical, perceptual, linguistic,
and interpersonal matrices that are meant by the term existence. Jung,
more clearly than Merleau-Ponty, reveals the body's imaginal matrices
which inspire structure, limit, and transform existence in all its dimensions (historical, perceptual, and so on).

We can see here the living tie of which Fredericksen writes, but that he does
not fully theorize, in the dialectical play mentioned earlier between secondary signification (semiosis) and primary signification (symbol). In this case,
the mutual articulation of intersubjective imagination in consciousness and
embodiment is a living/lived tie along which meaningfulness resonates. This
is, to reiterate, quite aside from the discrepancies and contradictory spaces
that arise through the processes of interpretation and elucidate for us the
potentiality of affective response caused through the act of film viewing.
For phenomenologists such as Sobchack, the 'wild communication' of pre-
existent signification systems ('The pervasive and as yet undifferentiated
significance of existence as it is lived rather than reflected upon' (1992: 11))
exists before the shared imaginal spaces of the social formation. At the
same time meaning is born first out of concrete sensibility, surface and
fleshly dialogue, and second out of the will to communicate. This will is, for
Jung, inspired by the objective subjectivity of collective unconscious experience as lived as social beings. We are, in other words, finitely situated in the
world as embodied beings and yet always informed by a decisive motility,
an 'imaginal matrix'. It is this imaginal embodiment that informs our sense
of subjectivity and, ultimately, our sense of existence as beings within the
social formation. Therefore, one might say that imaginal embodiment is
thus inherently political in an immediate and lived sense. As Sobchack goes
on to say, embodied existence always precedes 'natural language' or the
'natural attitude'. The natural attitude (of which the semiotic forms a part)
is the system of discrete instrumentality and objectification of existence that
enables us to negotiate the various orders of reality that exist for use in a
general sense in the everyday. It is from this 'natural attitude' that the
system of what Jung termed 'cultural symbols' evolved over time. These
orders of reality will be explored further in the next chapter, in relation to
filmic, subjective and phenomenological experience. In addition, there will
be a discussion as to how we may use the Jungian notion of cultural and
natural symbols for the study of film.

Part II

Applying key Jungian concepts in film theory

Chapter 5

Refitting the notion of the gaze

The 'I' that sees and the 'eye' that is seen

Nowadays more and more people, especially those who live in large cities, suffer from a terrible emptiness and boredom, as if they are waiting for something that never arrives. Movies and television, spectator sports and political excitements may divert them for a while, but again and again, exhausted and disenchanted, they have to return to the wasteland of their own lives.

Marie-Louise Von Franz, 'The Process of Individuation'

Terry Eagleton, in *The Ideology of the Aesthetic* (1990), notes that the cerebral aesthetic category of sensibility is also always-already engaged with the negotiation of the world through our 'creaturely existence'. In other words, there is an infinite play and reversibility between objectified, emotional meaning-making (semiosis) and subjectified, affective meaning (symbolism). The symbolic realizes, in terms of the expression of perception, a significance that pre-exists the signifying systems of linguistic expression that nevertheless inform it intimately, and is in turn informed by this creaturely existence. The understanding of this is crucial for theorizing the act of viewing a film, for, as Sobchack (1992: 11) suggests:

As an 'expression of experience by experience', a film both constitutes an original and primary significance in its continual perceptive and expressive 'becoming' and evolves and regulates a more particular form of signification shaped by the specific trajectory of interests and intentions that its perceptive and expressive acts trace across the screen.

This leads directly from the lengthy discussion in the previous chapter on the fact that we are finitely situated in the world as embodied beings and yet always informed by a decisive motility. This is a motility that has been engaged time and again in film theory, but articulated more fully in terms of specular and spectacular viewing activity. Although concretely grounded in what Fredericksen has described as the 'semiotic attitude', this articulation is worth outlining briefly, as it inevitably leads us to emphasize the 'living tie' already discussed, between the conscious and unconscious, so crucial to developing a robust post-Jungian film theory.

It may be said that viewing film is today a fundamentally different experience to that of the past where (usually) the point of access was either in a cinema theatre or a television broadcast. Much psychoanalytic film theory during the 1970s in articulating the filmgoer's experience of the film was therefore largely contingent on the context of the cinema theatre. There have been a number of interventions since, but here I quote from Sobchack, as a familiar source, to indicate the changes that occur at an embodied level, in the experience of film in other viewing contexts. She states that, 'With the help of consumer electronics, the spectator can both alter the film's temporality and materially possess its inanimate "body"' (2004: 148). A curious and contradictory example of this is the DVD release of Lucas Belvaux's *Trilogy* (2003). A trio of films with a common narrative arc, not unlike Krzysztof Kieslowski's *Three Colours* trilogy, *Trilogy* is much more than three separate film texts (and discs) and even more than the sum of its parts. The DVD box-set features a fourth disc that brings together the main narrative thread of all three films, omitting the extraneous subplot developments and secondary characters, and places events in chronological order. Thus, it creates a fourth text, following a single narrative thread, which gives an impression of control over the narrative arc of the entire trilogy.

I write 'impression' because it occurs to me that this illusory mastery that the viewer has over the material of the trilogy is diluted by the very fact that the narrative labour has already been exerted *for* the viewer. Indeed, such vicarious interactivity presents itself in even the most familiar and innocuous of home viewing functions. For example, Sobchack notes that the pause functionality found on most domestic audiovisual hardware (including PVRs, VCRs and DVD players) belongs to the ontology of the electronic and is not of the cinematic. This is because, even though the freeze-frame technique in film resembles the pause function of video and electronic media, the celluloid strip itself is still moving through the projector. 'The film always has to actively work at "arresting" its gaze' (Sobchack, 2004: 149), whereas the DVD pause is a physical interruption in the flow of the material. The freeze frame involves an arrested gaze rather than a fully autonomous interactivity, and, following Sobchack's phenomenology as discussed in the previous chapter, we might say that this arrested gaze features in both the viewing and viewed view of the film, and the act of viewing from the spectator. This formulation ontologically differentiates between media in terms of interactivity in the act of viewing. So, what is this 'arrested gaze', and how does it relate to the way that the gaze has been theorized in film scholarship?

Visual pleasure, scopophilia and 'to-be-looked-at-ness'

The most obvious point for discussion would be Laura Mulvey's seminal essay 'Visual Pleasure and Narrative Cinema' (Mulvey, 1999), published in 1975 in *Screen* with the explicit aim of applying psychoanalysis as a political weapon in the theorization of both cinema and society. Mulvey addresses the place of men and women in the economy of pleasurable viewing, stating that 'It is said that analysing pleasure, or beauty, destroys it. That is the intention of this article' (1999: 835). Her intention is 'to use psychoanalysis to discover where and how the fascination of film is reinforced by pre-existing patterns of fascination already at work within the individual subject and the social formations that have moulded him' (1999: 833). I do not wish to dwell too long on this particular essay, as the intervening years have seen continual debate on its premises. Indeed, crucial interventions from Mulvey herself (1989) as well as from several others have been drawn upon to critique her original position. The questions raised in her original article are, however, still relevant to film scholarship and Mulvey's 'gaze' embodies a number of characteristics that are of use to post-Jungian scholarship in addressing the act of viewing. I give a brief overview of these characteristics in what follows.

Mulvey states that woman stands in patriarchal culture as signifier of the male other: Woman is the bearer of meaning, bearer of the image; she is not maker of meaning, nor is she bearer of the look. 'The look, pleasurable in form, can be threatening in content, and it is woman as representation/image that crystallises this paradox' (1999: 837). It is essential to recognize troublesome representations of gender in narrative film as, semiotically speaking, images of the human form in narrative cinema are generally to be considered iconic and therefore *representative* of humans in the real world in terms of appearance. Although difficult to extend to diegetic characterization, this representation in its most politically explicit form is one of the principal ways in which meaning may be articulated in the re-telling of the film's story in the everyday.[1] However, the pleasurable act of viewing is not wholly contingent on meaning, as we have seen in relation to the phenomenological perception–expression of film. This is because phenomenologically speaking, pleasurable viewing is an affective element in the act and experience of viewing generally, whereas in the sense that Mulvey uses the word it is more akin to desire. Filmic desire is an emotional and discriminable object predicated on the signifying systems and encoding process that she describes in detail and, and therefore stands as a separate (although no less important) object for analysis, simultaneous to the affective potential of pleasure.

In all of this, the importance for the post-Jungian film analyst is fairly familiar. Following Von Franz's position on popular distractions such as film (see epigraph at start of chapter), it is clear that the curiosity and fascination in viewing outlined by Mulvey's key theory still stand as an indicator of alienation within a contemporary socio-political context. As stated by Jung and countless others after him, the disaffection and the disenchantment typical of today's collective and objective consciousness in the West are, ultimately, political in essence no matter whether articulated in paradigms of historical struggle, psychic distortion or thwarted individuation in the guise of shadow inflation. It is still a matter of regarding the participation in Von Franz's 'Movies and television, spectator sports and political excitements' as empty gestures and diversions away from the underlying poverty of everyday life. My point here is not altogether pessimistic, as there is a political potentiality in the act of viewing film – the affective potential of pleasurable viewing, aside from the desire engaged in Mulvey's articulation of curiosity and fascination. Film is, of course, not necessarily a special case in popular culture, but is a key resource in rethinking the place of ordinary subjects within a highly mediatized, late capitalist society.

There is little denying that, following Mulvey, looking itself is a source of pleasure, just as there is pleasure in being looked at. However, Mulvey here stipulates two Freudian takes on this pleasure of looking and being-looked-at. The first of these is scopophilia – simply put, Freud's term for an instinctual component where one takes other people as objects, subjecting them to a controlling and curious gaze. This relates back to childish, voyeuristic activity, especially found in the child's curiosity with the private, the forbidden or the taboo. For Mulvey, cinema is indifferent to the presence of its audience, producing for them a separation and play on voyeuristic phantasy (curious looking at an objectified other). It is almost as if cinema is itself a fetishistic space (in the 'magical' sense of the word) unfolding for the audience.

However, part of narrative cinema's convention builds up this world of the film for its audience but is utterly separate from it. The contrast between darkness of movie theatre and the play of light and shadow on the canvas screen lends itself to this separation and helps sustain the illusory status of the moving image. In other words, cinema thus satisfies the primordial wish for pleasurable looking but also develops scopophilia in its secondary, narcissistic aspect: 'Scale, space, stories are all anthropomorphic. Here curiosity and the wish to look intermingle with a fascination with likeness and recognition: the human face, the human body, the relationship between the human form and its surroundings, the visible presence of the person in the world' (Mulvey, 1999: 836).[2]

Another aspect of Mulvey's discussion is on the way that pleasure in looking has been split between active/male and passive/female. This is where the feminist agenda of Mulvey's work comes to the fore (although is not complete until she implies a notion of gendered division of viewing labour towards the end of the essay). On this aspect, Mulvey (1999: 837) is worth quoting in full here:

In their traditional exhibitionist role women are simultaneously looked at and displayed, with their appearance coded for strong visual and erotic impact so that they can be said to connote *to-be-looked-at-ness*... The presence of woman is an indispensable element of spectacle in normal narrative film, yet her visual presence tends to work against the development of the storyline, to freeze the flow of action in moments of erotic contemplation.

There are a number of familiar ways in which this is achieved in classical narrative cinema. One is through the initial introduction of character, framed in such a way as to emphasize certain body parts in isolation, intercut with the male protagonist's on-looking gaze within the diegesis. There are some interesting well-known examples of this. In the film noir *The Postman Always Rings Twice* (Garnett, US, 1946) for example, we are first introduced to Cora (Lana Turner) through a sequence of shots in which a lipstick falls to the floor and rolls towards Frank (John Garfield). Frank looks off-frame, and the camera follows the path towards the direction in which the lipstick rolled from in a tracking shot. The shot ends at a pair of feet and bare legs. Frank gets off his chair and picks the lipstick off the floor, and it is only after his actions that we see a full-length shot of Cora. The implication of this particular sequence of shots, according to the conventions of narrative cinema and continuity editing at least, is that Frank is gazing at Cora's legs, and the subjective nature of the tracking shot suggests that his gaze is not interested in her face. It is only after this lengthy track, followed by a cool exchange between the two characters, that we see Turner's face close up. The implication here is that the camera's gaze is standing-in for Frank's, and that, through a secondary identification with the male protagonist (and his gaze), we are sharing in his erotic contemplation of Cora/Turner as woman-as-image.

Another, much more recent, example comes from contemporary Indian cinema. *Devdas* (Bhansali, India, 2002) is a neo-noir remake of a classical Indian tale, and so shares much with *Postman* in terms of thematics and the role of the woman as *femme fatale* in the narrative development. We are introduced to the character of Chandramukhi (Madhuri Dixit) through a sequence of shots that concentrate on her (somewhat implausibly) voluminous hair, as she oils it in a mirrored room. Intercut with this, a shot of Devdas (Shahrukh Khan) looking on implies that he is viewing Chandramukhi with 'erotic contemplation'. The shots of Cora and Chandramukhi in the two examples just mentioned are, according to convention and by implication, subjective, i.e. from the male characters' point-of-view. This reinforces the position that Mulvey (1999: 838) takes on the look. She states that:

As the spectator identifies with the main male protagonist, he projects his look on to that of his like, his screen surrogate, so that the power of the male protagonist as he controls events coincides with the active power of the erotic look, both giving a sense of omnipotence.

In this way, woman as bearer of the image functions as spectacle on two registers: firstly, as an erotic object for characters within the diegesis and secondly, as an erotic object for the spectator. In this sense, then, for Mulvey narrative cinema reproduces the 'so-called' natural conditions of human perception. She states (1999: 839) that:

> Camera technology (as exemplified by deep focus in particular) and camera movements (determined by the action of the protagonist), combined with invisible editing (demanded by realism) all tend to blur the limits of screen space. The male protagonist is free to command the stage, a stage of spatial illusion in which he articulates the look and creates the action.

There are, of course, films that feature female protagonists as Mulvey acknowledges, but she notes that the strength of the female protagonist is often more 'apparent than real' and is therefore problematic. She does not dwell on this as her focus of discussion, however, citing the work done by feminist contemporaries such as Claire Johnston and Pam Cook. Her 'Afterthoughts on "Visual Pleasure and Narrative Cinema"' essay (Mulvey, 1989), published some 15 years after her original paper, acknowledged an oscillation in the female protagonist between passive femininity and regressive masculinity in the narrative development. I will return to this revision in Chapter 7, in the context of theories of narrative in film. For now, returning to our two examples, the eroticization of the female form in narrative cinema is multiplied through the fact that, very often, the female form is prostheticized through the techniques of edit and framing, leading to a fetishized emphasis on particular body parts. In our two examples, this involves the legs of Lana Turner and the hair of Madhuri Dixit. The latter example may be further complicated by three overdeterminations. Firstly, depending on viewing context, Madhuri may be subjected to an additional stage of objectification through the fact of her ethnic otherness. Writers such as bell hooks (1992), Stuart Hall (1997) and Jacqueline Bobo (1995) have commented at length on this in terms of the spectacle of (racial) otherness. I will not dwell on this here, although this is an important element in the film's semiosis. However, the erotic spectacle of Madhuri is more definitely and fully focused on a dismembered objectification rather than racial differentiation, in the way that she is introduced when bathing her hair. The sequence ends with Chandramukhi being aware of Devdas' presence and whipping her wet hair against the mirrored wall, causing it to shatter spectacularly to unnerve him. This is, in a physically manifest sense, an explosive end to a highly eroticized sequence, and masterfully bookmarks the scene as such. In part, this is thanks to a third objectification, in that Madhuri, as star of Indian cinema (a fact that compounds the fascination with her performance and image) is partly objectified through the conventions of a specific star system.

Returning to the notion of introducing (and thus, fetishizing of) the female figure as isolated/fragmented body parts serves to objectify further the female image. In Mulvey's formulation, this leads to a further pleasure in this objectification and separation of viewing subject and viewed object. It is, ultimately, a Lacanian aspect of the phantasy of the Real: the body-in-pieces; undifferentiated existence before the first stirrings of subjectivity in the infant during the 'mirror stage'. I return to these concerns in relation to the notion of synchronicity in Chapter 8. As previously stated, the difficulty in this scenario is that Mulvey is discussing the fundamental separation of the activities of viewing (the film's viewing view and the spectator's viewing) on a psychic level.

This theorization of the cinematic apparatus was expanded by several film theorists during the mid-1970s, most notably Jean-Louis Baudry, who wrote on the 'apparatus' of film and film spectatorship in the journals *Film Quarterly* and *Camera Obscura*. Among Baudry's most notable contributions to the debate was the emphasis on the startling resemblance of film to dreams. This followed closely Freud's metapsychological dream analyses, of which Baudry was not uncritical: Baudry stated that he did not wish to insist excessively on Freud's analysis. However, his commentary was largely predicated on an earlier psychic topography that entailed the conscious, preconscious and unconscious. He writes: 'We need only note that the dream wish is formed from daytime residues in the Preconscious system which are reinforced by drives emanating from the Unconscious . . . it is regression which gives dream its definitive shape' (1999: 769). This engaged a topography that Freud was to rework significantly in his later writing, but additionally rested largely on the assumption of the film/dream metaphor, a likeness that is curiously close to the problematic anthropomorphic assumptions of other writers such as Mulvey.

One should not be too quick to jump to accusations of anthropomorphism in the theory of likeness to human processes in psychoanalytic approaches to spectatorship. This emphasis was typically later taken to be much stronger than perhaps the original authors intended, and what was initially a re-imagining of the spectator–screen relationship at the level of the psychic can be read through its detractors as an immovable theoretical edifice. Such superficial thinking negates the metaphorical value of thinking through the cinematic apparatus as to an extent representative of psychic processes, and is a similar negation to that which I have already discussed in the light of recent interventions from phenomenology. In that case, however, it is more an analogy (an attempt to remove itself from the linguistic by avoiding metaphor and allegory) than a metaphor, and as such is a more flexible and less dependent likeness. What is most useful here is that the holistic approach re-imagines the separation formulated by the apparatus theorists as a suspension of the living tie between conscious and unconscious worlds, materialized as it is by the fundamentally embodied notion of the viewing and viewed view. As previously discussed, film does not represent phenomenology as much as present for the viewer its perception–expression. This, however, does not stop some commentators from exercising criticism. For Frampton (2006: 43), there is a major problem with translating phenomenology to film wholesale in this fashion:

> We are separate yet mingled with our world, but film 'is' its world. Merleau-Ponty remarks that films 'are particularly suited to make manifest the union of mind and body, mind and world, and the expression of one in the other.' The film-world and the film-intention are one.

Therefore, for Frampton (2006: 43):

> How can film have experience of 'separate things' when film is its things? The film-body and the film-image should be seen as one and the same. The result of this is the realisation that we need to give film its own terms, not second-hand phenomenological ones.

Film may be its own world, but exists of and for the real world: Its perception–expression is experienced through the other viewer (the audience) and is understood as expression of perception by anyone who has attempted the activity of expressing perception in the real world. As Sobchack (1992: 204) writes:

> As we engage it, the film is visible solely as the intentional 'terminus' of an embodied and seeing subject, as an intentional activity irreducibly correlated with an intentional object. That is, the mechanisms and humans who *enable* the correlation to visibly exist as vision are not themselves visible in the correlation – nor can they be said to function as mediating instruments or agents *within* that correlation.

Although this process is rife in narrative cinema, the conventions of that cinema are such that much of this activity is rendered invisible through the techniques of continuity. It is perhaps most apparent in those art films that emphasize the filmmaking process in their plot development. For example, in *2 or 3 things I know about her* (Godard, Fr, 1968) Godard's voiceover references both what is being shown and how it is being made to show in that way, in addition to stating its relevance to the story line. This simultaneously reveals a self-aware camera, an intrusive and subjective narrator and a description of the editing and framing process in words.

For Frampton, these techniques and the means by which I have described them would be more properly classed as a poetics of the cinema, a philosophical rather than theoretical endeavour. More useful than a phenomenological reduction, for Frampton, a post-phenomenological poetics of film would entail what seems to be a more idealist and holistic engagement. He writes that, 'An accurate description of the difference between optical and actual movement in cinema (zoom and track) may be clarifying for film theorists, but does it provide a way into the thoughtful and poetic usages of these forms?' (2006: 45). I find myself in disagreement with Frampton here, because I contend that the phenomenology of film experience provides us with an adequately poetic and thoughtful grounding for film experience. The movements mentioned (zoom and track) and their difference, especially when used in conjunction, may be expressively used simultaneously to mimic sensation and therefore be perceptive as well as expressive in an affective sense.

It is troublesome to assume a direct analogy between film and reality, or filmic images and inner thought processes in an anthropomorphic sense. However, we may say that the attempt to approximate human experience through cinematic representation and form elucidates the embodied, *felt* relationship between the spaces occupied by the film and the spaces occupied by the spectator. It constitutes the other subjectivity of the film's viewing view, for film is the eye that sees and is seen. It is also seen to be seeing, and embodies 'other seeing' – that is, another subject that sees. As previously stated, film is more than analogy for human vision: It is an embodiment of subjectivity, an object that is seen to be materializing an existential, embodied perception. This is further complicated when we consider the cinematic gaze. As Sobchack states, the 'here, where I (eye) am' of cinematic spectatorship, the place where vision is en visioned or imagined, is doubly occupied as 'here, where we see', and as 'there, where I am not' (1992: 10). It is, in short, the space embodied and inhabited by the cinematic other: Whether human-like or not, this *unheimlich* or alien aspect of cinematic vision is most palpably perceived–expressed in this way. Cinematic presence for Sobchack, then, is ultimately a presence and experience of being-in-the-world not congruent with the viewer's own. Therefore the secondary narcissistic aspects of scopophilia suggested by Mulvey as a recognition of sorts (leading to a specific identification with the protagonist) fall some way short of accommodating such subjective otherness. The 'visible presence of the person in the world' is merely the semiotic equivalent of the intangible-but-affective presence of the 'other' view. For Sobchack (1992: 10):

> Thus, while space and its significance are intimately shared and lived by both film and viewer, the viewer is always at some level aware of the double and reversible nature of cinematic perception. . . . The viewer,

therefore, shares cinematic space with the film but must also negotiate it, contribute to and perform the constitution of its experiential significance.

For Sobchack, the aim of semiotic phenomenology is not to arrive at essential or perceptive categories, 'but to address "thickness" of human experience and the rich and radical elements of incarnate being and its representation' (1992: 7): that is, signification and significance as immanent, *as given*, with existence, informed by it and understood with it and other to it. This 'otherness', far from being an element to be disregarded, should be thought of, semiotically speaking, as a secondary, yet always present, notion of systematic 'distortion'. It is enough here to say that ideological, rhetorical, and poetic modes of address may be employed to interpretative ends when analysing the representational elements of these distortions themselves. After all, these modes all affirm the experience of cinema. It does not fall to phenomenology to 'correct' these distortions remedially, nor to move beyond the contingencies and specificity of biased existence/ experience. However, in identifying the interplay of such contingencies in the enworldedness of the film, we can come to accommodate such 'distortion' as part of the analytical methodology of film criticism, phenomenological reduction, and post-Jungian holistic analysis in particular.

To summarize the phenomenological and analytical approach to the gaze, then, if perception is an equivalent to 'making sense', and expression is an equivalent to signifying this making sense, the viewer's vision, as an element of the perception–expression of viewer, viewing and viewed plays a major part. Sobchack (1992: 9) states that:

Through the address of our own vision, we speak back to the cinematic expression before us, using a visual language that is also tactile, that takes hold of and actively grasps the perceptual expression, the seeing, the direct experience of that anonymously present, sensing, sentient 'other'.

The 'here, where eye (I) am' of film experience that Sobchack identifies as crucial to the tactile viewing-viewed relation can thus be doubly occupied. 'It becomes the "Here, where *we see*" – a *shared* space of being, of seeing, hearing, and bodily and reflective movement performed and experienced by both film and viewer' (1992: 10, emphasis in original). The 'here, where eye am' is simultaneously available as 'here, where we see', but also stands against the viewer as 'there, where I am not'. It is the space embodied and inhabited by the cinematic other, whose presence and experience of being-in-the-world is not congruent with the viewer's. It is a 'present, sensing, sentient "other"' (Sobchack, 1992: 10):

Thus, while space and its significance are intimately shared and lived by both film and viewer, the viewer is always at some level aware of the double and reversible nature of cinematic perception . . . The viewer, therefore, shares cinematic space with the film but must also negotiate it, contribute to and perform the constitution of its experiential significance.

This is why the film has a specific ontology with which we must engage specifically. By thinking through our place as viewer in relation to the specific medium in question, we may begin to understand how films come to be seen as being meaningful, while at the same time producing for the viewer a sense of specific meanings, and specific intentions behind those meanings, for which both the semiotic and symbolic attitudes are crucial for engagement. On this, it is useful to turn once again to Terry Eagleton (1990: 18) in his discussion of the relationship between phenomena and aesthetics:

The body, even before it has come to think, is always a sensibly experiencing organism positioned in its world in a way quite distinct from the placing of an object in a box. Scientific knowledge of an objective reality is always already grounded in this intuitive pre-givenness of things to the vulnerably perceptive body, in the primordial physicality of our being-in-the-world.

Phenomenology and meaning-making in film spectatorship

Therefore, as discussed in the previous chapter, the main question that should be asked of film is not what films mean, but how they come to be seen as *meaningful* in a sensible, pre-given and intuitive sense. In other words, meaningfulness is the element of the spectator–text relationship that matters for the phenomenologist as for the analytical psychologist. This potential for meaning, as I expressed in Chapter 1 and discussed in the previous chapter, is important as it differs quite markedly both from the iteration of political content and from a notion of 'message' presence in-itself as social commentary. Such matters, as discussed in Chapter 3's analysis of *The Pursuit of Happyness*, are revealed through the most superficial of interpretative approaches and contain very little in the way of potential or illicit meaning. Our perception of the signification process, which tells the story of, for example, Chris Gardner's motivation and drive towards productivity, is itself arrested through the pointedly immediate social commentary of the film's narrative economy. Here, meaning, as a message from which we as an audience are presumably supposed to be able to learn something about ourselves, is to be found in the interstice between form and content. Form (in this case, resolution and denouement) and content (material success and individuation in the face of economic privation and racial prejudice, the American tradition of material pursuit embodied in the writings of Thomas Jefferson) are somewhat inseparable in this context. But to reduce interpretation of the film and its narrative image to this would be to render racial identity and social class status, for example, meaningless. Worse still, the explicit resolution proposed by such a film would ignore completely the very real struggles against economic adversity and institutional racism, sexism and discrimination that exist for all kinds of disenfranchized groups and sectors of Western society.

Meaning in cinema is volatile, and is engaged through several layers, or 'frames of perspective', problematics that impinge on options of interpretation in several ways. As we have seen, meaning-making is constituted at various levels of production and seen through various frames of perspective: for example, through prevailing ideology and the stylistic/signifying systems that support it, through film's simulational or abstraction capabilities, through hierarchical systems of technical virtuosity, and also through 'authentic' attempts to address the spectator through social commentary. It is virtually impossible to say for certain which of these 'frames' has more influence on meaning-making at any one time, as this would constitute a universalization of the worst kind: Films (both popular and art-house) mobilize different frames at various times, often simultaneously. I shall discuss these frames of perspective and reference momentarily, in terms of 'orders of reality'. For now, we need to consider how we arrive at a point where these frames actively come into play and impinge on meaning production. In other words, how do films come to be seen as meaningful in the first place? Is there something 'about' the materiality of a film that enables such accommodation for meaning? If so, how might this be apprehended by the spectator through the act of spectatorship?

Patrick Fuery (2000: 114) has written that in phenomenology, such questions are underpinned by 'quasi-judgements'. These are:

> distinctions made between those actions and events in the text, such as film, and those that take place in the outside 'real' world. We do not race out of the theatre and call the police when Norman Bates stabs Marion in the shower, yet our emotional reactions of horror and fear demonstrate that at least on one level such events mean something.

As discussed in the last couple of chapters, this famous scene is an exemplar of the way in which the imagination of the audience can be manipulated through the inner workings of film technique. As we have seen, this has much in common with Grodal's notion of 'enaction', when various psychosomatic dimensions in which mind and body working together are activated by the act of watching film, and supplemented by emotional and physiological reactions in the spectator. For Grodal, however, this 'mirroring' effect is metaphorical in the sense that the characters on screen are virtual stand-ins for our reactions to the events portrayed. We do not usually act in a way suggested by the on-screen participants in the real world, but imagine such acts, and to an extent our bodies prepare for them through physiological effects. We never actually *see* Marion Crane (Janet Leigh)'s naked body, although we think we do. In fact, there is a certainty to that image. We do not see the knife penetrate flesh, but are certain that this is what is being represented here – there is evidence in the amount of blood that is let, as well as the perceived pain that has been inflicted, and the distress evident in the victim's reaction (enhanced through the chilling Bernard Herman score). Through a series of ingenious cuts and imaginative camera positioning, a naked and vulnerable Marion Crane has been murdered in cold blood before our eyes, and yet we know that she has not. This attitude is somewhat linked to Grodal's term, 'reality-status': an evaluation that enables us to make distinctions as to whether apparent phenomena are reality, fantasy, fiction, dream, and so on. This reality-status of apparent phenomena presented to the sensory faculties is filtered through prior (worldly) knowledge, (reasonable) understanding and emotion.

In cinema, certain procedures for ascertaining the reality-status of phenomena based on these filters are rendered ambiguous through a variety of techniques peculiar to cinema, including, in the *Psycho* example, fast editing techniques, combined with multiple takes from several angles. The virtuosity found in Hitchcock's film adds to the uncertainty about the 'reality-status' of the images we encounter, contributing to the shock value of the film and its narrative conceits. However, whereas the notion of enaction is a useful one in determining emotional response as an effect of audience–text intersubjectivity, there are a number of ways in which the cognitive approach is found lacking as a holistic approach to film. This is largely because its schemata often do not reconcile the microcosmic necessity of close textual analysis with the macrocosmic context of production within the social formation, while simultaneously accounting for the intersubjective relation between audience and text. In sum, such reconciliation would contribute to a potential understanding of the world of the film as ascertained by audiences; that is, the potentiality of meaningfulness itself. There is, furthermore, a crucial difference between an approach like Grodal's, and an approach that incorporates phenomenology. While the former relies on reality-status as a combinatory presentation filtered through prior knowledge, (reasonable) understanding and emotion, the latter involves a complex analytical reduction process that assumes prior knowledge as an order of reality that must be isolated and, if necessary, eliminated. So that one may engage the primary signification of embodied perception–expression, this process is necessary in order to appraise the object of analysis as a thing-in-itself, as well as to acknowledge the complexity of determination and socio-cultural context and thus engage the process of meaning-making. This complex methodology, as we shall see, engages the notion of essence, while at the same time establishing an analysis of those essences as elements of a holistic, meaningful phenomenon.

Patrick Fuery has written an account of the orders or registers of reality on which phenomenological quasi-judgements may be made. For the purposes of making sense of these within the context of this book, I have chosen to recount three of these registers here – 'filmic reality', 'subjective reality' and 'phenomenological reality' – renegotiating them in existential phenomenological terms for the relationship between audience and text. This is also a practical demonstration of the practice of phenomenological reduction: the move towards the object of analysis as a thing-in-itself, our experience of which is most readily constructed through the orders of reality that supersede the thing-in-itself in shared cultural meaning. Although Fuery describes a number of other orders or filters, such as the psychical, the epistemic and the ideological, I choose not to outline these here, as they are the subject of much discussion elsewhere in this book, and underpin filmic and subjective reality in subsequent chapters.

Filmic reality – the world of the film

The first order, one might describe as the world of the film as apprehended most 'immediately' by the spectator – the 'movie' that we view. Essentially, this is filmic reality, constructed and experienced through two levels. The first is, for Fuery, an order that is made up of narrative, style, history, position in the industry, and so on. Presumably, this also crucially includes the aesthetics of the film itself – its aesthetic form enables the mobilization of perceived inner movement in the spectator, and relates dialectically to the psyche, subjectivity and epistemes (systems of knowledge, which often incorporate the promulgation of ideological positioning). This involves such phenomena as Grodal's enaction, as well as the activation of Münsterberg's imagination (and, to an extent, the activation of Lacan's Imaginary, to which we shall return momentarily).

For Fuery, this construction of the world of the film reveals something of its 'world order, and how that order in turn, is intertextually connected to lots of other films' (2000: 125). The second of these levels is the film's reality constructed out of the culmination of various elements from a combination of the other reality orders, which I outline below. It is important to reiterate that this world of the film as immediately apprehended is a *culmination* – a summation read through the filter of a number of frames of perspective and perception which anticipate cultural cues that collectively construct the 'natural attitude' towards the world of the film. Through a distillation, or a reduction of the impact of subjectivity, psychology, knowledge and politics, the constructed aspect of this natural attitude is revealed. This is one of the primary goals of phenomenological reduction: to move beyond constructed reality towards an appreciation of the thing-in-itself. In this way, the construction as well as the object may be negotiated in a more thorough, meaningful way.

This method has its own sympathetic resonance with that used by Jung and especially his immediate followers. For example, and as discussed briefly in previous chapters, the naturalization of phenomena known as cultural symbols in Jungian terminology plays on the immediate impact of shared cultural meanings that may be apprehended in an unproblematic and superficial manner, and the concomitant release and shared experience of emotion is palpable. These shared cultural meanings are often associated with rituals and pictorial representations that have evolved over many centuries, and which are inextricably linked to mass and/or religious phenomena, such as the incorporation of the deity, played out in the Roman Catholic Eucharist. A commonly asserted symbol of this kind in the analytical tradition, the swastika, has obvious and immediate connotations. Most explicitly, it is the symbol of National Socialist atrocity, an appropriation of the symbol of ancient Spartan martial authoritarianism. Subsequently appropriated by subcultural movements such as punk, the swastika came to signify the sacrilege of postmodern signification, and the shocking aestheticization of politics. It is also, of course, an ancient symbol from Hindu tradition, signifying enlightenment. That it can mean two or three things simultaneously not only is a confirmation of the arbitrary nature of signification, but also signals the way in which symbols have over-determined meaning within the cultural sphere. It may be interchangeable with any number of equally 'meaningful' symbols. This process is not just tied-in to Western culture, but also manifests itself forcefully as a global phenomenon.

The beautifully rendered opening sequence to Mahiro Maeda's *Animatrix* animated short, 'The Second Renaissance Part I' (2003), demonstrates this over-determination in global cinema perfectly. This sequence incorporates a combination of representations of technological matrices (microprocessors and networks of light formation) with traditional symbols of, and gestures towards, knowledge acquisition. In the director's commentary, Maeda states that he wanted to visualize a gate leading to visual archives. The audience is positioned as privileged to information that has been accessed in some way. It is an enunciatory technique typical of contemporary Japanese animation, although it may be found in any number of story-telling techniques. Mary Ann Miller (1998), for example, has written about the ways in which the enunciation of the story-world is much like a ritual. In the history of film theory, theorists have tried to describe this from different perspectives, often stumbling on the common metaphor of crossing a bridge and entering a space very different to that of everyday life. This is especially so in the case of the cinema theatre, as the exhibition space is set apart from the everyday via several simultaneous cues. Indeed, as discussed in the opening to this chapter, many theorists of the 1970s took this as one of their main points of analysis, especially in the context of viewing pleasure. For example, the shared, 'uterine' space of the darkened theatre and the 'undivided' attention given over to the cinema screen characterize cinematic viewing.

The rhetoric of cinema-going experience remains surprisingly robust. One has merely to think back to Gibbs and Pye's remarks (outlined in Chapter 1) that state the typical patterns of making sense of a film on departure from the cinema. This tends to happen to nowhere near the same extent after a shared televisual experience, for example. Although contemporary television sometimes emulates cinema in this regard, the fact that many pre-credit or credit sequences of popular feature films explicitly enunciate the story-world reinforces the experience that Miller discusses.

For Maeda, the transformation of the overtly technological into the overtly spiritual and traditional in the opening sequence of his anime short signals an invitation to the audience: to participate in the dissemination of knowledge about the pre-history of the *Matrix* story-world. Hindu symbolism, especially, is abundant in this sequence. The goddess-like keeper of the archive (and the story's narrator) sits in lotus position within a lotus flower of eight petals. This is a subdivision of the classical Jungian four-folded symbol of Selfhood. Tellingly, Maeda states that he had the mandala in mind when designing this sequence: 'Mandala is meant to be something that includes everything. I thought that it fits to the idea of this place where the knowledge is stored.' Although there are a number of problems with assuming director's commentary as 'authentic' – the central argument in Chapter 2 concerning the centrality of the author, problems with interpretation from the original Japanese into English notwithstanding – one need not resort to the director's commentary to engage Maeda's interpretation. A rudimentary knowledge of Hindu tradition or analytical psychology would tell the same tale of these representations. The point of this digression is that it serves to demonstrate, in cinematic terms, the ways that filmic reality and the world of the film may be apprehended in their most immediate representational state. The reference to other films, to anime culture, to Hollywood appropriations of existentialism, and to wide public consumption of Eastern/New Age philosophies are all present. All are engaged in this very short animated sequence, thus establishing within seconds the appropriate frames of perspective and reference through which an audience apprehends this particular filmic reality. It is not just the film's narrative, nor its aesthetic elements, nor its symbolic representation, but a combination of all of these, overtly mobilized as they are by prior knowledge. A phenomenology of film seeks to go beyond this first order of reality.

Subjective reality – having at a distance

The orders of reality that follow subjective reality (psychology, knowledge, ideology) impact on that subjective experience of reality, of how the world is, and how we think of ourselves, and apprehend, as coherent individuals. This is of course a big question, even within a specialized field of film, and therefore merits some lengthy consideration. As we have seen in Chapter 3, the imaginary (of various hues, both psychoanalytic and ideological) status of subject formation within the social forms the basis of a constructed set of interpretations. Subjective reality, then, may be viewed as deriving 'from the subject's position within all these other orders of reality, and the sorts of impacts that that has on how we construct, accept (or deny), and participate in the other orders' (Fuery, 2000: 125).

It may be taken further than this however, for experiential reality in its subjective sense reinforces a sense of the centrality of the individual subject, while at the same time allowing for a deconstruction of that subjectivity based not on difference, but on continuity. As we shall see, this approach to subjectivity as an adjectival term is very different to that of the notion of an ideal 'human subject'. The differences implicit in the terms 'subject' and 'subjectivity' stem from the way that the two notions are constructed. The first term is a construct based on specific Cartesian principles of dualism; the second is a construct that both underpins the phenomenon of experience and is created by it. The first is an ideal, cohesive form; the second is a fluid, social form that may or may not be linked inextricably to the first. This idea of fluidity and continuity in the social formation is the break from the psychoanalytic view of the acquisition of differentiation through language that underpins Lacanian thought. It seeks to engage a *material* experience of the world that connects the 'eye that sees' with the 'I that is seen' (and, conversely as we shall see, the 'I that sees' with the 'eye that is seen', underpinning the experience of intersubjectivity and inter-objectivity). Rather than a mis-re-cognition of self, this connection is based more exclusively on cognition: incorporating the imaginary in a worldly, or creaturely, existence more closely associated with existentialist phenomenology than post-structuralist psychoanalysis. It also engages the tradition in modern Western image production underpinning the evaluation processes associated with image culture, and of which cinema is a crucial development: that of central perspective. To situate this position more firmly within the context of film studies, I return to the work of Vivian Sobchack, and her phenomenology of film experience.

It is a commonplace in media and film theory to assume that photographic and cinematic optics are structured according to Renaissance theories of perspective, and Cartesian laws of perception. 'Such perspective,' according to Sobchack, 'represented the visible as originating in, organized, and mastered by an individual and centred subject' (2004: 142). For Stephen Heath, in *Questions of Cinema* (1981: 28), this was more a question of central projection – the Quattrocento, a system introduced in Italy, specifically by such key artists and thinkers as Alberti during the 1430s:

The possible exact match for the eye of picture and object, the deceptive illusion; the centre of the illusion, the eye in place. What is fundamental is the idea of the spectator at a window, an '*aperta finestra*' that gives a view on the world.

For Heath, the stress in this system 'is on the camera as a machine for the reproduction of objects (of solids) in the form of images realized according to the laws of the rectilinear propagation of light rays, which laws constitute the perspective effect' (1981: 28).

Notice here that Heath uses the term 'effect' – perspective as generally accepted in image production may be thought of, in a general sense, as a constructed realism. This may be thought of as 'correct' reproduction of reality, internalized as a value of rendering the image as realistic and 'correct'. The problem that appears in the commonplace assumption of central projection occurs when the observer's eye is not exactly matched to the centre of the projected perspective of the picture, resulting in a distortion of rectilinear perspective. This distortion is sometimes appropriated in image production to emphasize both 'subject' position and process implicit in image production itself. This is called anamorphosis: 'the recognition and exploitation of the possibilities of this distortion' (1981: 28). This technical process allows for marginality of viewer's position, and also for parody of the central projection system, e.g. Holbein's 'The Ambassadors' (1533) or the recent street art of Julian Beever. For Heath, 'What must be more crucially emphasized is that the ideal of a steady position, of a unique embracing centre, to which Galileo refers and to which anamorphosis pays its peculiar homage, is precisely that: an *ideal*' (1981: 29, emphasis in original). Does this not then suggest that Heath's subject is an ideal subject? That his discussion should be read in the context of a tradition of idealism that informs the very notion of a cohesive, singular empirical human subject? Note that Heath is not necessarily an idealist in this same tradition: His argument here emphasizes the differences implicit in the terms 'subject' and 'subjectivity'.

The de-centring that occurs through anamorphosis – a concomitant postmodernist thread of modernity, if ever there was one – is directly attributable to subjectivity without ever having to rely on 'the subject'. As Heath goes on to say, painting and image production adhering to the Quattrocento system does 'accommodate' alternative views, as well as a variety of marginal perspectives (e.g. again, Holbein), giving the viewer a reproduction of the fluid experiences inherent in modernity as a world-view, as an experience. If every person's experience of the modern world, in a cognitive sense, may be said to be different it is largely due to this very phenomenon. This is of vital importance, as it relates directly to Frampton's argument against Sobchack, in which she is accused of anthropomorphizing the camera. As discussed in the previous chapter, this is far from correct, but this misreading may be explained in terms of reference to the idealized human subject. True, the term 'experience' may be attributable as a human term, but it does not need to correspond directly to a 'subject' in the sense of a cohesive human individual. It may, on the other hand, be quite appropriate in its adjectival form to describe human sensibility brought to bear on the production of images and their meanings (that are, after all, contingent on the act of the film being viewed, upon spectatorship). For this to make sense, we need not consider the camera as a substitute for the eye, any more than we should consider the protagonist in a narrative film as the stand-in for the viewer in identification processes. Heath (1981: 29–30) takes his argument further, by suggesting the 'translation of reality' implicit in the dominant perspective system:

> A real utopianism at work, the construction of a code – in every sense a *vision* – projected onto a reality to be gained in all its hoped-for clarity much more than onto some naturally given reality . . . The Quattrocento system provides a practical representation of the world which in time appears so natural as to offer its real representation, the immediate translation of reality in itself.

Indeed, as already stated, such perspective persists even in contemporary postmodern image production. Given the increasingly unstable centring of the human 'subject' in modernity, and the revelation of the construction of subjectivity in existential and structural theory, this assumption of perspective has proved itself remarkably tenacious. Eugenie Shinkle (2006) has commented, for example, that the Quattrocento system perfected by Renaissance artists such as Alberti has since rendered the (real) embodied, physical nature of visual technologies, from painting through photography and cinema to digital environments, largely a redundant question. In new media technologies, however, the image-as-process is foregrounded primarily through immersive and physical, interactive engagement. It is clear in retrospect that if such interaction makes the qualities of *process* in image consumption more immediate in subjective experience than its semiotic function, then surely any kind of non-trivial interaction (e.g. film spectatorship) would also sustain this quality of process. Process in this formulation is a subjective phenomenon, whose principal characteristic is meaning-production. Again, it appears that what matters here is the potentiality for meaning, or meaning in the process of becoming: the ways in which films come to be seen as meaningful.

Contrary to Cartesian principles, Merleau-Ponty points out that a phenomenological description of subjective human vision is a form of apprehension: 'to see is *to have at a distance*' (cited in Sobchack, 2004: 143, emphasis in original). It is highly suggestive of a possession; of looking and fixing, and the subjective feeling of having at a distance, or apprehending the object, emphasizing the mediated nature of the gaze. This is a principle that, on the face of it, appears to share certain elements of recognition and identification often associated with Lacan's mirror stage. In short, the identification of the infant with the imago of the counterpart in the mirror results in the deflection of the specular I into the social I, evidenced through the acquisition of language, and Lacan's 'Law of the Father'. However, the subjective consumption of filmic images should not be conflated with these psychoanalytic accounts of human subjectivity, as they do not fully engage the construction of the ideal subject. Furthermore, Sobchack's approach plays with the notion of objectification not as a distancing effect as in Mulvey, but as an affective response to viewing the image. Far from alienating the spectator, this formulation suggests that photography and cinema bring subject-beings together in their object-state:

> This subjective activity of *visual possession* – of having but at a distance – is objectified by the materiality of photography that makes possible both a *visible* – and closer – possession. That is, the having at a distance that is subjective vision is literalized in an object that not only replicates and fixes the visual structure of having at a distance but also allows it to be nearer.
>
> (Sobchack, 2004: 143, emphasis in original)

Although Sobchack makes explicit reference to photography here, she later uses the difference between contemplation and lived experience to show the visual movement from still to moving image. This transformation demonstrates the operations of this object-status relation between the spectator and the image. For Sobchack, 'the cinematic radically reconstitutes the photographic' between 'the transcendental, posited moment of the photograph and the existential momentum of the cinema' (2004: 145). This is an idea to which we shall return, as it entails a remarkable transitional state of subjective apprehension between the two media. Vision, in terms of regarding the image, is the same in both media, but the experience of that vision as a lived phenomenon is radically different. Hence we return to the problems associated with transposing the formalist/realist schism from photography to film. The mobilization of still frames in the cinematic apparatus, traditionally 24 frames for each second, is, to the naked eye, a seamless transitional phenomenon and is experienced subjectively as such. However, the 'fact' of its periodical transition from one frame to another through mechanical transition momentarily allows each frame to become. The ontological status of film therefore offers a unique existential representation of lived experience as a causal and meaningful transition from one moment to the next – its almost imperceptible status of always-becoming stands as a remarkable document of subjective reality (even though, of course, it is only experienced as such).

It is interesting to note Sobchack's take on this in full, eloquently summing up this strange corresponding phenomenon between subjectivity and the cinema:

> The cinema mechanically projected and made visible *for the very first time* not just the objective world but the very structure and process of subjective, embodied vision – hitherto only directly available to human beings as an invisible and private structure that each of us experiences as 'our own'.
>
> (2004: 149, emphasis in original)

The analyst Pat Berry, in 'Image and Motion' (2001), points out rather significantly that film began around the same time as depth psychology, so that, for the very first time, the external world presented to its inhabitants coincided with the presentation of their inner worlds in fine detail. In turn, her approach to film is coloured with allusions to the simulational function of cinema as somehow embodying loss. That is, nature (an event) has been transformed into art (an aesthetic form), but in that transformation 'the life water, flesh, here-and-now tangibility of the actual event is sacrificed, creating perhaps a vacuum, an emptiness, in the event itself' (2001: 71).

This is a telling quote, as it reveals two problems in Berry's approach. Firstly, why, for example, does film 'perhaps' create a vacuum? The absence characterizing the Lacanian cinematic apparatus (via identity formation, and the act of misrecognition, for example) is itself enough ground to purchase a theoretical perspective on cinematic 'loss'. Secondly, it is unclear to what event Berry is referring: the event that was filmed? The event of spectatorship, perhaps? Certainly, several theorists, particularly at the height of 'Screen theory', emphasized a loss within the act of spectatorship, based as it was on the illusory nature of identification practices: The poverty of the image in comparison with the real object that is being represented is not a new idea. However, this is a highly problematic notion – even Berry herself (2004: 71) states:

> In return for this loss, the transformation into art provides form and an aesthetic level of excitement: pleasure. With film, this transformation occurs as the event is framed in the camera's eye. Essentially film is a series of such frames sped through a camera and projected onto a screen.

Well, yes, and no. Again, it is not clear whether Berry is suggesting that pleasure is a result of the transformation itself or the satisfaction in contemplating the aesthetic form. I would suggest that it is both, with an eerily powerful emphasis on the former, as this yield of pleasure is the very yield that returns to Freud's idea of infantilized intersubjective playfulness; the 'fort/da' game. It is a crucial part of normative mental capacity that allows for the successful negotiation of the world and its displeasures. I say 'eerily' as this emphasis on the transformative pleasure of cinema is difficult to pin down as an object towards which pleasurable response occurs. In other words, it is affective rather than emotional. This suggests an affective dimension of pleasure that is every bit as embodied as emotional, discriminable pleasure, but with the caveat that if there is at all an object towards which intention is directed, it is the playfulness of that yield of pleasure itself. This new level of excitement that Berry describes, the 'aesthetic level', is an embodying level. Aesthetics do not incorporate just looks and the visual, but also feelings (emotional and affective), politics (ideology, identity, and representation) and the bodily (institutional, civic, and human). Eagleton (1990: 9) describes aesthetics as at once:

> The very secret prototype of human subjectivity in early capitalist society, and a vision of human energies as radical ends in themselves which is the implacable enemy of all dominative or instrumentalist thought. It signifies a creative turn to the sensuous body, as well as an inscribing of that body with a subtly oppressive law.

Therefore, to dismiss aesthetics as a mere loss-provoking element of our emotional lives is rather like dismissing subtitled films as inferior products, relying as they do on a supplementary communicative form in order to tell their story. The feeling of excitement itself becomes a new object, and the act of spectatorship is the new event, partaking in significant facets of ideological, epistemological, and subjective reality. These are not the objects and events that were filmed, but are objects and events nonetheless. This is a crucial omission that Berry, along with countless other film theorists, takes for granted. But we should be careful to highlight both the differences and the similarities between the lived experience of the world-at-large and the lived experience of spectatorship.

Phenomenological reality – 'carnal thoughts'

One method that has proved itself useful in this regard is Sobchack's phenomenology of film experience. Sobchack points out that since the Renaissance, theories of perspective have formed the structural basis of optics and optical technology. One might even venture to say that this has had a knock-on effect on the development and ecology of contemporary visual culture, given the emphasis on the visual aspects of the act of film viewing. The perspective that Sobchack is discussing is the same Cartesian perspective by, in and through which the sense of subjectivity is commonly understood. Although some postmodernists have theorized that the decentring of the subject has caused a caesura in modernist notions of perspective, such perspective persists even in contemporary postmodern image production. Given the increasingly unstable centring of the subject in modernity, and the revelation of the construction of subjectivity in existential and structural theory, perspective has proved itself remarkably tenacious. This is partly as a result of the role of Cartesian perspective in what Heath has described as the 'impression of reality' in cinema: 'Cinema uses the images produced by photography to reproduce movement. Phenomenologically, the result is characterized as "neither absolutely two-dimensional nor absolutely three-dimensional, but something between"' (1981: 27, citation from Merleau-Ponty). It is worth quoting Heath (1981: 30) in full here, as his approach has had a lasting influence on the ways in which cinematic viewing and seeing have come to dominate thinking on the cinematic eye and the cine-subject:

> Eye and knowledge come together; subject, object and the distance of steady observation that allows the one to master the other; the scene with its strength of geometry and optics . . . In so far as it is grounded in the photograph, cinema will contribute to the circulation of this currency, will bring with it monocular perspective, the positioning of the spectator-subject in an identification with the camera as a point of a sure and centrally embracing view.

The image with a capital 'I': affect/imago/symbol/ archetype

However, the relatively recent intervention of phenomenology allows us to move beyond the naïve Cartesianism and abstracted central identification system that Heath identified. This last point is vital if we are to consider the affinity of Jungianism with film studies and the study of images. What one always has to bear in mind is that the study of film is not *just* the study of images. For a start, film is a form that engages, at a conscious level, both the visual and the auditory senses – it is a profoundly audiovisual medium. As we have seen in this chapter, this ignites a crucial question that has become increasingly important to film theorists during the past few years. The phrase 'the study of images' implies that the object of study is primarily visual. What we are dealing with when we study images, then, might concern what our eyes see. The 'audio' part of what we are studying is, hierarchically speaking, nearly always relegated to second place. However, suggesting that this is what Jungian analysts primarily deal with – that the study of images concerns what our eyes see – is plainly ridiculous. No matter how 'post-'Jungian analysts consider themselves to be, no matter how much of our highly mediatized, postmodern culture is driven by image, among the classical concerns of the clinical analytical psychologist, the facilitation of psychic growth, reconciliation and well-being seems to be primary. This raises some fundamental issues in our presupposition of the study of film.

By presupposing that the object of study is visual (and even with the inclusion of sound, merely audiovisual) we are denying the importance that should be placed on the affective responses of our other senses and, holistically, our bodies within viewing contexts. This crucial awareness of the importance of the body as site of both reception and feeling, of process and emotion, in fully articulating the experience of actually watching a film, indicates another affinity between film studies and analytical psychology. It is a highly contentious point within conventions of both analytical psychology and film scholarship, but one that should be made. Indeed, it extends throughout Jung's mid-period thinking, where he develops an emphasis on the impossibility of separating the imaginal from the embodied. For example, in his Seminar on Analytical Psychology in 1925, he noted that:

> Somewhere our unconscious becomes material, because the body is the living unit, and our conscious and unconscious are embedded in it: they contact the body. Somewhere there is a place where the two ends meet and become interlocked.
>
> (cited in Conger, 2005: xxx)

Perhaps Jung's non-committal stance towards locating or defining such 'somewhere' where the different elements 'contact' is less woolly thinking and more an awareness that this interlocking of world, body and psyche as lived and experienced is apparent, but almost impossible to pin down. This is because the interlocking of which Jung speaks is affective in its nature, and is not therefore a discriminable cognitive (emotional) object. The 'image' that analytical psychology deals with (hereafter referred to as the Image, with a capital 'I') is no more fundamentally visual than is the image that film scholars deal with in the discussion of film. It captures both the realms of imagination and the body, and is therefore to be thought of in a more holistic way, if it is to be of any use as a tool for analysis.

Certainly, there are visual elements that are engaged with, and these are just as affective in quality as are other elements. However, to reduce the Image to the merely visual would be to deny the resonance and power that these filmic images potentially have to make us feel in the reciprocation of mind, world and body. That which Fiona Ross describes as 'material' is ever-present in Jungian thinking, but is rarely acknowledged for its material basis, and, conversely, historical materialism has sometimes been guilty of overlooking its imaginative potential. In fact, Hauke alludes to this very possibility throughout *Jung and the Postmodern*, where he discusses the reversibility of semiosis and symbolism within contemporary life. This is ultimately expressed as the flux of signification in the quotidian, suggesting that this reversibility has given rise both to a crisis in meaning and to the potential for fresh forms of expression and engagement within everyday contemporary media production and consumption.

In discussing images in this way, and specifically labelling the object of study as 'the Image', I am of course alluding to archetypes. Again, turning to Roger Brooke's discussion of Jung and phenomenology, we are provided with an extremely useful definition and discussion as to the nature of the archetype within the context of its expression in the form of images. The archetype is, for Brooke, realized through different historical and cultural contexts. Image production rather inevitably reflects those contexts, and therefore the semiotics involved in the interpretation of images draws on a specific array of signs and cultural meanings. In a phenomenological sense, however, these contexts, reflections and interpretation processes are contingent on two factors: formative potentiality and adaptive emotional impact. Here I am referring specifically to Brooke's (1991: 16, emphasis in original) definition of the term 'archetype' as:

> A hypothetical construct, used to account for the similarity in the images that cluster around typically human themes and situations . . . anything said about the meaning of an archetypal image, or *symbol*, is only ever an approximation to this core.

Hence my use of the word 'Image' to distinguish from the merely visual, to describe the formation of powerful, affective images as a potential source of engagement, *and* their emotional impact on the spectator. Here I quote Brooke (1991: 16) at length, as his description of archetypal mutual contingency is useful to further the understanding of the fundamentally dialectical nature of what I describe as the Image:

> As potentialities the archetypes are formative of affects as well as images, and the relationship between affects and images is reciprocal. In other words, archetypal images portray the meaning of the affects, and they can also act as a cue for the release of those affects. On the other hand, affects or emotions (Jung uses these terms interchangeably) are the media through which archetypal images are realised. The closer an experience is to an archetypal core the greater its emotional impact and the fascinating power of its image.

There are a couple of problems with this formulation, not least the troublesome definitions of affect and emotion (terms that I have already defined). I would agree with the reciprocal nature of image and affect, in and through which the affective and emotional weight of the Image is articulated as not specifically visual, but embodied. However, it suggests outright that certain images are of themselves more powerful than others, and that they are *in and of themselves* archetypal. As we have seen, in Brooke's words, the term 'archetype' is 'a hypothetical construct' and therefore much rests on the constructive nature of hypotheses generally, based on effects that are not altogether observable but are rather inferred. This also presupposes an imaginal economy, where certain images are inevitably invested with more potential than others and are of more value for the Jungian analyst. In fact, Fredericksen (2006) outlined this value system explicitly when he spoke of popular film as 'not the most pregnant mode of filmmaking'. In contrast, however, both avant-garde filmmaking and animation are, for Fredericksen, very rich for Jungians, and these are assertions discussed in the previous chapter as rather problematic. What is more useful here is the way that the imaginal economy that is so characteristic of Jungian film studies returns time and again to the fundamental question of the production of meaning. In this regard, Fredericksen is incorrect in his assumption that most Jungian film scholars use the most popular texts because they value them more highly. It is more likely because of the way that popular culture is so prevalent that it becomes the most immediately 'meaningful' to a mass audience, that it provides Jungian film scholars with a readily available source of subject matter. This concerns the film scholar as a matter of course, a question that is ultimately unanswerable in a definitive way. Here I would reiterate a previous point because of its central importance to this argument: Film matters, because of its *potentiality* for meanings and feelings, because of its potential meaningfulness. Following the Archetypal School, interpretation in this sense is of secondary importance, content subordinate to form, and it is for this reason that the living tie between the conscious and unconscious needs to be suspended, and rethought within the reciprocal relationship of mind, world and body.

So, I describe the Image, following from discussions in previous chapters, as the sum of affective properties in a holistic, embodied sense. However, I am also aware that in using the term 'Image' like this, I am getting very close to a prototypical formulation of the unconscious in Jung's early work, before he had coined the term 'archetype': the *imago*. Very similar in nature to archetypes, imagos are structures common to us all, which are expressed most often in the form of natural symbols that are universal in scope, and tend to recur in myths and stories on a global scale. Highly affective in magnitude, and resonating meaning in dreams, tales and recollections, the imago was central to Jung's adaptation of Freud's topology of the mind, because of the emphasis on the generality of libidinal energy rather than its specific relationship to sexuality and aggression, as Freud insisted. This generality, we might say, manifested itself in the affective power of images and in the imaginary power of affect. At this point in Jung's career, the interpretative nature of analysis revolved around specific images and meanings. So much so, in fact, that in the case of dream analysis or art analysis of the analysand, the images produced were considered an effect of hidden desires and specifically related to an aspect of the lifework of the individual. In the move from the term 'imago' to the introduction of the term 'archetype' (in 1919, with the publication of *Instinct and the Unconscious*), Jung moved from a content-based analysis to one of form. In this formulation, the *structure* of the perception and apprehension – the archetype itself – was 'not strictly a psychological content, or phenomenon, but was on the ambiguous edge between the psychological and the organic dimensions of existence' and 'therefore, the archetype itself could never be experienced' (Brooke, 1991: 137). However, its effects can be experienced, realized in the form of the affective and emotional resonance that is both so familiar and so alien at the same time, provoked by the experience of engagement with an image. In sum, the experience of the image, and the image itself, make up the totality of the Image. This, in turn, foregrounds the importance of the materiality of the images themselves as cultural artefacts with which we may engage at an embodied level. To quote therapist Shirley Wheeley (1997: 60):

> In psychoanalytic thought the relationship 'between things' and 'between sets of things' is conceptualised as object relations theory. As with the archetypes, internal objects are not actual entities either, they too are regarded as hypothetical structures.

Once again, it seems that the hypothetical (the imaginal) and the experiential (the embodied) are caught in a mutually mediating relation, dialectical in character and infinitely useful in articulating the one in the other. It is with this notion in mind that this book will apply central concepts of Jungian thought to case studies in Chapters 7 and 8. These case studies are, significantly, chosen to reflect the current climate of film theory, in which we are obliged to consider how film relates to the outside world (politics in particular), to other audiovisual media (such as television), and to the very forms of films themselves (genre and space-time). The notion that space and time in cinema are relative because of cinema's illusory/spectacular nature will be explored further by considering cinema as an illusion of bodies in motion. In Chapter 8 I discuss the position of the moving image as being situated precariously outside space-time as normally experienced and perceived, further extending the otherness of cinematic vision. In the cinema theatre, for example, there is an impression of space, evidenced by the iconic image, which corresponds with our space in real life. There is also an impression of time, evidenced by the illusion of movement within the play of shadow and light on canvas, played out in a linear narrative. When film narrative (or anti-narrative, for that matter) highlights this 'illusory' relation between spectator and spectacle, there is a curious interplay between the quasi-physical image and the emotional alignment of the spectator, similar to how apparatus theorists such as Baudry imagined the relationship between dream-work and the cinema-going audience. Often contingent on the breakdown of causality within the narrative, or in the presentation of the image, this interplay is what Jungians might refer to as potentially *synchronistic*. Therefore, one of the most important and crucial elements of Jungian thought, synchronicity, will be discussed in detail in relation to film spectatorship, as a highly problematic theorization of inner/outer worlds, body/mind, subject/object and difference. In the next chapter, however, a number of key themes touched on here will be picked up and discussed at length in relation to another of Jung's classic theories: that of contrasexuality.

Chapter 6

Contrasexuality and identification

Difference, sameness and gender in film

> The mystical marriage with the queen goddess of the world represents the hero's total mastery of life; for the woman is life, the hero its knower and master.
>
> Joseph Campbell, *The Hero with a Thousand Faces*

> Psychoanalytic theories of identification used within film criticism have led to very narrow conceptualisations of cinematic identification, which have ignored the broader meanings of spectator/star relations and indeed have led to some overly pessimistic conclusions about the pleasures of cinema [. . .] What, then, does identification mean to female spectators?
>
> Jackie Stacey, *Star Gazing: Hollywood Cinema and Female Spectatorship*

There are a number of ways in which the archetypal structures explored by classical Jungian psychology appear not only in folktales, myths and antiquated legends, but also in contemporary cultural texts. Film is, arguably, the most prolific and dynamic contemporary example of this kind of cultural production for a number of historic, economic, industrial and cultural reasons explored elsewhere in this book. The form of narrative film is particularly suited to placing archetypal content within a narrative structure that overtly references character type, modes of story-telling, and individuation processes through the equilibrium–disequilibrium–resolution structure with which popular audiences are so familiar. This is, despite some claims to the contrary by some post-Jungian film scholars, a quite *conscious* use of archetypal motifs. However, film theorists have been dealing with the problem of intended meaning and 'unconscious' structure in film production for some time now.

As discussed in Chapter 2, the idea of 'auteur-structuralism', first developed by critics such as Peter Wollen in the late 1960s, engaged the idea that meaning-making comes from a production perspective and is therefore charged with a synergy activated by both authorial intention and the unconscious structure within the work. Through sustained critical engagement with this synergy, what Perkins called a 'hard core of basic and often recondite motifs' (cited in Wollen, 1999: 521) is revealed. This hard core was the element of the work that both defined it internally, and set it apart from other directors' work.

What is crucial to the application of the notion of archetypal material here is that it is a mistake to think that the use of archetypal imagery is anything more than the utilization of themes and motifs familiar to audiences in traditional story-telling strategies. In other words, we might say that much Jungian film criticism that makes use of this strategy does so superficially, reiterating a common visual language that exists on screen. In the above epigraph from Joseph Campbell, this is revealed through a specific emphasis: 'The mystical marriage with the queen goddess of the world *represents* the hero's total mastery of life' (emphasis added). That is, the archetypal imagery encountered through the tale of the hero and his union with an embodiment is a mere representation. The evocation of syzygy in the individuation process of the life of the hero is represented through the union of character types in a narrative, but this is not necessarily followed by activation of archetypal material. The activation of the archetype as a structure is a very different phenomenon: It is a non-conscious or partly conscious mode of engaging audiences that is affective in character and therefore very difficult to discern, not contingent on discriminable objects. This is particularly the case when, in phenomen-ological terms, the subjective reality of one's position as a viewer within a dominant film culture takes over the interpretative process. As Jung himself once wrote (1998: 99):

> By the 'subject' I mean first of all those vague, dim stirrings, feelings, thoughts and sensations which flow in on us not from any demon-strable continuity of conscious experience of the object, but well up like a disturbing, inhibiting, or at times helpful, influence from the dark inner depths.

What is interesting here is that Jung goes on to describe the self-perception of subjectivity as the perception of an 'inner object', thus entertaining the objectification of self-perception, and the implications that this might have for object relations and their impact on meaning. In other words, the appearance of an archetypal figure such as Obi Wan Kenobi in the original *Star Wars* trilogy is so obviously supposed to represent the Image of the Wise Old Man or Mentor structure that we tend, as objective viewers, to assume that this is the case. Thanks to the convention of auteurism that exists in film culture, when a director such as George Lucas admits that he has read and been influenced by Joseph Campbell, we also might tend to assume that this interpretation is the 'correct' one. As demonstrated in the following chapter, the use of 'archetypal' contents or character types in film criticism is simple shorthand for the filmmaker to move the plot along, and for audiences to engage with character types that are perhaps immediately familiar to them. Reading anything further into the text requires a critical understanding of the source material, the historic, cultural and socio-political implications of production and consumption contexts. I am not suggesting that popular audiences do not possess such knowledge, but the prevailing film culture, with its emphasis on magic and escapism, gives little freedom or need for the notion of such a viewing position. Furthermore, a critical understanding of one's own position in relation to these factors in terms of embodiment, and one's own field of experience in the phenom-enological sense, is crucial to the understanding of how Image and Material interact in film spectatorship.

Contrasexual archetypes, identity and feminist film theory

One of the most important and probably misunderstood archetypal structures in Jungian psychology also happens to be one of the most com-monly used: the contrasexual archetype. In simple terms, this represents those aspects of the personality that most typify one's gender opposite. For the male subject in Jungian terms, this is the feminine aspect or anima. For the female subject, this is the masculine aspect or animus. There is a very important point that should be stressed concerning terminology here in order that these different elements of the archetype are not confused. I use the words 'male' and 'female' to denote sex or biological difference, and the words 'masculine' and 'feminine' to denote gender construction. This is the accepted terminology in many disciplines of cultural study and marks out a crucial separation between sexual difference, with its concomitant normative biological fact, and gender difference, characterized by learned socialized attributes. Although this is not the place to go into a lengthy discussion, the point is nevertheless worth making, as the common mistake in dealing with contrasexuality is that it sometimes suggests polarization of gender, as well as a naturalized notion of equivalence between gender, sex and sexuality.

To an extent, these issues are central to recent work in the field of Jungian studies and feminist thought. Philosopher and psychoanalytic theorist Frances Gray has written at length about the philosophical tradi-tions associated with essentialist notions of sexual difference. Most notably, in her recent book *Jung, Irigaray, Individuation* (2008), Gray discusses the work of Jung, critiquing his conception of the feminine and its appropri-ation by and for the patriarchal symbolic. In this dominant system of signification, discourse and embodiment, women are reduced through the masculine imaginary to the role of inferior types. This is a critique that draws on the work of feminist psychoanalytic thinker Luce Irigaray to seek a feminine-feminine: a conceptual and lived femininity that is conceived of, and embodied by, women. At once, this position threatens both to subvert normative notions of women and to reproduce the very ideas of sexual difference in a progressive conception of gender construction. On the face of it, this is both Gray's strength and her weakness; for in her argument, a powerful understanding of embodied fact coupled with radical political discourse is equally imbued with a sense of matri-centric revisionism of the female essence. This last was the focus for a number of key American feminist film critics of the early 1970s such as Molly Haskell (1987 [1974]) and Marjorie Rosen (1973), who sought to reappropriate what they saw as a womanliness subsumed by a repressive patriarchal regime for its own interests. This was a key intervention in terms of putting the subject of femininity and women on the film theory map. It is of course vital that the patriarchal process and structure of gender division, stretching back at least as far as Plato, is renegotiated and Gray does this through critical and philosophical inquiry, as well as a great deal of poetic flair. This is particularly the case when she deals with the tradition of essentialism in Western philosophy, and it is useful here to quote Gray (2008: 130) at length:

> For a very long time individual instances of things were seen not as products of social and discursive practices but as effects of their internal makeup. And the importance of this view is realised when we consider the kinds of views that prevented women from taking up various occupations. Women were seen to be fit for motherhood and the caring services like teaching and nursing by virtue of the fact that they have the kinds of bodies that fit them for specific professions. Recall Plato's argument that one should do the one thing for which one has a particular kind of nature.

When transposed to socio-political practice, especially the agenda of the political right in many Western countries today, these essentialisms have been used to identify, classify and oppress all kinds of marginal groups, including women. A thread of this logic exists in the everyday transactions that occur in popular media texts. These transactions range from popular TV shows to Hollywood and beyond in film. Consider Jung's own words, that a woman 'can do anything for the love of a man' (1970: 243). This implies a heteronormative role that all women do, and perhaps should, perform. It is a role reproduced throughout narrative film history, and is a state of womanhood that extends throughout the social formation: culture, work, leisure, home, the church, and so forth. What is interesting to note about the discussion on contrasexuality here is that much of it centres on various critiques of Jung's psychological theory of contrasexuality, as an outmoded form of theorization. This alone is a perfectly reasonable justification for renegotiating his ideas. However, following Gray, this is not a matter of mere revisionism: Jung cannot be 'fixed' by the application of contemporary cultural studies approaches to sexual difference and identity formation to his theories. What Jung's analytical psychology does, however, as we have seen countless times already during this book, is to ask some of the more pressing questions concerning the choices we make in our personal, collective and creative lives. From this starting point at least, then, we may begin to re-imagine Jung from a new perspective.

A reproduction of the philosophical tradition of identifying and classifying types according to an equivalence of character tropes and the fact of sexual difference takes place within certain feminist cultural approaches. This includes the process of associating woman-ness with cultural practice – and importantly within feminist film studies of the 1970s and early 1980s, the reappropriation of woman-ness as a potentially radical creative force. This much is, arguably, a legitimate claim, as the mobilization of identities can be particularly empowering when considering the relations of production and consumption within, for example, film culture. It is a matter not just of powerful representations with which to identify, but also of the pleasures and desires that drive the supply and demand of films that cater for women: Women's needs and tastes as a specific demographic are both shaped and acceded to in film culture. For Gray, however, it is a matter of definition that essences of concepts, ideas or things are identified and fixed in the philosophical tradition. As such, the discourses that integrate the identity, definition, needs and taste of men and women as culturally specific audience groups are naturalized as the most relevant in film production, reception and criticism. In other words, identity formations such as 'women' and 'men' are located and mobilized by the fact of definition, whether in terms of gender, biology or both concomitantly, and engaged by producers, audiences and critics:

> What makes something what it is, in other words, is revealed in definition and definition therefore serves to point to the essence or the essential properties of any concept, idea or thing. An essence is what is necessary to something in order that it be what it is . . . Jung's uncritical adoption of stereotypical characterisations of women and men, couched in terms of collective unconscious pre-figuring, opens the door to reading him as ahistorical and apparently essentialising when it comes to women and the feminine.
>
> (Gray, 2008: 131)

Essential woman-ness (or man-ness, for that matter) is a powerful locus of film culture, and its place in Jung's psychology enables the film theorist to enter a discussion of contrasexuality in Jung and in film that engages a range of similar themes and discourses reproduced within the two paradigms. This is a matter for further exploration and I return to this issue throughout this chapter. However, I propose that further application of Gray's philosophical approach to film theory in a volume dedicated to this theme would be necessary to reignite some of the unresolved themes and currencies of feminist film theory that are now often considered outmoded or irrelevant.

Jung wrote that of all the archetypes, the three that have 'the most frequent and the most disturbing influence on the ego' are the shadow, the animus and the anima (1998: 91). As the shadow archetype will be discussed at length in relation to narrative in the next chapter, I will here concentrate on the contrasexual types. In classical psychology, these types have such frequent influence on the ego because they are (to borrow from one of Freud's psychic topologies) among the most 'pre-conscious' of the types. Anima and animus, for Jung, are very much associated with the shadow, and its twin image – the persona. The persona is important here, as it is the representation of that part of the personality that exists for and in the realm of the social. It is, in film narrative terms, that part of the characterization that exists for the audience to engage with, to discover and empathize with, and with whom to identify occasionally. It works in the real world as an identification point for subjectivity, and marks out the difference in experience between 'individual' and 'personal'. The persona is the 'personal' in this particular differentiation. Jung derived his ideas for this aspect of personality from his theories on character-splitting and personality dissociation – a clinical problem that had fascinated him throughout his career. In formulating the persona, he suggested that the particular pathology of dissociation was, in fact, 'a problem of normal psychology' (1998: 98), just as play had been a normal stage in the development of subject formation for Freud. Jung (1998: 98) defines the difference between individual and personal thus:

> Naturally he is individual like every living being, but unconsciously so. Because of his more or less complete identification with the attitude of the moment, he deceives others, and often himself, as to his real character. He puts on a mask, which he knows is in keeping with his conscious intentions, while it also fits the requirements and fits the opinions of society . . . This mask . . . I have called the persona, which is the name for the masks worn by actors in antiquity.

Personality disassociation becomes problematic when the subject identifies himself or herself with the persona to such an extent that they no longer know 'themselves'. As individuals, in other words, they have become 'lost'.

Jung notes in 'The Relations between the Ego and the Consciousness' that society expects and demands that each person play the roles to which they are assigned, and in this regard three interesting implications emerge.

Firstly, that the social dimension of identity and identification are the initial phases in the psychological mechanisms that involve identity formation. Secondly, that this identification mechanism involves a performance of some kind. Thirdly, that, according to Gray, Jung had explicitly 'introduced the idea of identification with a compulsory sexualised position within society' in his account of anima/animus, and that this formed part of the basis for his later work on individuation (2008: 16). These are useful implications to which I shall briefly return in the last section of this chapter. The reason for outlining the persona archetype here is that Jung himself had noted that the social and psychological implications of identity formation had a compensatory relationship with the contrasexual types. One may speculate that this is probably due to the crucial role that gender construction and performance have within the social sphere, and the implications for this in terms of the strategies employed in interpreting representations of gender in film are vast. These include playful notions of imagination and pleasure, as well as less optimistic notions of stereotyping and audience alienation.

Psychologically speaking, we may say that the contrasexual types are the interfaces between the 'individual' aspect of being and the 'personal' identity on view in our social interaction. For Jung, this interface that gives us a conscious clue to inner wellbeing is always represented by the contrasexual identity, so that in men this takes on the characteristics of the feminine. It is complementary to the persona, so that it:

> contains all those fallible human qualities his persona lacks. If the persona is intellectual, the anima will quite certainly be sentimental. The complementary character of the anima also affects the sexual character, as I have proved to myself beyond a shadow of a doubt.
>
> (1998: 101)

There are, of course, a number of problems with this theory, not least of which is Jung's claim that he has proved this beyond doubt. To himself, he may have done, but his following remarks leave much to be desired:

> The more masculine his outer attitude is, the more his feminine traits are obliterated: instead they appear in his unconscious. This explains why it is just those very virile men who are most subject to characteristic weaknesses; their attitude to the unconscious has a womanish weakness and impressionability.
>
> (1998: 101–102)

Again, the recurring problems seem to stem from Jung's rather blasé perspective on sexual difference. One must bear in mind, when reading Jung, that his thinking was 'in a long tradition in which the feminine voice and the voice of women is ridiculed and trivialised' (Gray, 2008: 12). In this example, it is almost as if he is attempting to 'excuse' the normative patriarchal model of masculinity. His words here are characterized most readily by a questionable treatment of women (here considered weak and easily led), and the sexual proclivity and destructive behaviour of certain men (here justified because women are impressionable and therefore, presumably, 'available'). If a Jungian psychology were employed in the amplification of this particular passage, one might be tempted to suggest that Jung was making his own excuses for mistakes made in his personal life. It is almost as if, in characterizing the anima of promiscuous or sexually pathological men as 'impressionable' – in other words, weak and feminine – he is suggesting a causal relation between inner passivity and outer recklessness. There is also a normative inflation of attributes associated with gender (essentialized through their association with the sexes) in which women are here doubly given the rough end of the deal. They are characterized as weak, and their treatment at the hands of reprehensible men is therefore largely excused.

There is something to be said for the celebration of both the masculine and the feminine, and the playful ways in which people identify with normative practices and assumptions associated with each. However, it is important to remember that these practices and assumptions are learned and are therefore cultural, and not natural. The kind of inflation involved in naturalization has been critiqued in recent years in film and television scholarship through various interventions, suggesting that, because of its constructed nature, gender difference in identification practices is highly mutable. This is the case in some feminist film theory, especially in the imagining of the female spectator. As Susan Hayward (1996: 100–101) argues of British feminist film critics such as Laura Mulvey, Claire Johnston and Annette Kuhn, there existed a vociferous objection to the assumption of a neglected female essence within the patriarchal order, an assumption characteristic of some US feminist film criticism:

> The essentialist debate assumed, first, that all women possessed an innate inability to judge the authenticity of the representation of women in film, and, second, that all women film-makers were feminists. Most critically of all, they pointed out that a belief in a fixed feminine essence meant legitimating patriarchy through the back door.

This led ultimately to the employment of semiotics, psychoanalysis and historical materialist analysis as theoretical and critical tools for the reinterpretation of film practices and audience address during the 1970s. Mary Ann Doane, in her influential *Screen* article 'Film and the Masquerade' (1982), for example, later employed Joan Riviere's model of performative gender identity in order to imagine a textual female spectator.

It is important not to confuse this textual spectator with an empirical spectator. The differences between the two theoretical spectator models were elaborated by Jackie Stacey in her book *Star Gazing*. Here, she states that the empirical female spectator is the actual spectator in the audience, the subject of various examples of ethnographic studies. This work, Stacey (1994: 11) writes,

> typically uses ethnographic approaches (including interviews with, or letters from, audiences) to analyse the consumption of popular cultural forms. What is analysed in these studies of how male and female spectators watch differently is thus not the unconscious pleasures of the viewing process.

These more scientifically oriented methods have their uses, and I return to contextual considerations in a discussion of female consumer culture below, from a theoretical consideration of female political economy. However, the focus on Freudian psychoanalytic models (for Stacey, still a dominant concern for feminist film critics in the 1990s) allowed theorists to engage with the notions of looking, pleasure and desire that popular film mobilizes in quite different ways in the address of male and female spectatorship. For Doane, the female spectator is not synonymous with the woman sitting in the theatre, eating popcorn. 'It is,' rather, 'a concept which is totally foreign to the epistemological framework of the new ethnographic analysis of audiences . . . The female spectator is a concept, not a person' (1989: 142). As a result, one could argue, an essential psychological difference both pre-exists and is embodied by biological difference in men and women in this model. What is perhaps more useful for us to consider, especially in relation to the currents within contemporary film theory, is the fact that there is very rarely an agreement within feminist film theory as to the definition of the 'female spectator'. Therefore we might say that the issue of essentialism is avoided by the narrowest of margins.

In reappraising this complex position, the four-part definition of female film spectatorship offered by another psychoanalytic film critic, Barbara Creed, addresses a number of relevant issues for us in re-imagining sexed audiences. She cites the diegetic (the woman on screen), the imagined (as a construction of patriarchal ideology), the theoretical (in film theory) and the empirical (woman in the audience) as different definitions operating within feminist film criticism. I would argue that these definitions in sum only perhaps bring to light the focal concerns of embodied, material spectatorship and may be applied equally (although differently, especially in problematic psychoanalytic forms) to 'male' and 'female' spectatorship as a concept. In considering these mutually sustaining definitions, we may avoid what Stacey has described as 'the use of psychoanalytic frameworks which collapse gender and sexuality into a totalistic binarism of masculinity and

Figure 6.1 Scene from 'Gilda'.
Copyright © 1946, renewed 1973
Columbia Pictures Industries, Inc. All
Rights Reserved. Courtesy of
Columbia Pictures.

femininity' (1994: 27). This is a subject to which I shall briefly return in the last section of this chapter.

As discussed in Chapter 5, Laura Mulvey's 'Visual Pleasure and Narrative Cinema' first articulated the notion of a male gaze in popular narrative film. This involved the female character fixed in the gaze of the male character, but also presented, through a series of conventions of framing, camera movement, and *mise-en-scene* arrangement, for the gaze of the (heterosexual) male spectator. Very often, particularly in films where spectacle is the site of pleasure for both audience and characters, such as the musical number phenomenon, the arrangement of character and audience gaze was plausibly conflated so that it was difficult to discern diegetic looking from the cinematic. Note, for example, the set-up during Rita Hayworth's 'Put the Blame on Mame' number in *Gilda* (Vidor, US, 1946) (Figures 6.1–6.3).

Many critics, including Stacey, have pointed out the general nature of such an assertion, claiming that pleasures other than the fixivity and default positioning of the spectator as male are to be found in such cinema. Mulvey herself has revised and commented on this a number of times since. Mulvey's notion of woman's 'to-be-looked-at-ness' involved both the mechanisms of scopophilia ('pleasure in looking at another person as an erotic object') and ego formation (identification) played out in an ideological arena benefiting and reproducing the patriarchal order (1999: 843). However, such is the power of her argument in relation to the objectification of women on film that one of the key factors that is sometimes overlooked in Mulvey's account of visual pleasure is the gendered economy employed in the address and act of spectatorship. She states (1999: 838):

> An active/passive heterosexual division of labour has similarly controlled narrative structure. According to the principles of the ruling ideology and the psychical structures that back it up, the male figure

Figure 6.2   Scene from 'Gilda'.
Copyright © 1946, renewed 1973
Columbia Pictures Industries, Inc. All
Rights Reserved. Courtesy of
Columbia Pictures.

cannot bear the burden of sexual objectification. Man is reluctant to gaze at his exhibitionist like. Hence the split between spectacle and narrative supports the man's role as the active one of forwarding the story, making things happen.

'Emotional' consumption and representation of (hetero)sexuality

What is so useful here is the way in which Mulvey employs turns of phrase to characterize discernible patterns in popular film. For example, note the singular here: '*Man* is reluctant to gaze at *his* exhibitionist like.' This is, generally speaking, the accepted heteronormative discourse within popular culture, in practice working through the proliferation of, for example, sexual fantasy numbers in popular films, featuring lesbians-who-aren't-lesbians, the use of table-dance iconography in music videos, and the reduction of queered readings to postmodernist inconsequentiality in jokey Oscars ceremony skits. Less useful, of course, is the absence of other marginal pleasures in Mulvey's economy. However, one might take this notion of spectator economy further, placing it within a more general context of exchange in late capital. The division of labour along lines of gender becomes one of the contributing factors towards the feminization of consumer culture in late capital, leading to specialist marketing towards men, ironically employing the same 'feminized' strategies, but within discourses of 'need' rather than 'want'. Hence, cars, sheds, tools, porn, shavers, and even women are all commodities that men need. Magazines, curtains, shoes, accessories, pets, sex toys and conversation are what women want. Arguably, this reinforces the popular notion of the disposability and trivialized nature of women's goods in Western society, discursively based as it is upon 'wants'. If the industrial development of popular cinema in the twentieth

Figure 6.3 Scene from 'Gilda'.

century is anything to go by, then surely this economy includes film consumption, as well as the way male and female audience demographics are courted in advertising.

Stacey has noted that the historical economic shift of the home as a centre of production to the centre of consumption coincided with the cultural shift of the definition of domestic space as a female space. Henceforth, women steadily became the managers, if not financiers, of familial consumption. She states that 'By the time women attended cinemas in the 1940s and 1950s, then, their position as consumers had already been shaped in specific ways through other forms of consumption' (1994: 178). Also, popular film culture and Hollywood cinema in particular, as the dominant form, 'has been a key source of idealised images in this culture. The cinema combines the exchange of looks with the display of commodities' (1994: 9). Doane echoes this to a certain extent when she notes that 'The cinematic image for the woman is both shop window and mirror, the one simply a means of access to another' (cited in Stacey, 1994: 9). As a massively global industry, with Hollywood as its dominant hub and model, the cinema has traditionally associated itself with other consumer practices and media forms. Indeed, in this age of multinational corporation takeovers and mergers, it is unlikely that such industrial film can exist outside such spheres of interest, even if it is politically subversive and anti-corporate in content.

In her discussion of the development of a general consumer culture and the associated shifting of gender roles, Bowlby states that:

The transformation of merchandise into a spectacle, in fact, suggests an analogy with an industry that developed fifty years after the first department stores: the cinema. In this case, the pleasure of looking, *just* looking, is itself the commodity for which money is paid.

(1985: 6, emphasis in original)

As already discussed in detail elsewhere in this book, the act of spectatorship involves more than just looking: It is a fundamentally embodied process. In *incorporating* the general consumer culture into the creative process of popular filmmaking, popular film culture has become, in Janet Wasko's words, 'the vehicle and inspiration for the display of brand-name products' through practices such as product placement, cross-promotion, and merchandising in the public space of the cinema foyer (1994: 217). In other words, not only is popular film a commodity, but it is a commodity that acts as a platform for other commodification processes. The privileged position occupied by the visual in the act of looking suggests that, in reappropriating the gaze for female spectatorship, women film spectators re-enact the commodity–identity/consumer relationship that already exists in the general consumer culture. Wasko (1994: 217) goes on to say that:

> In sometimes disturbing ways, both individual and cultural identities become bound up in this type of consumption. Indeed, the way in which these 'real world' commodities are introduced in the fantasy world of film is another disturbing element that deserves more attention.

Popular film, then, mobilizes a tightly bound reversible commodity–identity relation that not only is palatable to audiences (and female audiences in particular) but is actively encouraged as desirable at an industrial level. The importance of Bowlby's statement in relation to this is fourfold. Firstly, it reproduces the reversibility already discussed elsewhere that exists in postmodern culture, whereby symbol and semiosis (in this case, a sense of Self and a sense of the image respectively) become both mutually sustaining and negating. In other words, identity is confused with possession: We are what we consume. Secondly, it recounts a cultural difference in the ways in which men and women consume and the problematic emphasis in late capital on desire as an emotional object on which to fixate at the expense of affective experience. Thirdly, there are implications in terms of the targeting and exploitation of women as a specific cultural demographic that is more likely to engage in certain types of emotional- and object-oriented consumption. Finally, there is a pleasurable experience in the very act of looking, although to my mind this exists for men and women both – occasionally in very different, learned ways, sometimes mobilizing remarkably similar strategies of viewing. This last implication is by far the most intriguing, as it suggests the potential of an *affective* response that is less gender-specific than the first three *emotional* responses. This difference has been addressed in film theory terms of a gendered gaze, already discussed above. The *sameness* of affective response, however, is a contradictory force that employs some of the same embodied processes that are engaged through the infinite reversibility of semiosis and symbol – a phenomenon with both positive and negative dimensions, as discussed in Chapters 4 and 5.

One way to think this through, especially in relation to moving away from the essentialization of gendered viewing, is to consider the popular assumptions about pornography. This is a highly controversial and complex area of film scholarship: one that as a genre has been discussed in greater depth elsewhere. I refer the reader to three exceptional scholarly overviews of porn film and culture here: Linda Williams' *Hard Core* (1991), Lawrence O'Toole's *Pornucopia* (1998) and Tanya Krzywinska's *Sex and the Cinema* (2006). It is useful to challenge some of the more general assumptions surrounding the pornographic film here, namely that it is made by men, for men, that it is principally violent against women, and that (therefore) most women dislike viewing it. Indeed, one might say that these assumptions are based on material practices.

It is evident that most mainstream pornography is less to do with the act of sex and more to do with the exchange of power, often between men and women. This is both personal and economic: The commodification of the body on screen and the reification of the audience as active or passive viewers are partly the result of the industrialization of straight pornography as a generic form. It is also evident that there is a curious contradiction in terms of gender representation here: The men are often reduced to objects in that emphasis lies on their sexual performance and size of genitalia; the women are often reduced to fragmented body parts through generic framing and camera set-ups. Although active in the sexual act, the men are little more than stuntmen, whereas the women in mainstream porn films frequently fulfil the role of the 'lusty and busty' or dominant/submissive stereotypes, depending on the subgenre.

However, the assumptions outlined above in relation to gendered viewing practices of porn take on a very interesting slant when other, related issues are raised. Anna Span, for example, is one of the principal directors of porn in the UK today. As shown in the documentary *Sex Films for Girls* (Channel 5, 2003), she is from a film school background, and writes, produces and edits her films. So the assumption that porn is made by men is one that is firstly auteurist, and secondly false. Indeed, Span is not the only female porn director. That it is all made for men is also a false assumption. Once again using Span as an example here, many porn production companies are seeking to address a specifically female market, and the attempts to make such products are most often characterized by a shift in content. These 'made-for-women' adult films tend to have more emphasis on plot and characterization and the women performers are frequently active in the production of fantasy scenarios. Also, production values seem to be significantly higher than those found in mainstream porn, and the whole thing is 'tastefully' done, usually in monogamous contexts, conforming to popular discourses of acceptable (hetero)sexual behaviour, especially of women. However, Anna Span does not make 'sex films for girls', as the title of the documentary suggests. This title itself conforms to the auteurist assumption that a director's connection with the audience is far more immediate than it really is. It also reproduces the same essentialist argument put forward by many of the original 1970s US feminist film critics that women are the best judges of female representation and that all women directors are feminists.

Furthermore, it also suggests that women want something other than the mainstream fare. This is not necessarily the case, as Span contends when she states that the 'made-for-women' category of porn is not very successful because people (of both sexes) watch porn to get the full visceral experience of intense, sometimes edgy, sex on screen. Instead, Span makes porn for a generic audience. From a superficial Jungian position, one may critique this in contrasexual terms, for example by speculating that women who seek such visual pleasures have an inflated animus and that the 'masculine' aspect of their personality is somehow overcompensating for a very feminized persona. Indeed, such an assertion could be critiqued itself as reinforcing the gender bias that exists in terms of cultural value. These are traits that are often seen as undesirable in women in Western culture, but one could argue for various historical reasons why this might be the case. Conversely, just because Span is a woman this does not necessarily suggest that she is making feminist films or a radical statement in political terms. Nor does it follow that she is making films specifically for women: For a start, her films do not display any of the indicators that 'made-for-women' pornography does. It fact, she states at one point in the documentary that she specifically wants to make films that can be enjoyed by men, women, couples, and people of various sexual preferences. Her casting of male performers that she regards as attractive to women and refusal to shoot scenes that condone violence towards either sex seem to be the main criteria to achieve her finished product. Her films are very much a part of the mainstream porn landscape, and so any attempt to create a feminist–auteurist dialogue with Span's films is, to an extent at least, frustrated. In fact, the orthodox view employed by much feminist film theory since the 1970s has been criticized from various quarters as lacking on two counts, and Span's directorship is an interesting case in point. As Lapsley and Westlake (1988: 25) have noted of orthodox feminist film theory:

> The most fundamental reproach was that it proceeded either explicitly or implicitly on the basis of a presumed feminine essence that had been repressed under patriarchy and that it was the task of the women's movement to emancipate from its state of alienation.

Therefore, to reiterate, a twofold problem associated with orthodox feminism was that it rested on two presuppositions.

1   Women possessed an in-built knowledge of femininity (thus essentializing the experience of womanhood and conflating it with the empathic 'essence' of femininity).

2   Any film made by a woman was therefore feminist in some respect (although of course, in retrospect, one may acknowledge the pluralism inherent in feminist responses).

It has often followed in feminist film criticism that an elision occurs in equating female authorship with social activism. The only conclusion that should be made to counter this is the rather simple, though often overlooked, reality that not all women are feminists, and not all feminism is radical. Indeed, psychoanalytical feminist thought, itself sometimes fairly radical in its notion of overturning the patriarchal normativity embedded in Freudian models of gender, is often itself critical of this assumption concerning the essentialism of femininity, feminism and womanhood. As Elizabeth Wright has noted, 'much of feminist criticism has been a concerted effort to challenge the representation of woman as constructed within a patriarchal symbolic' (1998: 173). Nevertheless, it does not necessarily follow that female practitioners of psychoanalysis are naturally and ideally placed to critique this, nor in fact is this necessarily the automatic response from women. Such a suggestion would imply a default 'original' position from which to comment, something that psychoanalytic critic Luce Irigaray (1991) indicates is possible in the social formation only from a dominant masculine perspective, and from which constructs of 'woman' and femininity spring. She interrogates the underlying assumptions of psychoanalysis, maintaining that they are masculine assumptions. I would contend that these assumptions, reproduced large within the social apparatus, are in fact patriarchal rather than essentially masculine, and that within that dominant form of patriarchy certain norms of masculinity and femininity are privileged. It follows that other forms of gender are marginalized or discouraged.

In this light, it becomes increasingly difficult to sustain the above-mentioned 'original' position, while at the same time reinforcing the notion that gender construction processes, as well as the constructs themselves, are fundamentally based on relations of power, deference and insubordination. As Elizabeth Grosz has stated about Irigaray's work, she 'poses the question of sexual enunciation: of who speaks, for whom and with what interests' (1990: 177). The feminist perspective employed here certainly emphasizes the notion that women and their interests are subordinate to men within this enunciatory system. However, it should be noted that this discursive formation of power should be extended to include more general relations, within which men are also caught to their own denigration and to which other identity formations such as sexuality, age, race and class are also subject. From a certain point of view, there are traces of liberal feminist discourse in Span's filmmaking practice, for example. The fact remains that – whatever the predominant view is on mainstream pornography – her refusal to produce images of violence and degradation (against women in particular, but also, importantly, against men) makes a welcome change. In fact, her film style and articulation of engagement with the general film culture (as well as the pornography genre) should be, in practice, seen as progressive in general. However, her participation (and the participation of porn directors generally) in an industry that insists on the promulgation of a perceived availability of women remains problematic. It ensures that her filmmaking can never be considered emancipatory, no matter how empowering its representation of women. In other words, in the mode of filmmaking within which she operates, Span's films to an extent necessarily reproduce the relations of power, deference and insubordination that exist within the patriarchal symbolic. As a corollary, this affects the representation of both men and women within this system, in turn limiting the emancipatory effects of insubordination and transgression.[1] We need to return to the issue of representation and the problematic perception of essential qualities that exist in the representation of women within films in order to address this question fully.

Of course, it is not just pornography that employs shorthand character types: Christopher Vogler describes these contrasexual types as 'shape-shifters' and cites the femme fatale of film noir as an example of the anima. He states (2007: 60) that:

> An important psychological purpose of the Shapeshifter archetype is to express the energy of the animus and anima . . . The animus is Jung's name for the male element in the female unconscious, the bundle of positive and negative images of masculinity in a woman's dreams and fantasies.

Note the confusion of terminology in Vogler's statement. There is no clear separation of gender construction and sexual difference here. This is symptomatic of an unclear differentiation between conscious uses of Jung's ideas (Vogler's book puts these to use dramatically, as a scriptwriter's guide) and the archetypal structures that pre-exist image and consciousness, and are therefore inexpressible themselves. The representations that exist in embodied Images coalesce around certain themes, and Vogler's use of these themes, undeniably well intentioned, happens to be incorrect. This is further blighted by a comment he makes later: 'It's natural for each sex to regard the other as ever-changing, mysterious' (2007: 61). Although it is easy to think about gender in this way, and the pleasures that are created and experienced through the frisson of mystery, this is not necessarily a natural order of things. It is a notion undermined by the variety of representations and contradictory identity practices that are perhaps most visible in gay and lesbian culture, but in fact also exists abundantly in straight culture. The way that one may take a secondary meaning from

Vogler's comment, to essentialize the differences between men and women in an unequal manner, further complicates this approach. This is an issue that feeds into the context of discussions of contrasexuality and gender representation, and in particular considers the troublesome position within which women often find themselves in what may be considered a highly patriarchal, gender-divisive society.

In Campbell's statement above (see epigraph), there are a number of immediate themes connected to the notion of contrasexuality. To unpack this statement is to question some of the founding assumptions that underpin our daily interactions with members of the opposite sex: *We* are fundamentally different to *them*. Campbell's statement is no doubt intended as a celebration of difference, and of the way that men and women seem to embody aspects of humanity that act as counterparts in the greater scheme of things. Many of the myths and folktales employed by Campbell to demonstrate this centre around the reproductive power of women and the potency of men in bringing that power to fruition. Indeed, many of the key players in Hollywood today, principally George Lucas, make no secret of using Campbell's ideas to troubleshoot their stories; make them archetype-tight, as it were.

One of the principal reasons that the study of film has become so important in recent years is that its tendency to represent stereotypical gender constructions as well as their subversion and deconstruction has allowed students from a growing number of disciplines to engage with such complexity. Even the section heading under which, Campbell's statement appears is telling: 'Woman as the temptress'. It describes the phenomenon of representing woman as a personality type, while at the same time feeding into one of the most fundamental assumptions of how women should be perceived both by men as potential heterosexual partners and by women as potential heterosexual rivals/allies. One need only be reminded of the discourses employed in daytime television chatshows such as *Jeremy Kyle*, *Maury* and *Tricia Goddard* to find examples of how these assumptions are reproduced and proliferate in everyday life. Further to this, the phrase 'Woman as the temptress' implies a negative connotation in the kind of roles that are assumed by women in society. Even when the Temptress 'type' is assumed for playful or empowering purposes, there are problems. The ways in which this role is often commodified, to the extent that there are whole niches of pornography and an industry in consumable goods devoted to playing the role, seem to amplify the emphasis on power exchange rather than pleasure. This complex issue can only ever be partially addressed in thinking through the identity and gender politics of film culture. Furthermore, the phrase 'Woman as the temptress' arguably mobilizes the very notion that there is, or perhaps should be, a 'battle of the sexes'.

I would like to qualify some of the reasons for specifically addressing this in relation to the notion of identification. To me, the term 'identification' is embodied in the notion of identity, and is therefore an externalization of the idea of self. As discussed in the next chapter, this idea of self is useful in determining some of the narrative choices made in the construction of cinematic and televisual storytelling. It feeds into the notion that a primary motivation for staying with the film as we watch, and our continued (or indeed, discontinued) empathy with a character in the film, derives from this subjective feeling of self that is superimposed upon the characters being watched. The implications of any theoretical model of identification in cinema should be obvious when it comes to thinking about gender construction. Gender is most often presented as a projection of the difference between men and women in popular cinema, and is therefore popularly viewed as an accurate representation of the differences between men and women in the real world. Furthermore, characterization of male and female characters is structured to cater for male and female audiences, and therefore characters are often simplified into types broadly along the acceptable/ normative lines of gender difference and sexual preference.

Often, the most well-known transgressions of gender roles are the subject of recuperation through other means. For example, rugged frontier woman Calamity Jane wears men's clothes, can drive a stagecoach and down a tequila shot with the best of us, but has a beautifully feminine singing voice, a set of pearly white teeth emphasizing her cleanliness, and happens to look like Doris Day. In *Barb Wire* (Hogan, US, 1996), Hollywood's favourite 'rock chick' Pamela Anderson plays a post-apocalyptic deadly assassin who hates being called 'babe'. Later in her career, she demonstrated a flair for marketing the bimbo side of her image by agreeing to have a soft drink named after her because the bottle had an hourglass figure, and starred in as well as produced a sitcom ironically called *Stacked* (Fox Network, 2005–6). The fact that *Calamity Jane* (Butler, US, 1953) is still seen as groundbreaking in terms of its subversive representation of womanliness, or that Anderson's postmodern self-deprecation in *Stacked* has won her critical and popular plaudits, suggests that any recuperative effects may be outweighed by the success of the stars and their screen personas.

What is interesting to note is that as film theory has developed, it has incorporated reading strategies from various disciplines to unpack this complex of textual meaning and audience reading. These recently developed strategies both challenge heteronormative stereotyped representations that mobilize ideology and engage alternative viewing practices employed by audiences (made up of both men and women, incidentally) that 'look beyond' any preferred or intended meanings. What briefly follows is a discussion of text-based interpretation, which both considers and critiques the notion of intended meaning (while retaining the concept of 'meaningfulness' in its critical sphere), before moving on to consider alternative viewing practices and the problems that can arise through placing too much emphasis on reader-position. Throughout, the discussion is placed within a context that negotiates these problems in terms of gender identity and identification in film.

'Looking beyond' in text-based interpretation

The following statement from John Izod (2006: 5) outlines the importance of French literary critic and cultural commentator Roland Barthes within the realm of cultural studies:

> It seems to me that a measure of inflation has occurred to the extent that we post-Jungian film readers have ignored Barthes's arguments about the ideological function of myth. We have not sufficiently accounted for ideology in our work, and the two modes of understanding myth have been implicitly taken as diametric opposites. However, they should be employed to complement each other. Jung himself, always conscious of the cultural dimensions of symbols and their location in social discourse, would not have found this strange.

There are a number of reasons why Barthes is considered so important in cultural studies, not least the fact that much of his work in the 1950s and early 1960s was published in French newspapers and magazines. It was a pioneering effort to seriously examine popular culture within a popular medium. Many of the essays that he published, on subjects as diverse as wrestling, Garbo, advertising and striptease, were published in English in a collection called *Mythologies*, along with arguably his most influential essay, 'Myth Today'. In 'Myth Today', Barthes attempts to take account of the secondary meaning of cultural texts that exist beyond the primary, more literal meaning. His starting point for this approach is in his use of Swiss linguist Ferdinand de Saussure's ideas about the formation of language, and thus meaning, in everyday communication. For Saussure, any communicative sign is made up of a representation (or signifier), and the mental concept of the thing being communicated (the signified). In sum, the signifier and the signified make up the sign, and thus a denotative or literal meaning is communicated and understood. This idea may be taken in very detailed, close readings of language and the way it is used. For our purposes, we may entertain the notion that films can also work linguistically, although, as noted in previous chapters, a film text should be noted for its material, as well as linguistic, basis.

A filmic example of literal or denotative signification, which also happens to be an important incident of Hollywood's representation of women, is in the musical number from *Calamity Jane* titled 'A Woman's Touch'. This sequence features two female characters Calamity Jane (Doris Day) and Catherine (Allyn Ann McLerie) singing a song about how good women are at home-making, while demonstrating this through various acts of light housework. The twin signifiers of the lyrics of the song and the act of housework, plus the signified concept of women in general performing this task and fulfilling the role outlined in the lyrics, form the desired communication, and primary meaning – domestic spaces benefit from a woman's touch. Of course, this is a very general reading of this sequence, and serves to remind us that almost immediately this primary meaning starts to unravel. The textual realm does not exist by itself, nor indeed does it exist for itself: It exists, for the audience, within the cultural realm. The strength of Barthes' approach to signification is that he suggests that the linguistic sign is merely the starting point, the signifier, for a secondary meaning production, or connotation. This comes into play almost immediate to the denotative primary meaning, effectively wiping the primary meaning away, and emptying it of its particular history. Therefore, in our example, the secondary signifier is that domestic spaces benefit from a woman's touch, and this is the *starting* point. The signified mental concept at this level requires a cultural 'filling-in' of the gaps that are left by the signifier, so that in this example the secondary signified might be that spaces other than the domestic benefit from male intervention. The sum of this, the secondary meaning, is that spaces are gendered according to each sex's abilities, and that there is a natural division of labour that separates men and women according to domesticity and non-domesticity.

Again, I should emphasize the general nature of this example and its analysis. However, taking the mythological reading of 'A Woman's Touch' further, we may speculate tertiary meanings that are, in fact, quite reasonable given the context in which *Calamity Jane* was made, and that make up the mythology of the phrase 'a woman's touch'. The post-war anxiety of returning soldiers, coupled with a booming economy and rising consumption, the embryonic phenomenon of the teenager, and the return of women to domestic life in the United States, are reflected in the kind of statement that the film is making here. This is not an 1890s frontier domicile being made before our eyes, but a typically suburban, white, 1950s American home. The delicate gingham curtains, the bouffant hairstyles, and long dresses – utterly impractical for frontier life – all stem from the same cultural presence. This is not the stuff of the Wild West, and yet it does feed into another very important mythology of how America represents its own history. In effect, the Western film and the United States as it has been conceived since the closing of the frontier in the 1890s share a remarkably similar timeline, closely following one from the other in a cultural exchange that stretches through to this day. In filmic terms, then, the mythologies of the West and of America itself are intertwined, and this will be a subject for discussion in the next chapter.

Aside from larger politics, we may discern a specific address of sexual and identity politics in our example at the tertiary level. The star persona of Doris Day, and the ways in which she has been received within film cultures in the past half-century or so, are quite specific. If we regard a secondary meaning of two women setting up home and painting their names in flowery letters on the door as a reinforcement of gender roles, then surely we would expect these gender roles to be fulfilled normatively? There is something peculiar about the women's gender performance during the number and the implicit sexuality of their lyrical as well as physical exchanges that works in a subversive way. Catherine teaches Jane how to dress properly, despite Jane's claims that 'I knew I weren't no lady. Least ways, ever since I saw you in that dressing room in Chicagee.' It seems that the home is not the only thing that benefits from a woman's touch. Jane's burgeoning awareness of her own femininity (in the normative, 1950s sense) is amplified through her experience of Catherine's body, and also through Catherine's guidance in knowing her own body. This is not necessarily a lesbian subtext as such, as contemporary women's culture is saturated with references to exploration of sexual prowess through mutual exchange of experiences, methods and ideas. It should be said, however, that Doris Day's status as an icon in gay and lesbian culture is partly the result of her appearance in such scenarios, as well as her importance in the development of romantic comedy performance – another key element in post-war gay and lesbian culture.

The point and strength of conducting mythological analysis is that it supports Barthes' notion that mythology exists not only in historical fantasy and fable, but also for us in the everyday. It also has a strikingly ideological dimension – one that may be analysed itself to produce several tertiary meanings of various kinds. Izod's understanding that this mode of thinking about myth should be used to complement the more classical Jungian mode is something of a revelation for post-Jungian approaches to film. It strikes a blow against woolly uses of archetypal standards whilst at the same time acknowledging the power of myth in the realm of culture, and thus, the collective psyche.

Syzygy: Alignment of anima and animus in film, and the looking 'affect'

I have previously discussed Barbara Creed's re-imagining of sexed audiences through the critique of feminist film criticism. What Creed identifies as the diegetic, the imagined, the theoretical and the empirical, we may assume to negotiate through various methodologies in order to ascertain what the object of inquiry actually is. It is fairly certain, however, following several more recent interventions in feminist thought, that what we are not dealing with is an essential womanliness or femininity when engaging female representation and spectatorship. I have argued that Creed's definitions bring to light the focal concerns of embodied, material spectatorship and may be applied equally to both 'male' and 'female' spectatorship as a concept. In doing so, we may avoid what Stacey has described as 'the use of psychoanalytic frameworks which collapse gender and sexuality into a totalistic binarism of masculinity and femininity' (1994: 27). This binarism has been noted in post-Jungian theory to inform and problematize Jung's classical notion of contrasexuality. For example, Frances Gray notes that 'Jung's uncritical adoption of stereotypical characterisations of women and men, couched in terms of collective unconscious pre-figuring, opens the door to reading him as ahistorical and apparently essentialising when it comes to women and the feminine' (2008: 131). What is largely missing from many such accounts (although, notably, included in Gray), one of the most illuminating ideas in Jung's *oeuvre*, connects these contrasexual elements: syzygy.

Syzygy is, for John Izod, 'the conjunction in opposition of the sexes', characterizing 'many images of the unified self' (2001: 142). Although Izod acknowledges that syzygy is only one image of this kind of deep unification, there is a case to be made for the power of this specific conjunction that is both overwhelmingly other and yet utterly reasonable. As many commentators have noted, post-Jung, there is a general consensus that both men and men should be considered to have both anima and animus aspects of the psyche present. This makes sense in terms of the overall consensus in cultural theory that gender is performative, is not static within identificatory practices, and is a social construction. However, this conjunction flies in the face of normative assumptions surrounding the sex/gender alignment that have changed little since Jung, in popular representation.

It is important to note here that Jung's association of masculine and feminine with body-type is not unambiguous, and is, following Gray, a problematic affair. She notes that 'Men's and women's understanding of themselves as men or women arise through their conscious and unconscious experience of their bodies and how they figure their bodies by virtue of their experiences in their communities or collectives' (2008: 52). This is connected to that aspect of identity acquisition within the social formation that this book has occasionally referred to in both psychoanalytic and materialist accounts of the cine-subject. Crucially, it is also fundamental to the aspects of phenomenology of experience discussed in the past couple of chapters that deal with the self-identity of felt subjectivity, in contrast to the felt otherness of the film-subject. To my mind, this is similar in practice to the aspect of the persona, the psyche's presentation of itself within the realm of the social. In cinematic terms, it may be thought more concretely in terms of how sexed audiences are addressed according to specific aesthetic practices and creative sensibilities. This does not necessarily address specific needs of audiences, but maps out and re-presents to the audience notions of gender-specific experiences of what it feels to be in the world as men and women.

For example, the British heritage film, popularly considered a woman's genre, has nothing extrinsically feminine about it other than its general concern with women's issues and politics in historical periods. This should be of interest to male audiences too, although the story-telling strategies employed, such as the romance tradition, and sometimes references to the gothic novel, say, help to engage the tastes of female audiences more directly, perhaps. This admittedly is a generalized statement, but in its address, such practices tend towards generalization anyway, in order to maximize impact on both specialist and general audiences, with specific tastes and general attitudes in mind.

What is interesting to note in terms of identification here is that this cinematic other, this film-subject, this 'persona', has something of the kinetic about it, in that it mobilizes sensibilities that are often gender-specific, and accordingly engage our experiences of being men and women. However, this is not a straightforward projection and identification mechanism, as in the illusory sense of taking human representation on screen as us at an unconscious level, *à la* Metz or Baudry. Gray (2008: 54) writes:

> Unconscious identification with the persona, which we saw as mimetic, causes a man to generate a 'false' sense of himself as an individual: the persona seems to be him, the I that he is, but actually turns out to be something from which he can distinguish himself, a not-I in the same way as the anima feminine is not-I. A man can therefore be both not-I feminine (anima) and not-I masculine (persona).

However, the transposition of the Jungian persona to that of film-subject is not so straightforward. In previous chapters (1 and 3 especially), I have discussed how the transposition between inner and outer forms in cinematic spectatorship is not a straightforward mimetic relationship. The relationship between the audience's viewing practices and the viewing and viewed view of the film is characterized more directly by kinesis, and not memesis. That is, film has the power to move and this movement is not mere physical movement, but more fundamentally embodied in an affective sense. Its expression may ultimately become emotional in the cognitive sense, enabling such gender-specific associations and identificatory practices to emerge during, for example, the plight of the female protagonist within heritage film narrative. It is clear from Jung's original writings, and many post-Jungian thinkers since on the subject of identity and persona, that gender is tied-in to such an extent that it is impossible, particularly in a culture seemingly obsessed with gender production, for us to separate the two. It is also clear, therefore, that gender is fundamental to the understanding of film as a creative enterprise and a viewing practice. More work is needed specifically in this area, and this would need a dedicated volume to itself, however there are one or two related matters that I wish to discuss before moving on.

Gray's reading of Hegelian dialectics suggests that the recognition of the other is simultaneously the recognition of self in self-consciousness. She states that: 'Hegel's Master/Slave Dialectic assumes difference as a founding moment of identity, and the expression of that is desire. Since self-consciousness requires the recognition of an other who is not itself, that other must be different from it' (2008: 8). What is interesting to note here is that the notion of emotional objectivity (in this case, that of desire) is an objectivity that is present in many classic apparatus theory articles, and characterizes an often debunked attitude towards cinematic identification from such theories of the 1970s. Karin Littau (2008) has recently commented on such theories in her keynote address at a conference on *Philosophy and Film/Film and Philosophy*. She stated that above all, cinema is kinesis before it is mimesis, because we inhabit the media that we engage. Cinema does not copy identification and projection mechanisms present in the psyche (such that there are) any more than film is itself anthropomorphic. It does, however, *move* us, conceptually, and is, in Sobchack's words, anthropocentric: it exists as a mode of perception–expression within the human realm of creativity and imagination – it could therefore not be otherwise. It is this element that allows us to entertain the possibility of films' morphology as a gendered and engendering machine. The ability for recognition in cinema is based partly on its specific phenomenology and partly on its ability to engage certain psychic aptitudes for recognition present in human psyche and in viewing practice itself. As Gray (2008: 7) states:

> The notion of recognition embraces affirmation and denial, acknowledgement, the gaze of the other. This fluid engagement of self-consciousness traces the dynamics of interpersonal, personal/social and intersocial relationship as our original condition: we are always already in the world, in social relation, and this has a profound existential impact on us.

However, it should be noted that Gray goes on to say that this condition highlights the importance of heightening awareness of the Dialectic as it 'subtends the binary nature of human being'. In thinking of human social being as a binary form, Gray loses the dynamic of dehiscent reversibility that exists in social being and cultural practice, towards which Hegel nods (while perhaps never fully articulating) and which ultimately finds its articulation in both Jungian thinking and existential phenomenology. As outlined in previous chapters, this has been explored extensively by writers such as Roger Brooke, so I will not comment further here, except that a corollary may be of use in relation to film theory. Gray (2008: 8) suggests that:

> In going out of itself, we can see that self-consciousness as a mode of psyche collapses the boundaries between self and the other so that it

can eventually return to itself . . . Self-consciousness achieves identity through dissolving the projection: its going out of itself.

The projection mechanism within the cinematic apparatus that writers such as Baudry state as fundamental to the identification of self in cinema is undermined through the sudden rush of self-awareness that occasionally erupts when a film refers to itself, its production process or its culture. This identification of self is a form of recognition by and for which identity is bound, and, in the cinema theatre, may announce to its presence for an audience, or in sometimes breaching the diegesis of the hermetic story world to make self-awareness present. There are several examples of this in popular cinema. *Be Cool* (Gray, US, 2005) has as its subject matter a gangster-turned-movie-producer (John Travolta) who calls into question the MPAA rating system by mentioning that a film can only use the work 'fuck' once, or it will be classed NC-17. This would affect its performance at the box-office, and indeed would stall distribution to entire chains of theatres. The word is not used again in the film, thus fulfilling the implied brief.

Blazing Saddles (Brooks, US, 1974) uses several strategies of self-awareness to comic effect, especially in the scene where the mass brawl leaks from the Wild West and into the studio lot in which the film's story-world is being staged. *A Cock and Bull Story* (Winterbottom, UK, 2006) seems to do all these things almost constantly throughout the course of its duration. This curiously self-reflexive British satire usurps the conventions of cinematic diegesis and space-time to such an extent that its political statements become almost immediate to the audience from the first few scenes onwards. This kind of self-referentiality and coincidence will be the subject of much discussion in Chapter 8. For now, we will turn to matters relating to narrative, myth and self in film and television, in order to develop further some of the ideas discussed during the course of this chapter.

Chapter 7

Narrative and myth, heroes and villains, film and television

It seems to me that a measure of inflation has occurred to the extent that we post-Jungian film readers have ignored Barthes's arguments about the ideological function of myth. We have not sufficiently accounted for ideology in our work, and the two modes of understanding myth have been implicitly taken as diametric opposites. However, they should be employed to complement each other. Jung himself, always conscious of the cultural dimensions of symbols and their location in social discourse, would not have found this strange.

John Izod, *Screen, Culture, Psyche*

It's difficult to avoid the sensation that the Hero's Journey exists somewhere, somehow, as an eternal reality. A Platonic ideal form, a divine model. From this model, infinite and highly varied copies can be produced, each resonating with the essential spirit of the form.

Christopher Vogler, *The Writer's Journey*

The NBC hit TV show *Heroes* (NBC, 2006–) is ostensibly built around various characters' sudden discoveries of latent superhuman abilities. There is a moment in the second season when, after taking a job as a fire fighter, D. L. Hawkins (Leonard Roberts) steps into a burning house and rescues a child. It is fairly safe to state that this is an act of heroism. What makes this an act of heroism? D. L.'s special ability is that he can walk through walls, and can transfigure his body's constitution so that matter passes through him and those with whom he is in physical contact. He is therefore doubly configured as a hero: by the fact of his generic 'super-ness', and by virtue of his acts of heroism, or how he puts these abilities to use. As Joseph Campbell (1993: 17–18) has stated of the hero:

The first work of the hero is to retreat from the world scene of secondary effects to those casual zones of the psyche where the difficulties really reside, and there to clarify the difficulties, eradicate them in his own case

... and break through to the undistorted, direct experience and assimilation of what C. G. Jung has called 'the archetypal images.'

It is, in other words, the role of the hero to go on a journey of transformation. He confronts his own inner demons, so to speak, and in doing so (through performing certain acts and making certain choices in the narrative) transforms the narrative experience of the story's audience.

Heroes' premise is based on the ways in which ordinary people's lives are utterly transformed by their self-discoveries, and is an attempt to move beyond the comic book fantasies of Marvel and D. C. towards a more realistic and sympathetic portrayal of fully rounded characters. The show's ability to do this differentiates it from the proliferation of big-budget comic franchise movies of contemporary popular cinema, which pay lip-service to character interiority but actually foreground their own mode of caricature through emphasis on action, spectacle and special effects. Franchises such as *Spider-Man*, *X-Men* and *Fantastic Four*, for example, serve specific commercial needs, and as such fulfil generic standards far more easily than they do the need for rounded character interiority.[1] Superficially, this might suggest that the films exhibit the cartoon and caricature of their basic subject material, the comic book – so often thought of as a trivial and adolescent medium. On the contrary, one may easily argue that the comic book itself is a heavyweight medium when it comes to social commentary and subversive politics – the work of Alan Moore springs to mind here particularly. Although *Heroes* uses special effects, and features fantastical science proposition, its televisual setting provides a specific grounding for 'ordinariness' that comic franchise films miss entirely. Its episodic structure and the narrative feed from its paratextual add-ons (such as the online virtual comic book, and making-of TV show *Heroes Unmasked*) help to contain the visual and narrative excesses of the movies' form. The commercial imperative of a TV show is very different to that of a movie franchise, dependent as it is on ratings, simultaneous competition and casual viewing. Any evaluative or qualitative comparison between the media in question, therefore, is a complex issue for another discussion.

For the benefit of readers who are not familiar with the show, D. L. is an African-American man, who is in a long-term relationship with Niki (Ali Larter), an ultra-slim blonde woman who possesses super strength. Their union was engineered by a shadowy organization, known only as the 'company', consisting of people both with and without their own super powers. The fruit of their marriage (felt by the couple to be a real love affair) is a son, Micah (Noah Gray-Cabey), who has the ability to control machines of all kinds telepathically. In addition he possesses an uncanny empathic faculty, although this is never figured in 'super' terms. To define heroism within the context of the series is a complex business. For example, Micah's empathic faculty means that he has a seemingly unconditional fondness for humanity. This faculty, to my mind, is a 'heroic' expression of one's own condition, and yet Micah's super powers are only ever figured as a technological empathy (he uses his mind to 'talk' to machines to ask them to do his bidding). His empathy with people is only expressed in his desire that his family use their special gifts to help people, just like the heroes in the comics he reads.

The 'ordinary' heroism embodied in Micah's humanitarian world-view is occasionally expressed in other characters' actions, however. D. L.'s act of rescue, for example, seems one of self-sacrifice, except that he knows that the fire will not harm him and his ward. Neither his co-workers nor the general public know this about D. L., and he is featured on news reports as a hero. Indeed, although Micah knows of his father's ability, he still regards him as a hero whatever his abilities – and this feeds off the mythology that all sons find heroism in the acts of their fathers. This raises a philosophical dilemma concerning D. L., and indeed, all of the characters in the show, for the moral status of a hero by definition entertains the notion that people who act out of selflessness beyond their immediate needs and abilities, sometimes with great personal sacrifice, are heroes. Indeed, even the head of the company, Mr Linderman (Malcom McDowell), has made a sacrifice in that he has given up his capacity for differentiating between healing and destruction. He plots to 'heal' the world by causing the death of millions of people in a nuclear disaster, and perhaps millions more in the bloody counterterrorist aftermath. Under this definition, Linderman's Nietzschean ability to look beyond good and evil grants him the moral status of hero. This is a question quite apart from the fact that his politics are reprehensible, his actions psychopathic and his ethics redundant.

Race politics is also a key issue in the show, and the many allusions to the War on Terror carry the proviso that terror has a face of otherness in some form or other. In the real world, this specific otherness has a racial dimension, after all, but there are several ways in which race is represented in *Heroes*. D. L.'s family background offers the producers of the show an opportunity to explore African-American race politics in some detail. After D. L.'s demise in a shooting in LA, Niki leaves Micah safe with D. L.'s family in New Orleans. Micah's cousin Monica Dawson (Dana Davis) is going through a crisis because of the lack of jobs and opportunities in the wake of the Hurricane Katrina disaster. There are numerous references to this as we are introduced to the family, but it is rarely if ever acknowledged that the African-American community of New Orleans has traditionally suffered from social deprivation at the hands of a complacent and uncaring series of administrations.[2]

It is refreshing to see that the fact of D. L. and Niki's mixed-race[3] relationship is not an obstacle, although there are hints of prejudice when, in the first season, Niki is confronted by D. L.'s mother. However, as in the previously discussed example, *The Pursuit of Happyness*, what is clear is that the real discriminatory practices exercised against those who engage in such relationships is never really addressed. A pity, as the walls that the couple would have to surmount every day would require an effort of 'heroic' proportions, and the representation of this would constitute a more definite move towards social realism, and a more thorough definition of the term 'hero' in the show. This is because these two characters are clearly working-class/underclass, and both Niki and D. L. have very troubled backgrounds, a social stratum in which race is not an identity barrier apparent to overcome, but often one that is upheld. This is related to the myth of meritocracy, that one's work ethic will overcome any such barrier, reinforced by a discursive political equity. Monica's own burgeoning powers (muscle memory) come with a self-belief that she was destined for something special, by God's grace. Such self-belief and manifest destiny in contemporary popular media will be the subject of further discussion later in this chapter.

One of the more interesting things about Niki is that she suffers from a form of multiple-personality disorder, which causes her identity to literally fracture into separate personas. It is implied that this has been brought about by the abuse she suffered at the hands of her father as a child, and the subsequent death of her twin sister Jessica, whom she was protecting from the abuse. In the course of her life, Niki associates strength and courage with Jessica. As her super strength develops, so does her identi-fication with 'Jessica' until Niki is trapped in a world of mirrors, unable to break free and take control again. This is further complicated when, following Jessica's reintegration, it emerges that Niki has a third persona fighting for control – 'Gina'. It is Gina's appearance as the dominant personality that results in D. L.'s death in a nightclub.

I bring up this interesting example of dissociation because in relation to both the popular representation of such disorder and its relationship to race and race identification, it highlights an overlooked aspect of this discussion of heroism more generally: double-consciousness. I use this term advisedly, as it engages several meanings at once, all related, but ultimately linked to Jung's mechanism of identification with persona and the emergence from persona amplification into the trajectory of individuation. This is seen in not only *personal* histories and narratives, but also *collective* ones, and *fictive* ones. Although one must be careful not to conflate these three narrative manifestations, the resonance between all three in the popular imagination is self-evident. In comic-book culture, we see it frequently: the 'secret' identity; the masquerade and costume; the split personality; and, the battle between heroes and villains who often mirror or complement each other in temperament. It is the aim of this chapter to discuss this resonance in terms of the representation of the hero in popular narratives, and its articulation in both the personal and the collective in Jungian psychology.

Double-consciousness and self-consciousness

Frances Gray discusses the 'bi-conditionality of human self-consciousness' as a theme within nineteenth-century traditions of philosophy and psychology on subjectivity. She states (2008: 4) that:

> Each self-consciousness preserves itself and the other in its respective action, while at the same time acting as one. Hegel refers to this as the double movement of self-consciousness: it is itself through another yet is not the other even in the exact imitation of the other.

This should come as little surprise to the Jungian reader, especially in Jung's classic formulation of Selfhood, characterized as it is by doubling. To reiterate briefly a point from Chapter 3, Lacan suggests that the image of internal selfhood (within, and from which, the ego and the sense of subjectivity are formed) is characterized by an internally verifying ego-identity that acts as a self-sufficient structuring presence. For David Tacey, 'The ego is the centre of consciousness, the focus of our personal identity, whereas the Self is the centre of the entire psyche, conscious and unconscious, and thus the focus of our transpersonal identity' (2006: 47). Beyond this ego-identity lies a fourfold structure of the archetype of Selfhood, in the Jungian topography a totality of wholeness or Self/God image, a realization of inner wholeness. Again, for Tacey, 'the Self is an archetype which expresses the totality of the psyche', that includes both ego and the unconscious (2006: 25). It is also 'a transcendental concept, and it cannot be known directly by the ego, but only indirectly through symbol, dream and myth' (2006: 48). In the Hegelian view, self-consciousness as an ego-identity is always already dependent on an other: that is, self-consciousness constituted by the presence of another self-consciousness. As Gray describes: 'In finding itself in an other, self-consciousness moves out of itself but it also has to over come or to supersede the other in order to see its own self' (2008: 4). Therefore, self-consciousness always has within it the constitution of the other that enables its own existence. In many philosophical approaches, this carries a particular meaning: a doubling in consciousness brought forth through tension, struggle and contradiction. It is, in other words, a double-consciousness. This has specific resonance for the politics of identity when applied to the figure of the hero, and especially to the hero of colour.

One meaning of the term 'double-consciousness' stems from the work of W. E. B. DuBois, the African-American activist and intellectual who pioneered dialectical thinking on black and mixed-race identity in the late nineteenth and early twentieth century. His most famous work, *The Souls of Black Folk*, originally published in 1903, contains the frank and moving account of his first-born son in which he describes his first meeting with the infant. It is worth quoting this description at length:

How beautiful he was, with his olive-tinted flesh and dark gold ringlets, his eyes of mingled blue and brown, his perfect little limbs, and the soft voluptuous roll which the blood of Africa had moulded into his features! . . . Why was his hair tinted with gold? An evil omen was golden hair in my life. Why had not the brown of his eyes crushed out and killed the blue? – for brown were his father's eyes, and his father's father's. And thus in the Land of the Color-line I saw, as it fell across my baby, the shadow of the Veil.

(DuBois, 1999: 131)

DuBois' work foregrounds the material history and conditions of existence of people of colour. Although his efforts are specialized on a discussion of the state of African-Americans at the turn of the twentieth century, his work is peppered with allusions to a second problem – that of miscegenation, and the ontology of mixed or dual racial heritage. This was eloquently described in the above passage on the birth of his first-born son, but finds its ultimate expression in DuBois' (1999: 11) first statement on double-consciousness:

It is a peculiar sensation, this double-consciousness, this sense of always looking at one's self through the eyes of others, of measuring one's soul by the tape of a world that looks on in amused contempt and pity. One ever feels his two-ness, – an American, a Negro; two souls, two thoughts, two unreconciled strivings; two warring ideals in one dark body, whose dogged strength alone keeps it from being torn asunder.

Note DuBois' terminology here, and its similarity to that found in Jungian psychology. It seems clear that Jung's questions are being answered from another perspective, focusing on a specific problem in order to engage a more general problem of consciousness. The use of the term 'sensation' for example, suggests an affective awareness, if not also a cognitive one specifically engaged in a lived and embodied consciousness. Here, DuBois' immersion into German philosophy, Marxist politics and Hegelian dialectics as a young man left an indelible mark on his thought and is the key to his uniqueness in political thought. DuBois' dialectic opens up the possibility of the complexity of double-consciousness as a dehiscence; a flowering of self-consciousness lived, felt and thought by the person of colour. This is why 'one ever feels his two-ness': It is lived in the fact of unreconciled belonging/otherness, and kept in play by a society that polices its political boundaries rigidly, and discriminates, often abhorrently. The aspect of 'looking at one's self through the eyes of others', suggests both a default and privileged act of looking from a specific stratum of society (namely white, middle-class, male). In theories of spectatorship, this became the object of criticism for Manthia Diawara and others, as noted in previous chapters.

Jung regarded subjective persona identification as 'normal' or at least normative pathology: He derived his ideas for this aspect of personality from his theories on character-splitting and personality dissociation. He suggested that the particular pathology of dissociation was, in fact, 'a problem of normal psychology' (1998: 98). For Jung, personality disassociation becomes problematic when the subject identifies himself or herself with the persona to such an extent that they no longer know 'themselves'. This regularly finds its popular representation in superhero narratives. Bruce Wayne lives a lonely life thanks to the over-identification he has with his 'secret' identity of Batman. The identification is stronger with this aspect of his personality because of its associations with revenge and attrition. It is mirrored in his constant battles with villains who display similar disorders – Two-Face, the Joker and the Riddler are all characters who have two sides to their existence. The villainous personas are, in Jungian parlance, inflected with the shadow archetype, a juvenile and insidious aspect of consciousness that is so close to ego-identity that it becomes difficult to acknowledge consciously the misplaced identification. In *Spider-Man 3* (Raimi, US, 2007), for example, this becomes physically manifest in the shape of Venom, a parasitic life form that takes on and perverts the characteristics and attributes of its host, in this case, the Spider-Man (Tobey McGuire) himself.

For Niki in *Heroes*, this identity crisis is played out as a tool with which she is manipulated by the company, for her insecurities about her own past are revealed as being just as potent in the here and now as in her childhood. The fear is that Micah will be the ultimate victim of her condition, should he ever be exposed to this side of her personality. His position in terms of narrative function is curious: At the beginning of the first season, Niki is seen performing for an adult webcam service in order to pay off a debt to the mysterious Mr Linderman. When Micah later tells her that he is aware of what it is that she is doing (and more importantly, *why*), we get the first inkling that this child is more than he first seems to represent. He plays a special role in the show's narrative conceits, his selfless heroism serving as an example for others to follow. He is also soon aware when Jessica takes over Niki's consciousness. His role is that of the eternal youth, whose innocence teaches the wise the folly of complacency and pride. Of course there are many interpretations of this figure's narrative function, even within Jung's body of work. Narratologists such as Northrop Frye and philosophers such as Paul Ricoeur share with post-Jungian thought a common approach to archetypes as they persist in popular narratives. Archetypes are, for them, recurrent narrative elements that persist because they are so communicatively effective of the literary experience as a whole.

In certain instances, such as in the case of Micah, the function of such figures is to instigate inspiration in other characters within the story. The specialism of Micah's role is expressed through the exoticism of his racial make-up. There are many such mythological figures in the popular imagination, where racial ambiguity has a beauty other than convention, an emotional object of pity or scorn. The figure of the 'tragic mulatto' has been thought of in similar ways, and I refer the reader to Donald Bogle's work (2001) on this matter, in relation to traditions of racial stereotype in American cinema. I use the terms 'figure' and 'narrative function' here, specifically avoiding the term 'archetype', as there are a number of issues that need to be dealt with in terms of narrative structure and character type, for which the symbolism of archetype and semiotic image of stereotype become intertwined. This intertwining, one might say, is characterized by the way in which mythology and history work together to produce particular narratives, told time and again.

Theories of narrative, Jungian mythology and historicity

In literature, 'we are confronted with a product of complicated psychic activities – but a product of that is apparently intentional and consciously shaped'. In contrast, the source of dreams is 'obviously autonomous psychic complexes which form themselves out of their own material' (Jung, cited in Jones, 2007: 58). This statement echoes a reservation that I stated in the opening chapter of this book, which concerns the often-cited reason for the affinity that psychoanalysis and analytical psychology have with film, namely that films are said to be like dreams. To reiterate, films are not dreams. Indeed, narrative films can only really be said to be like dreams insofar as their assemblage is prototypical of the way that people often recount dreams in a narrative way. We do not necessarily dream like narrative films, but we certainly tell stories verbally in a similar fashion, often evoking imagery in a certain narrative order to elaborate our tales. In other words, dreams are narrativized in their telling or retelling in order that we make some sense of them. Otherwise they are, as Jung states, formed out of their own material, residual of thoughts, thought processes and memories. Film experiences and is experienced differently to dreams. The likeness comes through in terms of retelling the narrative. Story-telling and recounting are crucial to subject formation and self-identity, in that narrative shapes and informs our experience of the world in the most general sense. As Charles Taylor, in *Sources of the Self* (1989: 47), states:

> It has often been remarked that making sense of one's life as a story is . . . not an optional extra; that our lives exist also in this space of questions, which only a coherent narrative can answer. In order to have

a sense of who we are, we must have a notion of how we have become and of where we are going.

In the retelling of narrative in particular, we insert our experience of the narrative and emplot with the narrative as part of an empathic process that involves ideological world-views, as well as a micro self-awareness. This is one of the reasons why a film is never the same when we watch it for a second time: The story has been told, and then retold.

I shall return to this issue presently in relation to narrative and audio-visual media, but for now, it is worth putting Jung's assertions to further investigation. For Raya Jones, Jung's discovery of archetypes seems to rest on the misunderstanding that certain regularities in narratives of all kinds repeat themselves as universal moments. Jung once wrote that they are 'Forms or images of a collective nature which occur practically all over the earth as constituents of myths and at the same time as autochthonous, individual products of unconscious origin' (Jung, cited in Campbell, 1993: 18, note 18). For postmodern theory this is problematic, because 'The classification into types robs each one of those dreams, fantasies etc., of the uniqueness of its actual and effective performance' (Jones, 2007: 59). What is important for us here, in terms of Jung's organization of creative activity around repeatable and constant elements (archetypes), is the next question that Jones poses, namely 'the question of how experiences become *organized* (hence meaningful), not merely expressed or let out by means of creative acts' (2007: 59, emphasis in original). It is this question that enables the film theorist to scrutinize the value of critical interpretation of instances of creative practice – for example, the films of a single director as a body of artistic work, or the specifics of relationships between characters reflecting or contradicting real world relationships.

By thinking through meaningfulness as a resonant, alive element of the act of viewing (and indeed, making) films, we can move towards a more productive and open reading of what films come to mean, and why. As stated throughout this book so far, that films are meaningful should be enough to suggest that their power lies in the experience of that meaningfulness, and also is indicative of the plethora of meanings that producers, critics and audiences bring to bear on films as texts. Of course, part of this meaningfulness, particularly in popular narrative film, is experienced through the narrative structuration that is peculiar to the form of film itself. Not necessarily formalist, my approach to this aspect of form nevertheless has in its sights the formal methodology that Jung had in mind around the period of his break with Freud. This I have already stated in Chapter 1, but as Jung himself insisted much later in his career:

There are as many archetypes as there are typical situations in life. Endless repetition has engraved these experiences into our psychic constitution, not in the form of images filled with content, but at first only as *forms without content*, representing merely the possibility of a certain type of perception and action.

(Jung, 1936: para. 99, emphasis in original)

That form, I have suggested, is the Image – the reciprocation of symbol and affect, as potentially experienced in the act of viewing film. An incorrect assumption on the part of many of Jung's critics, the assertion that archetypes are 'inherited representations' is symptomatic of a more general conflation that has occurred in the theorization of Jungian narrative structure.

It is true that, following Jones, there is a difference in definition of narrative functionality between that found in narrative psychology and analytical psychology. The former 'assumes an open-ended construction of personal identity (by means of narratives)', whereas Jung 'assumes the unfolding of a common-to-all psychic configuration (by means of images)' (Jones, 2007: 72). However, although his approach to archetypes evolved throughout his working life, Jung did not suggest that stories or myths as conventionally conceived are stored somewhere in the unconscious. On the contrary, his approach may be thought of more productively as dealing with the ease with which we tend to form symbolic representation through meaningful interaction. As Jones states:

> To Jung, the psyche is unequivocally the organizer, the nothing-therein, whence meaning emerges. In contrast, postmodern psychologists locate the organization of experience in the narrative itself. Meaning is said to emerge from *how* something is told; that is, not only what is said, but also from how it is structured and its other stylistic, grammatical and linguistic characteristics.
>
> (2007: 59, emphasis in original)

My own approach is not so much a synthesis of these two perspectives as an integration, in principle, of two formal methodologies for thinking through meaningfulness in narrative. For example, meaning emerges from the embodied and existential reciprocation of story and audience, through how it is told, and how that telling is experienced. Fundamentally, in film spectatorship, this experience is also shaped partly by the film's experience as a viewing view and a viewed view – its perception–expression as a film-subject, that 'other' subject in the phenomenology of film experience. Rather inevitably, this would also involve cine-subjectivity and the formation of a cine-'self' (in Jungian terms) as characterized by narrativity, but also a reconstituted narration that is partly contingent on and partly informed by the human act of viewing film.

For Jones, 'Like Jung, narrative psychologists are seldom interested in the literary as such but describe the process of selfhood' (2007: 59). For example, according to Jones, Dan McAdams defines self-identity 'as a way in which the self can be arranged or configured, and which takes the form of a story, complete with setting, scenes, character, plot and theme' (2007: 70). I wish to expand on this, by engaging the notion that film has a different narrativity to that found in literature. While it is not strictly text, popular film has textuality, and employs convention in a way that is often likened to literary convention (in, for example, genre). In popular film this is partly achieved, perhaps most consciously so, through the work of narrative.

There is a sense, from a classical Jungian perspective, that narrative forms found in literature and elsewhere are emulated somehow in personal narratives, adding to the notion that narratives and myths may effect self-understanding. This is sometimes taken quite literally. Christopher Vogler, for example, clearly states that there is an essential form, or at least there is a 'sensation' of certain repeatable forms such as the hero in folklore. From this position, an endless series of hero-types may be cultivated for creative purposes, and these mirrored types resonate with the 'spirit of the form'. Well-meaning, but vague, Vogler does not translate what this spirit might be, although he uses this Jungian-style analysis of 'spirit' in his creative practice in order to communicate such essential forms. In another example, James Hillman has generally described plots as myths, making a direct comparison between the two, much in the way that the literal translation of the word 'plot' in classical Greek is *mythos*. However, he goes on to say (1983: 11) that:

> A mythos is more than a theory and more than a plot. It is the tale of the interaction of human and the divine. To be in a mythos is to be inescapably linked with divine powers, and moreover, to be in mimesis with them.

This is perhaps all well and good when making direct comparisons between literary forms and interior narratives. However, when dealing with film, an audiovisual medium of perception–expression, one must take this a step further to consider this 'divine-ness' to be nothing more mystical than an embodied relation between viewer and viewed. In other words, there is a *kinesis* involved in the mythos of interaction between narratives of the human and narratives of the divine.

In addition, from a literary perspective, Richard Chase's *Quest for Myth* makes for a slightly different view of mythmaking as creative practice, while nevertheless reinforcing the common direct comparison between forms of literature and myth. Chase states that 'myth is literature and must be considered as an aesthetic creation of the human imagination' (cited in Wheelwright, 1955: 155). I would take issue with the claim that myth is literature – it is so much more than this. Joseph Campbell (1993: 382) has explained in *The Hero With a Thousand Faces*, and it is worth recounting in full here, that:

> Mythology has been interpreted by the modern intellect as a primitive, fumbling effort to explain the world of nature (Frazer); as a production of poetical fantasy from prehistoric times, misunderstood by succeeding ages (Müller); as a repository of allegorical instruction, to shape the individual and his group (Durkheim); as a group dream, symptomatic of archetypal urges within the depths of the human psyche (Jung); as the traditional vehicle of man's profoundest metaphysical insights (Coomaraswamy); and as God's Revelation to His children (the Church). Mythology is all of these.

We might as well add, 'and more', for mythology is also, following Roland Barthes, the manifestation, through consent to dominant systems of signification and representation, of ideology: Specifically, we might say ideology that serves the interests of certain individuals or groups within society, and that which presents itself as serving the interests of all that exist within that society. Mythology is, in phenomenological terms, the natural attitude, the way the world intends towards us, as we intend towards it at the level of culture. This is what makes mythology, and the affective, reciprocal form of Image so potent for contemporary visual culture.

Mythology operates as 'all of these' things, and more. Even when thinking through the formal differences between written, filmed and oral storytelling, we may say that myth is more than literature alone. However, it is interesting to note the logic of endeavour that colours Chase's statement here, in that the human imagination takes primary credit for the aesthetic creation of myth. This is key to understanding the way that the experience of narrative is ultimately reciprocal for, as previously stated, Terry Eagleton's take on the cerebral aesthetic category of sensibility is that it is always-already engaged with the negotiation of the world through our 'creaturely existence'. In other words, there is an infinite play and reversibility between objectified, emotional meaning-making (semiosis) and a subjectified, affective meaning (symbolism). Myth, it seems, is also therefore of fundamental importance to our understanding of meaningfulness.

As stated in the last chapter, from Barthes' perspective, mythology may be understood as embodying ideology in a narrative form. Indeed, as Jones (2007: 64–65) has commented:

> A myth distorts by disconnecting something from its historical becoming and regards it instead as a manifestation of an essential order. Jungian psychology indeed distorts social history and the historicity of the myths told by ancient and aboriginal peoples into manifestations of essential human nature.

Indeed, Jung is able to do this because of a presumed isomorphism of 'primitive' culture, and his evolution of consciousness – a problematic position, and yet very much in line with modernist presumptions of Western civilization and its relation to the Third World. What is pleasing to note from Jones' account, is that she is addressing the theoretical gap that John Izod identifies in the epigraph above. That 'cultural dimensions of symbols and their location in social discourse' have now become so important in post-Jungian thought is a telling development, as reflective of post-Jungian appropriations of postmodernist thinking as it is of the general phenomenology of symbol and semiosis, as discussed in Chapter 5 of this book. However, Jones' statement that 'Barthes' footnotes on myth legitimate a new myth, according to which expositions of historicity are myth-free' (2007: 65) is slightly misleading. Barthes himself noted in his essay 'Myth Today' that, 'The world enters language as a dialectical relation between activities, between human actions; it comes out of myth as a harmonious display of essences' (2006: 301). It seems that the operation of human action/interaction is foremost in the account of the production of narrative, this time 'mythological' narrative. There is a loss of historical quality perhaps, as history is put aside in favour of an induction into the myth itself. For, as Barthes (2006: 301) notes:

> Myth does not deny things, on the contrary, its function is to talk about them; simply it purifies them, it makes them innocent, it gives them a natural and eternal justification, it gives them a clarity which is not that of an explanation but that of a statement of fact.

However, there is no loss of ideological value, even if one reads myth's intentions as being 'naturalized' (Barthes, 2006: 300). This is the peculiar effect of the concept of historicity itself. To round off this matter, Richard Campbell describes historicity as a thought that 'through our actions we constitute who we are' (1992: 1). In other words, historicity is the condition of human action and interaction, and underlying this, there 'is a new sensitivity to our own historicity, which requires us to take seriously the contingent character of what we ordinarily say and do. That calls into question any system which purports to present necessary truths concerning what there is' (1992: 3). Although principally a philosophical matter beyond the scope of this book, this is interesting as historicity engages not only 'truths concerning what there is', but also the constitution of who we are. These are pressing questions for Jung, who, as already discussed, used narrative psychology to describe the process of selfhood more than in the active critique of literature. Historicity then, can be thought of as a historically aware image of selfhood, and in film culture constitutes the same reconstituted narration that is partly contingent on and partly informed by the human act of viewing film, mentioned earlier in the chapter. As the historian Simon Gunn (2006: 26) writes:

> One of the simplest ways to define history is to say that it is a narrative about real events that happened in the past. By narrative is meant the arrangement of events in a sequential order, with characters and a plot, in the manner of a story. Thinking of history in this way connects it with earlier literary forms such as the epic and the saga.

Clearly then, there seems to be a relationship between history, narrative, the experience of time and the experience of oneself. This lends itself neatly to the idea of personal history, and to Jung's conception of identity formation, which, as we have seen, engages a normal or normative pathology of double-consciousness. It also engages the notion of causality in specific ways.

Hypostasis and individuation: the 'One'

The teleological process of identity formation and individuation in classical psychology also has close ties to the philosophical concept of hypostasis – final causality – which typically manifests in hero narratives in the form of a dilemma. This dilemma is one of tension between *choice* and *inevitability*: a tension that informs and underpins the narrative of many popular films. It seems to be particularly prevalent in the *Matrix* trilogy. This apocalyptic vision of the Wachowski brothers engages hypostasis in both characterizations, in that Neo (Keanu Reeves) frequently has to confront this dilemma throughout, and emplotment, in the question 'Is my life predetermined, or do I have a choice?' Indeed, one of the more interesting things about the *Matrix* films is that they leave this dilemma unresolved. Near the end of *The Matrix Reloaded*, for example, Neo makes the choice to leave the Architect's room through a door that his predecessors (the champions of humanity in previous incarnations of the Matrix system) could not. This choice, we are led to believe, will pre-empt humanity's destruction by machines. However, as an aspect of freewill, this is a choice that is invested with the value of fate in that Neo's position in relation to the oppressive Matrix as a system is anomalous. His position, his being, is motivated by love towards a particular individual – Trinity (Carrie-Ann Moss) – rather than mere general love for humanity. This is a factor that the Architect of the Matrix did not anticipate, and therefore is a defining trait of this particular hero manifestation. In this, Neo is exerting personal choice (and thus expressing free will) while at the same time fulfilling his duty and fate as the saviour of humanity: The machines are stopped, the characters succeed against the predetermination of the Matrix programming, but at great personal cost. Therefore, this narrative negates the central problem that Vogler defines in the individuation of the hero character.

For Vogler, 'Ultimately, a Hero is one who is able to transcend the bounds and illusions of the ego, but at first, Heroes are all ego: the I, the one, that personal identity which thinks it is separate from the rest of the group' (2007: 29). This is an internally contradictory position, as many Hollywood narratives seem to privilege this separation as a form of active, individuated hero. As with Neo's 'hero-individuation' trajectory, this contradiction entertains the notion that human life is ruled by destiny but also, paradoxically, by our own choices. The narrative of hypostasis, or final causality, reiterates the tendency of Western media to represent meritocratic 'individuation' as a natural phenomenon, while disengaging from what Jung has described as the move from adolescence to maturity through individuation or what might be described as an accommodation of the Self. The fact that meritocracy is most often framed within discourses of both freedom of choice *and* manifest destiny reveals the disingenuous relationship of reality and representation that I have already discussed in relation to both *The Pursuit of Happyness* and *Heroes*. Vogler's version of the Jungian individuation, therefore, is represented by the hero's journey: 'The ego, the Hero thinking she is separate from all these parts of herself, must incorporate them to become the Self' (2007: 30).

Sean Cubitt, in 'Digital Filming and Special Effects', claims that recent films such as the *Matrix* series have, within their narrative and spectacular story-telling strategies, certain common themes. He says that 'These and many other such narratives . . . of recent years devolve upon the recognition and acceptance of fate, a fate that is entirely against the concept of history as open-ended evolution and change' (2004: 27). Massively popular, these films are undoubtedly packed with the kind of moments that Jungians might call 'numinous'. Indeed, the very experience of cinema itself supports a powerful argument suggesting that the essentially religious experiences that Jung returns to time and again in his classical formulae are still very much a part of everyday engagement with our stories and myths. *Star Wars* plays on this discernibility. George Lucas fundamentally understands his audience as he builds up contemporary myths around his texts that draw off, and reflect, contemporary political and cultural exchanges. *Star Wars* was a key moment, after all, in what Ed Guerrero (1993) describes as the 'Cinema of Recuperation', a tryst between neoliberal political fantasy and consumer-led supply-side economics. Along with franchises such as the *Jaws*, *Superman* and later, the *Rambo* films, *Star Wars* began a cycle of recuperation that was to find its Millennial expression in the *Matrix* franchise. *The Matrix* latched onto the same imagination that Lucas so skilfully tapped. The Wachowski brothers are as adept as Lucas in their role as contemporary storytellers, not so much through the words that are spoken by the various characters as through their closeness to the audience in terms of need, demand and want. However, whereas the traditional practice of story-telling is a cathartic experience, whereby the journey of peril, enchantment and redemption works as a guide towards healing,[4] this is not what these films do. And yet, elements of this narrative unwinding can be found, layered within the fabric of the texts through the exploitation of technology, cinematic tradition and merchandising. This finds its most acute form in the exploitation of narrative.

As stated, the dominant theme running through the narrative of the *Matrix* trilogy is the tension between *choice* and *inevitability*. It is a central concern for much Jungian thought, in the sense that there is an archetypal tension in the dyad involved in journeying, and the character transformation that occurs as a result of choices made along the way. This tension is central to the narrative arc of the original film trilogy, and I would argue that it is also central to the hypertextual narrative closure located in the franchise as a whole. By this term 'hypertextual' I refer to the way in which contemporary film franchises are able to deliver a bounty of choice for the consumer in terms of the ways they engage with the texts.[5] This has the knock-on effect of enabling meaning in a number of ways, without necessarily contributing anything to meaningfulness. It is primarily articulated in what Paul Lunenfeld has described as the 'sheer plenitude of narrative, exemplified by the glowingly accessible archive of everything' (2004: 151). Note that 'plenitude of narrative' in this sense does not necessarily equate with 'more meaning'. In fact, such proliferation of textual material would constitute a foreclosure of meaning, in that interpretation has already been set up for consumption, particularly through documentary and commentary features on DVD releases.

For Vogler (2007: xxii), the notion of narrative and personal journey in popular media takes on a deeper resonance when thought of in terms of consumer access to these paratextual or incidental media:

> Interactivity has always been with us – we all make many nonlinear hypertext links in our own minds even as we listen to a linear story. In fact, the Hero's Journey lends itself extremely well to the world of computer games and interactive experiences. The thousands of variations on the paradigm, worked out over the centuries, offer endless branches from which infinite webs of story can be built.

Vogler takes his cue from structuralist theories of narrative, and this is clear when he states that 'All stories consist of a few common elements found universally in myths, fairy tales, dreams, and movies' (2007: xxvii). In this, he shares common ground with the likes of Levi-Strauss and other structuralists briefly discussed in earlier chapters, but chiefly follows the influence of Campbell, a comparative mythologist enamoured of the classical Jungian school. As Vogler (2007: xxviii) states of his approach to feature film narrative:

I worked with Campbell's idea of the Hero's Journey to understand the phenomenal repeat business of movies such as *Star Wars* and *Close Encounters*. People were going back to see these films as if seeking some kind of religious experience. It seemed to me these films drew people in this special way because they reflected the universally satisfying patterns Campbell found in myths.

In the case of *Star Wars* as well as *The Matrix*, we have an original film text that has been expanded in the established strategy of sequelization and franchising, which ultimately destroys any sense of a hermetically sealed cinematic narrative once and for all. The *Star Wars* franchise, for example, although phenomenal in terms of box-office receipts, was largely built on the renegotiation of merchandising rights between Lucas and 20th Century Fox. Whether this is ultimately a positive or a negative phenomenon is a question in itself, and I have explored the political economy of such effects elsewhere.[6] Here, I am concerned more with the effect this has on narrative, as well as the ramifications of these cultural phenomena in terms of archetypal themes within the narrative, and within the techno-culture in which the narrative expresses itself.

In the archetypal dyadic tension between fate and freewill in *The Matrix* (or, for that matter, *Star Wars*, or *Heroes*) there are strong thematic and conceptual similarities to Jungian psychology, and in particular, Marie Von Franz's approach to the individuation of the Self. Let us consider the main character of *The Matrix*, Neo, and his journey. This type of reading, however, should be qualified with the proviso that this book has argued for throughout: that, following Hollwitz (2001) and his critique of straightforward applications of analytical constructs to literary processes (see Chapter 1), one must be careful not to universalize personal interpretations in cultural texts.

Much like Luke Skywalker in *Star Wars*, Neo is clearly an expression of the archetypal hero, itself arguably an image of the ego formation, and this is confirmed by his status at the beginning of the narrative when he is seen to be waiting for his 'calling'. He is young, naïve, unassuming and curious. Throughout the films, he is given a series of choices to consider, and is mainly guided, and one might say manipulated, by Morpheus (Lawrence Fishburn), a typical Wise Old Man figure. Morpheus, a specifically Judaic character, whose belief in Neo as a messianic figure is unswerving, stands as a curiously overdetermined image. He is positioned as an Africanized Moses-like figure, leading sacred rituals and offering revelation to the people of Zion. This leaves us in little doubt as to his place in the intention of the production process: the representation of a zealot and racial other, with a pathological religious condition and fanatical belief in apocalyptic prophesy.

Significantly, Agent Smith (Hugo Weaving) refers to Morpheus as a terrorist in the first film, further confirming the overdetermination of such characterization, and reflecting the undercurrents of race and religious politics in terrorist rhetoric. When he gives Neo the choice of the red pill or the blue pill, Morpheus is allowing him to leave behind for ever the carefully constructed persona of Thomas Anderson, to begin his journey of Self-discovery. Therefore, his function in Neo's individuation process within the narrative is, like the role of the Wise Old Man, ambiguous. He offers wisdom and guidance through the choices that Neo must face (and, for all we know, gives Neo the opportunity to take the blue pill and forget his enlightenment), but is ultimately conservative in his ways and believes that all choices lead to the path of the 'One'.

According to Michael Palmer in *Freud and Jung on Religion*, representations of outmoded Christian and religious concepts have been 'drained of libidinal energy and have thus become valueless' (1997: 157). This is a highly contentious issue, however, for Palmer is clearly employing a value system based on a semiosis/symbol dichotomy. This I have critiqued at length in Chapters 4 and 5, in relation to the works of Fredericksen and Hauke. Aside from the issue of libidinal energy (a highly debatable quantity in itself), texts such as *The Matrix* offer familiar reproductions of psychologically and culturally privileged images, which work at an ideological level. Far from valueless, these images are *loaded* with value – as we have seen, mythology is not just about epic journeys, but is also concerned with the contemporary crux of personal, collective and fictive history. Such histories thrive on evaluative notions of cause and effect, and in particular on causality in its most final aspect (hypostasis). In addition, as Melanie Withers (2003: 208) states:

> Ideology, whether sacred or secular, offers explanations, meaning and structures within which to work and to understand life's events. It also offers illusory control – for if the explanations are correct, outcomes can be predicted. Believers therefore contend that ideology will prevail and lead to a better tomorrow.

Ideology is not a neutral entity, nor is it entirely visible. It offers explanation insofar as it engages belief systems, some of which have more cultural currency than others and are, therefore, 'valued' above others. Self-reliance and individualism, for example, are prized more highly in contemporary Western cultures than are community and collective action. As Roger Brooke states, 'In modern Western society expansion tends to be wilful, utilitarian, and heroic, and thus tends to empty the primordial powers and meanings of the self into the literalisms of contemporary life' (1991: 118).

The character of Trinity is an illuminating case in the ways that ideology can inform the value-system of an entire narrative. As we know, Jung devoted much of his career to the interpretation of religious structures and belief systems. In particular, in his essay 'A Psychological Approach to the Dogma of the Trinity' (Jung, 1988), he discusses the causality found in the Christian godhead. In the *Matrix* franchise, the character of Trinity is ambiguous in this context because of the curious masculine nature of the Trinity structure as explained by Jung. She is far closer to the Magdalene figure in both appearance and narrative function. Whatever the particular interpretation, the resonance with Christian mythology is obvious. Appropriating a post-Jungian model to examine religiosity in film texts is highly useful, as it can be used as a non-reductive approach to investigating how symbols are in a continual flux of divestment and investment of meaning. But it is also troubled by its own dogmatic clause. Melanie Withers suggests 'Jungian thinking as a dynamic to understand and potentially integrate what is disavowed and denigrated about religious belief by secular academic thinking' (2003: 203).[7]

Jung describes the first stage of the Trinity as the Father-stage: a representation of the first stage of the Individuation process, infancy, 'primitive religion', God-images, and most importantly Father as *prime cause*. He states that 'If we posit "Father," then "Son" logically follows'; in other words, a figurative procession from one to the other (1988: 27). This conjures up crucial existential and philosophical questions around the function of hypostasis and final causality – the ultimate expression of narrative in that its teleological aspects are elevated to the status of inevitable cause-and-effect. No matter how much the narrative seeks to emphasize freedom to choose in this case as its *raison d'être*, it cannot help the finality of its cause-and-effect retrospection. In the rhetoric of meritocracy, we are agents of our own free will, able to accomplish anything, if this is our choice. By the same token, however, its dialectical opposite – fate, or inevitability – is irresistible, and it is through the appropriation of such values as divine will, fate and manifest destiny that we see the absolute reproduction of the American Dream in many popular films, including *The Matrix*. As contradictory as this seems, it is not uncommon to encounter such paradoxes in Jungian thought. For example, in the case of the representation of the Trinity, the logic of figurative procession from the Father is complicated. Jung continues:

> 'Holy Ghost' does not follow logically from either 'Father' or 'Son'. So we must be dealing here with a special factor that rests on a different presupposition . . . What it really denoted was the *anima*, which, as its name shows, is a breath-being (*anemos* = wind). Although an activity of the body, it was thought of as an independent substance (or hypostasis) existing alongside the body. The underlying idea is that the body 'lives,' and that life is something superadded and autonomous, conceived as a soul unattached to the body.
>
> (1988: 27, emphasis in original)

For Jung, then, 'The Holy Ghost is hypostatized procreative power and life-force' (1988: 28). A number of questions are raised here. Is Jung using the term 'anima' in a slightly different way to his conventional use (that of feminine contrasexual archetype), or is he formulating a fundamental contradiction within the Trinity, in that the 'archetypal ideas' that return do so in a transubstantiated form? That is, can the feminine principle be the mitigating life force but also be excluded from the 'body' of the Trinity? Jung states that in all rituals associated with such mysteries, the feminine is taken out of the realm of godhead, sometimes physically, as women are banned (in Christianity and elsewhere) from such ritual. It seems that this internal contradiction cannot be resolved in its representation either. Therefore perhaps the Trinity character of *The Matrix* can be read as an embodiment of the Trinity dogma in Christian mythology after all: She is the principal cause of the particular way that the narrative is played out in the trilogy. She is the object of love for Neo, and therefore a motive behind his actions, the Father ideal. She is the double of the Son in that her abilities, even appearance, mirror those of Neo. She is also the life force in that her love for Neo acts as catalyst for his individuation at the end of the first film.

It should be reiterated that the symbolic expression of archetypes is a mere image of the internal archetypal structure – one can never know the archetype itself. Throughout his work, Jung would make statements such as 'Archetypal ideas are part of the indestructible foundations of the human mind. However long they are forgotten and buried, always they return, sometimes in the strangest guise, with a personal twist to them or intellectually distorted' (1988: 26). However, he would add qualifying remarks (in this case, on the same page) such as 'The special emphasis I lay on archetypal predispositions does not mean that mythologems are of exclusively psychic origin. I am not overlooking the social conditions that are just as necessary for their production' (1988: 26, note 4). This did not stop many psychologists of the classical school from overlooking these necessary social conditions, but this is an oversight that post-Jungian scholars have sought to address more recently. The problems in superimposing archetypal mythology on narratives that draw from and are informed by particular historical instances of mythology are obvious and manifold: not least the phenomenon of dehiscent semiosis–symbol reversibility that occurs, as discussed in Chapters 4 and 5, and the tertiary signification processes that Barthes envisaged as primarily ideological, as discussed in the previous chapter. I will return to the problem of Trinity and Jung's discussion of Plato's quaternity formulation of matter, specifically in relation to sychronicity, in Chapter 8.

There are several other characters in *The Matrix* that one might describe as archetypal – characters that, in the trajectory of individuation, seldom hinder the inevitable rise of Neo and his path towards individuation. As 'effects', these characters typify what may be described as a form-based approach to archetypes. Looking at archetypes in this way can, for Vogler, explain how characters become complex, and reflect the attributes of more than one archetype throughout the narrative, in order to progress plot. Characterization in this sense becomes over-determined through archetypal interaction. Returning to our *Heroes* example, Sato Nakamura (George Takei) is a shadow type, a 'threshold guardian' for Campbell and Vogler, and mentor at a thematic level to his son Hiro (Masi Oka). In his turn, Hiro variously plays the part of hero, trickster, shadow and split Self (especially in his role as 'future Hiro'), as do Kensai (David Anders) and Ando (James Kyson Lee), given the different plot twists and temporary roles performed.

Of specific note in *The Matrix*, the Oracle and Smith characters seem particularly archetypal in the classical sense. For example, the Oracle, exhausted from her efforts to keep the dark side of the Self (Smith) from corrupting the Matrix, is transformed from an Eternal Mother figure (played by Gloria Foster) into guardian of the sun (Mary Alice). Both figures are aspects of the goddess to whom religions around the world devote their worship. It is interesting to note here that the sun is not represented by the Christ figure Neo, as is frequent in Christian and proto-Christian myths, but by a little Desi girl called Sati in the final film (Tanveer K. Atwal). In itself, this has cultural significance in an age of multi-culturalism and endless media reference to cultural otherness – just one of the 'social conditions' that Jung implied in relation to archetypal develop-ment. Her appearance is a species of Orientalism and hybridity that also characterized Micah's role in *Heroes* – that of the Eternal Youth, an exotic and enlightened other, a bringer of peace whose coming is facilitated by the hero's sacrifice (D. L., and ultimately Niki). In *Heroes*, Micah performs the role in two ways. He is both a moral guide to those who would be corrupted by their power and the keeper of their humanity, a moral status that often assumes one must know right from wrong and act accordingly in order to qualify. In the *Matrix* films, Sati performs a similar narrative function. At the end of *Matrix Revolutions*, the guardian of the sun (the Oracle) is put in charge of the child who is the personification of a pro-gramme that makes the sun rise. She is the protocol in the Matrix system that allows this to happen, and so must be brought into being. Neo's function as hero is to make this happen through sacrificing himself.

The splitting of the totality of Self, a Jungian theme, creates for Smith and Neo extraordinary God-like powers with which to commence battle for the survival of both machines and humans. Smith not only has the power to reproduce, in the endless replication of himself, but also manages to *create* in that his consciousness pushes out of the machine world and into real life. Complementarily, Neo also takes his Matrix powers into the real world of humans. However, when he loses his eyes (a conscious nod to Freud and Ernest Jones's work on the uncanny and the myth of the Sandman, perhaps) he is given a second sight and is able to manipulate the machines through some sort of golden aura. This has its final manifestation in the bright light that emanates from his body at the end of the final battle, when he declares, in a direct New Testament reference, that 'It Is Done.' The Christ figure, often superimposed on hero characters in Western and other mythologies, is something of a favourite theme for the classical school. Jung (1988: 30) states that:

> The Son, the revealed god, who voluntarily or involuntarily offers himself as sacrifice as a man, in order to create the world or redeem it from evil, can be traced back to the Purusha of Indian philosophy, and is also found in the Persian conception of the Original Man, Gayomart . . . He is the prototype of the Gnostic redeemer-figures and of the teachings concerning Christ, redeemer of mankind.

For Louise Von Franz, the Purusha in Hindu tradition is perhaps more closely related to the Holy Ghost than to the Christ, but is ultimately personified as Cosmic Man. She states that 'The Purusha lives in the heart of every individual, and yet at the same time he fills the entire cosmos' (1964: 215). He is the place from where humanity flows, and towards which we strive to return, inevitably. It is a circular teleology that once again entertains the notion of hypostasis, a final causality except this time, it is identified with the Son rather than the Father. The Son, through his actions as the hero, is therefore *the cause made flesh* – a sentiment that would sit in ecumenical councils as well as it might in contemporary Hollywood films. As Von Franz (1964: 215) continued:

> In our Western civilization the Cosmic Man has been identified to a great extent with Christ, and in the East with Krishna or with Buddha. In the Old Testament this same symbolic figure turns up as the "Son of Man" and in later Jewish mysticism is called Adam Kadmon . . . Like all symbols this image points to an unknowable secret – to the ultimate unknown meaning of human existence.

The cosmological view of archetypal Christ-figures is problematic. If indeed archetypal, at what point is it possible to say that the 'cause made flesh' manifests itself in consciousness? Vogler (2007: 24) gives a throwaway line concerning Campbell and archetypes. It is perhaps most interesting for the fact that he does not attempt to theorize Campbell's position on this:

> Joseph Campbell spoke of the archetypes as biological: as expressions of the organs of the body, built into the wiring of every human being. The universality of these patterns makes possible the shared experience of storytelling.

This certainly tallies with the phenomenology of archetypes in film spectatorship as an embodied notion that engages affective response, emotional objectivity, and the resonance between audience and film. It informs the production of meaningfulness. However, from the terminology and sentiment employed in his approach, Vogler would not make the differentiation between these elements. Note his use of the built-in, 'hard-wiring' metaphor. We have already encountered this in Torben Grodal's problematic cognitive approach to film spectatorship. This is countered by the interdisciplinary nature of comparative mythology itself. Take, for example, James G. Frazer:

> The resemblance that may be traced . . . between the religions of the East and West is no more than what we commonly, though incorrectly, call a fortuitous coincidence, the effect of similar causes acting alike on the similar constitution of the human mind in different countries and under different skies.
>
> (Frazer, cited in Campbell, 1993: 18–19, note 18)

His terminology is telling: 'the *effect* of similar causes acting alike *on* the similar constitution of the human mind'. In Frazer, then, the causality of archetypal structure appears to be a reversal of that found in Jung until we are reminded of his note that social conditions 'are just as necessary for their production' as psychic and organic causes. When applied to the hero archetype in particular, this would have implications for 'identification' processes in cine-subjectivity. As Campbell notes, 'The hero . . . is the man or woman who has been able to battle past his personal and local historical limitations to the generally valid, normally human forms' (1993: 19–20). It is not entirely clear what Campbell means here by 'normally human forms', but one might make the informed guess that he is talking about moving beyond culturally accepted norms of individual heroism, a subjective development underpinned by collective forms of accepted behaviour. In Campbell's view, heroic visions, ideas and inspiration are not dogged by the disabling forces of society and psyche, but are defined through an 'unquenchable' spring of pre-existent energy of human being. This is the mythological hero, whose second task is transformative not only of his personal self, but also of his/her society. Campbell is, ultimately, writing about an ideal: a religious figure; but a religious figure representative of all religiosity in a more general sense.

   As Campbell notes in common with many post-Jungians, this has become increasingly difficult to understand in modern life. For, in 'the democratic ideal of the self-determining individual . . . The social unit is not a carrier of religious content, but an economic-political organization . . . In hard and unremitting competition for material supremacy and resources' (1993: 387). Indeed, this emptying-out of humanity for the sake of the particular mode of production (in neo-Marxist terminology, advanced or late capital) is a signifier that has no potential for meaningfulness outside itself, other than as a representation of the empty relationship between labour and its products.

Arguably, this is one of the reasons why heroic narratives and contemporary mythologies of rugged individualism in the face of insurmountable adversity proliferate in popular culture. Following a neo-Marxian or Weberian reasoning we may assume that these narratives offer a distraction from the meaninglessness of labour and its products, including the ennui that sets in with patterns of consumption. This discontent does not permeate all aspects of the hero narrative, however, and there are glimmers of meaningfulness to be found in figures such as Micah, who have yet to discover the full savagery of alienated capital. It should be made clear that this does not mean that there should be some sort of 'return to innocence', a return to nature before The Fall. It does mean, however, that we (in academia) often overlook such insights, no matter how fleeting, reducing them to interpretations of doom. Although strictly a matter for the existentialist, what we see in a 'truthful' interpretation of innocent intention towards humanity in figures such as Micah permeates the moral reality of everyday life. We are what we watch, in this respect, and we coincide with our objects in meaningful ways. The next chapter will be dedicated to an analysis of what this might mean for the post-Jungian and the film scholar: synchronicity, or a meaningful coincidence in time.

Chapter 8

Synchronicity and space-time transgression in film and video

Case studies in time sculpture and capture

Heaven has become for us the cosmic space of the physicists, and the divine empyrean a fair memory of things that once were. But 'the heart glows,' and a secret unrest gnaws at the roots of our being.

Carl Jung, 'Archetypes of the Collective Unconscious'

The dynamic structures of matter . . . all contain and unfold out of their own meaning, as opposed to static structures that are created according to the design of some external agency. Likewise the essence of the collective unconscious lies in the meaning of its archetypes, those dynamic patterns and symmetries that maintain its internal structure. Meaning, therefore is the kernel of both material structures and of the collective unconscious.

F. David Peat, *Synchronicity: The Bridge Between Matter and Mind*

The film *Twins* (Reitman, US, 1988) may be thought of as a pure fantasy, a shallow farce in which a series of unlikely comical events culminates in the familial reunion between two genetically engineered twin brothers, Julius (Arnold Schwarzenegger) and Vincent (Danny DeVito), with their birth-mother. However, there is one particular moment that stands out among all the other 'twin' jokes in the movie. At one point, Julius is wandering around the city in search of his twin brother, whose existence he has just discovered. Meanwhile, Vincent is wandering around the same city, in ignorance of the existence of his brother, trying to get hold of funds through criminal means in order to pay off a gangland debt. Throughout the movie, the two are seen mirroring each other's body language – a conscious attempt to represent their genetic connectedness: information to which only the audience is privy. However, in this particular moment they are seen framed in the same shot, unaware of each other's presence, and scratch their backsides at the same time while looking around at their surroundings. What does this mean?

The shot represents connectedness that is not conscious. Neither character is aware of the other's presence in the frame, and only one has partial knowledge of the other's existence. They are engaged in very different activities, although both are on quests of some sort, and their physical differences are staggering. This physical difference is, of course, one of the featured jokes throughout the movie – both actors are often employed for their capacities to produce different human special effects. However, the connection of shared genetic material in the narrative is represented through similarities in bodily expression, and also in affective response. Vincent feels Julius' pain in a climactic scene which sees him overcome his own selfishness and appropriate the higher ethical sensibility of his brother. Guilt at leaving his brother to die at the hands of bounty-hunters is triggered by a physiological effect, produced through common genetic material. Yet this material is not connected physically in space. It therefore represents not just an unconscious connectedness but also a physical acausality. *Twins* attempts to represent, in other words, a kind of synchronicity: Jung's acausal connecting principle.

So far, this book has taken into consideration a number of themes of relevance to both contemporary film theory and the theories of post-Jungian psychology. The effort to bring these two theoretical traditions together was not exerted in order to create a synthetic analytical psychological theory of film, but to map the common ground in the two fields. One of the key themes persisting in the writing of this work is that of meaningfulness. As Peat says in the epigraph above, meaning is the kernel of material structures and of the psychic processes. Meaning is, one should add, a key ingredient in the questions of film scholarship, whether we should say what films mean or not. However, that meaning has been a key concern in Jungian psychology is a slightly different matter to that of meaningfulness, as I have already discussed in relation to the act of film viewing and affectivity. Meaningfulness and popular film go together, as films resonate with the real world and our experience of it. This is not to say that films necessarily reflect reality (as epitomized in the fantastic example of *Twins*), but rather that they engage the viewer in a number of ways that can be recognized as meaningful works of art, entertainment and cultural reference.

The special place in Jung's psychology, in particular of the classical school, accorded to meaningfulness may be justified through a number of key ideas and writings throughout his career. It is perhaps one of his more controversial ideas – that of synchronicity – that I wish to focus on here. Synchronicity, or a meaningful coincidence in time, is a theme rarely tackled by post-Jungian film critics. Possibly due to its complexity, or its strong associations with Eastern mysticism and parapsychology, this is an idea that is sometimes thought of as best avoided in order to retain scientific objectivity. In fact, scientific objectivity is one of the targets of the theory more generally, and is a modernist principle that is left wanting.

There are three questions that I wish to address in this chapter in relation to synchronicity. Firstly, what is synchronicity, and can it be represented in a film? Secondly, can the concept of synchronicity be used productively to further our understanding of the act of viewing film? Lastly, as an acausal connecting principle, how does it relate to the representation of subjective reality in moving pictures? In order to help answer these questions, I will be referring to the work of three very different directors who work on the fringes of popular independent film, and who have distinctive approaches to the representation of subjectivity. In addition, all three are cult directors, thanks in part to their peculiar takes on realist and surrealist techniques, quirky styles and idiosyncratic choice of subject matter. The directors under consideration are Andrei Tarkovsky, Wong Kar-Wai and Michel Gondry.

Synchronicity: Some ground rules in causality

As discussed at length in relation to the hero archetype in the previous chapter, narrative and the way it is usually told (linear, cause-and-effect, etc.) has a specific place in popular film. The maxim employed at the Disney studio for example, 'Where Story is King', is telling, as it utilizes the rhetoric employed by the industry to reinforce the ideology of certain forms of story-telling as more natural or universal than others. Christopher Vogler worked as a professional script consultant in Hollywood for many years and, as we have seen on a number of issues, employs this normalized rhetoric in his discussion of archetypes. However, the act of viewing film engages our subjectivity (and sense of subjectivity) in much less discreet ways. It is a sensuous and affective act, connecting as it does the intimacy of perception–expression and our experience of it. In other words, what we see and hear *out there* is very difficult to separate from what we feel *in here* in any meaningful sense. Connectedness seems to pervade the experience of film, and it is this curiosity that also pervades the Jungian and post-Jungian concerns with normative subjectivity.

David Tacey envisages the future task of psychology as 'to rediscover the totality of life, and not to be content with exploring fragments of it in specialist disciplines' (2006: 6). This is an important statement to make, as it suggests that psychology needs to embrace the idea of meaningfulness as an aspect of normative psychology and identity formation rather than as a marginal curiosity. Often existentialist in its language and its goals, Tacey's approach is useful in engaging the psychological processes involved in the way people interact with their culture on an everyday level.

It is also crucial to further the understanding of how we determine and express our subjective reality. As discussed in Chapter 3, Lacan's approach to the acquisition of identity is useful in reinforcing the appropriation of the imaginal in and for embodied experience, establishing 'a relation between the organism and its reality – or, as they say, between the *Innenwelt* and the *Umwelt*' (2004: 83). Lacan goes on to suggest that 'to break out of the circle of the *Innenwelt* into the *Umwelt* generates the inexhaustible quadrature of the ego's verifications' (2004: 83). This suggests that the image of internal selfhood involves an *internally* verifying ego-identity which acts as a self-sufficient structuring presence – problematic in terms of a pre-existing subject that perceives itself in order to form itself. However, 'internal selfhood' may also be conceived as a fourfold structure of the archetype of Selfhood, which is almost fully unconscious in the Jungian topography, standing as it does for the totality of wholeness, a Self/God image. As seen in the previous chapter in relation to the narrative of individuation, the archetypal structure that Jung imagined lets us rethink the relativity between inner and outer worlds as experienced subjectively and connectively, and adds to the importance of meaningfulness in everyday experience.

The felt connection between inner and outer worlds in the realm of cinema has been theorized in various ways. For example, in previous chapters I have described the possibility of integrating a phenomenological approach with an analytical one, to engage aspects of subjective reality as an affective dynamic in the act of viewing film. The act of viewing film can be described as anthropocentric, engaging as it does both sensory appropriation and meaning in a dialectical dehiscence, but it also engages the possibility of moving beyond idealistic forms of subjectivity. Here I would argue that even in classical Jung there are elements of moving beyond the dualism of inner and outer worlds, towards something more akin to a phenomenological approach to being. A post-Jungian notion of film experience as a perception–expression is an extremely useful cultural example of this, but there are other examples in classic Jungian thought. As F. David Peat identifies in his book *Synchronicity: The Bridge Between Matter and Mind*, 'Synchronicity involves strong parallels between interior and exterior events that are emphatically endowed with meaning' (1987: 25). It is this parallel between inner and outer forms that needs to be re-examined: it is an age old philosophical problem that leaves a strong idealist legacy embedded in Jung's concepts of both individuated and collective identity.

In 'A Psychological Approach to the Dogma of the Trinity', Jung discusses the philosophy of the union of opposites as a relative form that differentiates according to whether it is conceived in the abstract or in the real world. This relativity is typical of Jung's affinity with idealism, but even in this discussion he is intimating an empirical aspect of opposites. For example, in writing an account of the abstract in the *Timaeus*, he states (1988: 17) that Plato:

> begins by representing the union of opposites two-dimensionally, as an intellectual problem to be solved by thinking, but then comes to see that its solution does not add up to reality. In the former case we have to do with a self-subsistent triad, and in the latter with a quaternity.

The reliance on triadic forms (which are in the abstract) without the incorporation of a fourth term therefore does not translate to physics in this approach. I do not wish to go into the details of the metaphysics and dialectics here, as this would mean a digression away from the main problem. However, it is worth mentioning that Jung's work does anticipate the need to move towards a fourfold dialectics of being, while at the same time somehow accommodating the Platonic ideal. He discusses (1988: 17) the needed fourth term of consciousness, and refers to:

> the opposition between the functions of consciousness, three of which are fairly well differentiated, while the fourth, undifferentiated, 'inferior' function is undomesticated, unadapted, uncontrolled, and primitive. Because of its contamination with the collective unconscious, it possesses archaic and mystical qualities, and is the complete opposite of the most differentiated function.

This engagement with metaphysics proves crucial in the Jungian framework of linking interior and exterior, not as opposites, but as fundamentally connected elements of consciousness and intention, of being-in-the-world. Consciousness is at first a seemingly abstract framework of being, until one regards consciousness as a state of being-in-the-world. It is here that the fourth term of consciousness, 'feeling' in the Jungian typology, is crucial to its own definition. Not only is consciousness associated indirectly and immediately with stimulus–response, but also it associates itself with subjectivity and the felt notion of what it means to be 'I'. It is connected with both ego-identity and the identity of physical being within an environment. Consciousness in this sense, then, commensurably draws from both inner and outer worlds.

Caution is advised here in relation to the terminology used, however: The 'inferiority' of the fourth term is problematic, as feeling is often regarded as a feminine aspect of typology and the problems associated with the gendering of personality types are manifold. However, if this is not regarded as a gendered aspect of identity, then it becomes a much more flexible model. If 'inferior' were replaced by the word 'interior' as a non-gendered example, we would have a four-way dialectic that works in both a semantic and an affective sense. The fourth term, in dialectical language, is the negation of the negation, the 'interior' of the first term. In fact, Jung already makes this dialectical leap: 'If the most differentiated is thinking, then the interior, fourth function will be feeling' (1988: 17–18). Feeling is classed as 'inferior' only in that its motivation is, in Jung's model, located in the collective unconscious, a more 'primitive' element of psychological functioning. I would reiterate an earlier point, that one of the problems associated with Jung's use of the term 'feeling' is that it often contradicts itself throughout his work, or encompasses several different terms, employed in different ways.

Peat identifies the problem of metaphysics and consciousness as one that mirrors the physical sciences. He states (1987: 2) that:

There appears . . . to be an unbridgeable gap between the objective and the subjective approaches to the question of the universe and our role within it. There seems at first sight, to be no way in which the theories of science can be spiced with the flavor of human experience or that a poetic insight can be transformed into the rigor of scientific objectivity. These two worlds appear to be simply too far apart.

This is not an unfamiliar notion in post-Jungian thought, and the problem of this subject/object dualism has been tackled by several writers who deal with it, one might say, as a defining problem of Cartesianism. Frances Gray, for example, devotes a whole section to subject and object in her book on Jung and Irigaray. She notes the philosophical notion that objects are the furniture of the world, stating that 'From this point of view, human beings are *at least* objects, *at least* part of the furniture of the world and, as such, objects that are the recipients of projection' (2008: 88, emphasis in original). She goes on to say that conferral of the status of subject is 'a first active projection that begins the constitution of a collective member as both a subject *and* object of that collective'. In this sense, then, the causality of subjectivity in a post-Jungian framework has much in common with that found in existential phenomenology, in that 'Subjects are always *inter*-subjects; and subjects are always potential objects for other subjects' (emphasis in original). The emphasis on the collective as the locus of subjectivity and conferral of status has, for Gray, resonance with the thought of Merleau-Ponty, and his emphasis that the site of collectivity is what gives place in the world, the world of subjects-with-subjects. In other words, 'Fleshy being with its bio-social origins guarantees an arcane individuality with the further potential to resist total identification with any collective' (2008: 89) and thus for the identification with subjective consciousness.

The world of subjects and objects, and subjects-as-objects, is central to the idea of synchronicity and its links with causality, and has its basis in Jung's fascination with mechanical physics, that every action has its equal and opposite reaction in physical energy. His collaboration with the renowned physicist Wolfgang Pauli developed this fascination in his work. For example, in his essay *Synchronicity: An Acausal Connecting Principle*, Jung states that:

The philosophical principle that underlies our conception of natural law is *causality*. But if the connection between cause and effect turns out to be only statistically valid and only relatively true, then the causal principle is only of relative use for explaining natural processes and therefore presupposes the existence of one or more other factors which would be necessary for its explanation.

(1999: 7, emphasis in original)

Indeed, for Peat, Jung's correspondence with Pauli produced a train of philosophical discussion that considered what these 'other factors' might be, leading to the possibility of discovering an underlying reality common to physics and psyche. Peat (1987: 103) states that:

> Pauli believed that this dualism between objective and subjective was particularly significant and indicated that a much deeper unification existed between matter and mind. As the structure of matter is probed in finer and finer detail, it dissolves into the indeterminacies of the quantum world.

Furthermore, sychronicity's strength lies:

> in its power to address the subjective side of experience and its value therefore involves the possibility of combining the subjective meaning of phenomena with objective explanations. By combining the subjective and objective elements together, synchronicity has something to say to both the artist and the scientist.
>
> (1987: 114)

This is a key example as to why the postmodern turn has caught such a foothold within post-Jungian thought: For many postmodern theorists, the postmodern condition has flattened the duality of subjective meaning and objective explanation. This leaves more space for the kind of relativism found in both the cosmology of modern physics and the intersubjectivity of contemporary phenomenology. As David Tacey has written, 'The postmodern turn is a move away from reductionism to more speculative models . . . Above all a time when the "margins" come into visibility, when centre and margin are likely to change places' (2006: 8). Causality as it is commonly understood, therefore, needs to be supplemented with 'other factors', as Jung put it. Peat puts it slightly differently: 'An "acausal connecting principle" clearly flies in the face of a very compelling worldview that is based on a causally dominated universe in which nothing takes place that does not have an ultimate cause' (1987: 35). As we have already seen in the previous chapter, the issue of final causality, or hypostasis, is troublesome, and yet populist accounts of narrative and world-building as typified by Vogler, for example, employ hypostasis in narrative as a causal principle of determination. Such popular narratives in mainstream cultural texts therefore reinforce what Peat describes as a 'compelling worldview' of causal domination. 'Strongly based on earlier notions of determinism, causality, and the linear unfolding of time', for Peat, the dominant scientific worldview, 'leads to the belief that all difficulties can be resolved through a process of analysis which leads to control or reorganization' (1987: 113). This is ultimately a political issue centring on a modernist notion of progress over nature and the containment of the determining effects of fate.

Awareness of this notion presents us with certain problems concerning the retrospective nature of meaning, however, as synchronicity and its affective elements are often recounted *a posteriori* the phenomenon itself. Mark Bould, in a terminological sleeve note to his book *Film Noir* (2005), makes an important distinction between determinism and determination on the one hand, and cause-and-effect on the other, as different species of causality. He states that 'Determination argues that the state of a system at one moment gives rise to the state of that system in the following moment' and is therefore causal in its nature. However, causality as is commonly understood, works in a more direct sense within narrativized accounts of a system. As Bould continues: 'Cause-and-effect is a narrative technique by which we make sense of the transition of a system from moment to moment. It is always a retrospective and partial account, an abstraction that marginalizes or ignores the totality of a system'. It is therefore possible for one to retrofit causality onto a system by superimposing a narrative on it, without engaging or critiquing that system, nor giving an account of its causality in determinist forms. In its refiguration, however, narrative gives the impression of determination and thus, meaning. It is to misinterpret determinism as fate or fatalism, and, according to Bould (2005):

> The ability to construct cause-and-effect chains implies that it should be possible to extend their construction into the future; this is an error based on forgetting that cause-and-effect is a retrospective abstraction. A deterministic system does not require fate, inevitability, predictability or cause-and-effect.

However, fate, inevitability, predictability or cause-and-effect are contingencies and variants of prerequisites for meaning and meaningfulness. Synchronicity is therefore not a deterministic system in which one state gives rise to another in the following moment, but is meaningful in terms of the retrospective (or spontaneous) attribution of fate, predictability (or unpredictability) and causality (or acausality). Cultural traditions, art objects and subjective identification practices may not by and of themselves determine human consciousness, with its contingency of meaning. However, this does not negate the deterministic relation between culture, art and human proclivity. It instigates a deterministic relation that occurs spontaneously, not directly. This is a crucial factor in the understanding of the phenomenon of synchronicity in popular culture and the popular imagination. For, as Peat states:

> From within the perspective of a living being, synchronicity, or the meaningful coordination of events, may be a more appropriate description than causality alone. The organism is concerned with its internal meaning, with *the way things happen together* and with the

integration of events that support its dynamic form and so maintain its meaning in the world.

(1987: 62, emphasis in original)

Indeed, Peat acknowledges that it was left to Jung to emphasize that what differentiates synchronicity from mere coincidence is its inherent meaning: It is not determinism, but the experience of such acausality, that instigates a *feeling* of determination at work in the system of experience. This feeling, this meaningfulness is, for Peat, the whole point of synchronicities as phenomena. They play a role in a person's life, sometimes of such significance as to change it, or a person's values and world-view, or to instigate change through prompting acts of agency. He proceeds to write on the nature of synchronicities:

> Characterized as being *acausal, meaningful, unique events* and involving some form of *pattern* . . . we must consider the limitations of our current worldview with its notions of causality, the arrow of time, objectivity, the separation of mind and matter, and the emphasis on reducibility rather than on unique, single events.
>
> (1987: 32, emphasis in original)

This is the by now familiar variant on 'pattern' discussed in previous chapters – a notion that Fiona Ross uses to describe the reciprocity of mind, body and psyche. In existentialist terms, we may simply describe this as a dehiscent phenomenon of being-in-the-world. However, for post-Jungians such as Ross and Peat, there is still a hangover from the mind/body dualism inherited from the classical school and ultimately from Descartes, which necessitates the kind of description that characterizes much post-Jungian writing. Such examples include having to construct a 'bridge that spans the worlds of mind and matter, physics and psyche' (Peat, 1987: 2).

Buried within such accounts, however, a seed is planted from which morphology between acausality and the dehiscent phenomenon of being-in-the-world may find a common vocabulary. As Peat describes it, synchronicity could 'be said to involve the meaningful unfoldment of potential' (1987: 81). Ultimately, this unfoldment flies in the face of Cartesian duality. Peat's project to 'inquire into the whole order of matter and the order of mind and in this way determine if these two orders . . . lie within a common spectrum of orders' (1987: 153) suggests that Jungian thought and existentialist phenomenology both lend themselves productively to this possibility.

Meaningfulness, sculpting in time, and recapturing 'lost' time

So far, we have examined what the term 'synchronicity' means in post-Jungian thought: a meaningful coincidence in time. It is a far from conclusive discussion, as definitive examples are not easily explained. My favourite example, Flammarion's tale of M. de Fortgibu and the plum pudding, is both a touching and a comic account of synchronistic events. It has been told by Jung himself (1999: 21, note 27) and recounted by Peat (1987: 8), and so I will not repeat it here. The tale told is a retrospective of meaningful coincidences, the meaning of which is conveyed only through their telling. Yet, the narrative form inherent in the story is in common with that found in popular narrative film and therefore raises the possibility that synchronicity may be recounted through the medium of narrative film. By Jung's own admission, synchronicity is a 'highly abstract and "irrepresentable" quantity . . . The "absolute knowledge" which is characteristic of synchronistic phenomena, a knowledge not mediated by the sense organs, supports the hypothesis of a self-subsistent meaning' (1999: 123–124). This immediately presents itself as troublesome, for how can one take such irrepresentable abstraction and invest in it some relevance to the field of film scholarship, concerned as it is largely with modes of representation?

In moving towards this end, we should first consider the possibility that an irrepresentable undifferentiated state may be figured as psychically as well as physically relative.[1] Take this example: If events were ordered according to some pattern within an undifferentiated state, and then appeared in linear, causal time, their appearance would be characterized by an aperiodical, acausal feature. It would be as if something utterly alien had dipped in and out of existence at random, but coinciding with certain moments in life, charging those moments with significance. According to Anthony Storr, Jung believed that 'there was a realm outside of space and time from which individuals become differentiated' (1998: 24). Jung borrowed the Gnostic term *pleroma* for this realm, describing it as a nothingness or a fullness, experienced only partially in causal space-time. For Jung, the *pleroma* implies 'a perfect interplay of cosmic forces, but with Creation – that is, with the division of the world into distinct processes in space and time – events begin to rub and jostle with one another' (1998: 342). Implied in this division of the world, of course, is the intrusion of language, of measurement, imposed on a state of plenitude. Additionally, Jung's penchant for dramatic Creation and Fall metaphors, as well as his emphasis on the Platonic ideal, characterizes such matters.

Returning to the idea of synchronicity, and its appearance in normative space-time, we can see that the idea of *pleroma* has a use in studying attempts to visualize space-time disruption in the experience of film. For Jung, what appears in a kind of eternal order within the *pleroma* 'appears in time [as it is generally conceived] as an aperiodic sequence, that is to say, it is repeated many times in an irregular pattern' (1998: 343). Thus, causal agents within an undifferentiated *pleroma* state can never be experienced as such in a reality ordered by language and measurement. They appear as acausal agents in synchronistic phenomena. For Storr, there are 'striking similarities' between Jung's thought on this matter and Schopenhauer:

> Schopenhauer considered that the very notion of individuality, the *principium individuationis*, is dependent on the human, subjective categories of space and time which force us to be conscious of individual objects, and prevent us from seeing the original unity of the Will of which individuals are a manifestation.
>
> (1998: 24, emphasis in original)

Although this is not the place to detail the theological implications of Schopenhauer's philosophy, we can say that the peculiarity of his dialectic between subjective, individuated time and absolute Time has much in common with Jung. This is especially given the instances when such irrepresentable material appears in subjective time and is accorded meaning. Attempts at representing these glimpses of an irrepresentable, undifferentiated state create for the film spectator an uncanny, incommunicable feeling. This is not unlike Lacan's Real order, which, for Malcolm Bowie, is 'that which lies outside the symbolic process, and . . . is to be found in the mental as well as in the material world' (1991: 94). The Real is a world order of archetypal material and structure in this formulation, as much as it is in the Jungian *pleroma*. Any form of measurement or tangibility is a construction partially superimposed on the demands of the Real, and instigated in the Jungian framework, by the resonance brought forth through activation of the archetypes.

As Storr notes, 'Jung came to think of archetypes as existing in this reality outside space and time' (1998: 25). Therefore, as previously mentioned throughout this book, archetypes themselves should be thought of in this framework as irrepresentable. The images and affects produced physiologically and psychically, and the representation of such effects (the totality of the Image as an experience of archetypal structures in cultural contexts such as film) are therefore difficult to apprehend in any singular visual sense. What is more, for Jung 'Archetypes, so far as we can observe and explain them at all, manifest themselves only through their ability to *organize* images and ideas, and this is always an unconscious process which cannot be detected until afterwards' (Jung, cited in Storr, 1998: 25). Archetypes are, therefore, related fundamentally to the narrativization of experience as discussed previously in connection with causality and meaningfulness, and are not necessarily contingent as deterministic principles at all. The 'absolute knowledge' embodied in synchronistic phenomena of which Jung writes is therefore impossible to judge in its naked state, as it is never experienced as such.

Is there evidence of such 'self-subsistent meaning' in film? By this term, Jung is presumably referring to archetypal structure as self-subsisting, creatively independent as it is from personal consciousness. Therefore, such meaning could pre-exist individual intention and yet also be activated through the very fact of social being within a collective culture, through a common or shared artistic production and consumption practice such as popular film culture. As Peat puts it, even though archetypes cannot be experienced directly, they 'leave their footprints in the mind and project their shadows across thought. While it is not possible to observe the archetypes directly, their movements can be sensed through the numinous images, myths, and happenings that enter consciousness' (1987: 106). Although I would not choose to use this particular terminology (projection and myth metaphors are confusing in the context of film theory, as we have seen), this does support the notion of the conveyance of meaning as a shared commodity within a common culture. It also supports the notion that meaningfulness is self-subsistent, if only in the sense that it is what seems to matter most about film at its most resonant.

There are certain filmmakers who touch upon the thematic of synchronicity, and who attempt to represent something like it (in the guise of meaningful coincidences, and human time as a motif). The Soviet filmmaker Andrei Tarkovsky is one such artist, whose work, although not popular film in the conventional sense, is fairly well known. As both director and commentator on cinema, Tarkovsky possessed an acute awareness of the mechanics of space and time, as represented in the world of the film and manipulated by the medium. Several of his films also demonstrate time and again both the fragility and the irrepressibility of the experience of cause-and-effect.[2] In his book *Sculpting in Time*, he states that cause and effect 'are mutually dependent . . . one begets the other by an inexorably ordained necessity . . . The link of cause and effect, in other words the transition from one state to another, is also the form in which time exists' (1989: 58–59). Such understanding of the laws of causality would be necessary in order to manipulate them in creative practice, and helps to explain the deftness with which Tarkovsky subjected the film medium to a systematic flaunting of temporality.

For example, his film *Mirror* (*Zerkalo*, USSR, 1975) flits with ease from one level of consciousness to another, and indiscriminately between historical and present contexts within the world of the film. This is done using a decidedly subjective/autobiographical presentation, yet, despite the confusion resulting from the indiscrimination, the meaningfulness that is intended is rendered through the disruption of privilege in the film's temporal hierarchy. Tarkovsky says of temporality that 'In a certain sense the past is far more real, or at any rate more stable, more resilient than the present. The present slips and vanishes like sand between the fingers, acquiring material weight only in its recollection' (1989: 58). The rhetorical language that he uses here concerning the present as an ephemeron is interesting, as it is highly suggestive of his film practice. Aware of the fleeting nature of the present, Tarkovsky often depicts past events as being in the present, without prior notice or audiovisual signifier to indicate the switch. It is only in retrospect that the film viewer makes the connection of transition between temporal states. Additionally, the transition is often not strictly causal: It is a matter of the film narrator's present represented as a repeat of something in the past, with no direct causal link. The repetition factor is lent more weight when, for example, in *Mirror*, the mother and the wife of the narrator appear as pivotal figures in both past and present, and are played by the same actor (Margarita Terekhova). This is one of the reasons why there is an eerie, uncanny feeling at the moment of transition between temporalities – a hesitation that one might describe as synchron-istic, or at the least meaningful, but acausal.

Mirror is a complex work, layered with repetition, coincidence and mysticism, filmed in an organic realist way with the use of sepia tones and earthy colour schemes. Peter Green, in *Andrei Tarkovsky: The Winding Quest*, describes the use of mirrors in the film as a 'transitional device' through which 'time is refracted' (1993: 80). In the film, we find (Green, 1993: 80) that:

> Generations are confusingly telescoped into each other, not least because elements of their histories repeat . . . Complexity of form is compounded . . . by the use of two persons to portray a single figure at different ages, and by casting one actor to portray two persons in successive generations.

It is all too tempting to suggest an Oedipal reading of *Mirror* here. For example, Mark Le Fanu in *The Cinema of Andrei Tarkovsky* has said of the film that 'The narrator, it would appear, chooses his model of womanhood too faithfully, and his marriage breaks up as a consequence. Repetition, beyond a certain limit is neurosis' (1987: 74). He is referring, of course, to a Freudian reduction in his reading of the physical similarities between mother and wife. However, in this reductive interpretation, Le Fanu misses the filmic instance of meaningful coincidence lying outside the constraints of time, and also misses the sensibility for this meaningfulness of memory that Tarkovsky possesses and wishes to express in his filmmaking. In *Mirror*, time disruption is not merely a plot device, but is crucial to understanding the symbolic representation of memory and (especially) women in his films. Disruption exists alongside the experience of causal time, subjective time, as it moves along within but sometimes also intersects the undifferentiated space-time of Jung's *pleroma*. As Maya Turovskaya observes, 'In this scheme of things, all moments in time are co-equal, existing alongside the ostensible plot' (1989: 87).

One may recall a remarkable example of this in *Mirror*, which may help to exemplify a cinematic representation of synchronicity. The young

Ignat (Ignat Daniltsev) is in a house with an elderly woman (Tamara Ogorodnikova), whose relationship to him remains ambiguous. She tells him to read aloud a letter written from Pushkin to Chaadayev. The fact of the letter being what it is (a historical document, written in pre-Soviet Russia; an artefact within the world of literature and the arts) is an intertextual device, certainly. However, the over-determined identity of this reference compounds the next series of events. During his reading, Ignat is interrupted by a knock at the door. He answers. His grandmother (Maria Vishnyakova) is standing before him in the doorway, but neither character recognizes the other. The woman hesitates before realizing that she has actually knocked on the wrong door anyway. Such unacknowledged coincidence is not so uncommon, even in mainstream film. However meaningful in itself, this event is complicated by the events that follow. Ignat returns to his letter to discover that the elderly woman is no longer at the table where she was sitting. All that remains is a ring of condensation on the table from her hot teacup, and as this fades, it is accompanied by a crescendo of voices, singing wordless notes in a dissonant chorus. The effect is quite staggering, and leads to a hesitation or ambivalence as to what has occurred. Did Ignat hallucinate the woman's presence? If so, then how does one explain the condensation ring? Was her presence down to supernatural means? What is the characters' relationship and what was the significance of that particular letter? Such hesitation, reminiscent of Tzvetan Todorov's first condition of the fantastic – 'the integration of the reader into the world of the characters' – is a world 'defined by the reader's own ambiguous perception of the events narrated' (1975: 31). Perhaps, yet again, it does not matter about interpretations and meaning, but such events, however inexplicable, are meaningful, and that is what Tarkovsky is attempting to express.

Indeed, meaningfulness and time seem to complement one another as inherently filmic phenomena when coinciding as representations of complementary inner and outer states. Tarkovsky is by no means the only filmmaker whose work engages such concerns throughout his *oeuvre*. The Hong Kong filmmaker Wong Kar-Wai is, to my mind, highly reminiscent of Tarkovsky in his principal concerns with the subjective experience of time and repetition. An early and simple example of this is *Chungking Express* (*Chung Hing sam lam*, HK, 1994), with its repetition *ad nauseam* of the Mamas and the Papas' 'California Dreaming' throughout the film. This repetitive technique is taken much further in Kar-Wai's later films. The sophisticated use of music is a telling take on the cultural hybridity that exists in the international film market, both as a knowing postmodern statement on globalization and in the filmmaker's narrative conceits. *In the Mood for Love* (*Fa yeung nin wa*, HK/Fr, 2000), and its sequel, *2046* (Ch/Fr/HK/It, 2004),[3] are full of audio references both to nostalgia and to the notion of globalized alienation. In a similar vein to the sensibilities of Tarkovsky, Kar-Wai is aware of the resilience and persistence of memory.

In his films, as in Tarkovsky's, he often depicts past events and imagined scenarios as being in the present, without notice or signifier to indicate the switch. Again, it is only in retrospect that the transition between temporal states may be recognized. It is worth briefly recounting the plots of *In the Mood for Love* and *2046*, as readers unfamiliar with the films need to be aware that this switching extends into both character name and action, often with actors being employed to depict two or three characters. Additionally, the action moves without notice from reality to fantasy within the world of the film.

In Hong Kong, 1962, a young man named Chow (Tony Leung) and a young woman, Su Li-zhen (Maggie Cheung) happen to move into the same apartment building. They are both married, although we only ever see their respective partners from behind, and only hear them through doorways or on the telephone in conversation. Su Li-zhen's husband is away on business in Japan most of the time, and Chow's wife works awkward shifts and so is also often absent. Through various developments, it turns out that the partners are having an affair. In their absence, Chow and Su Li-zhen spend more time together, sharing a passion for martial arts novels, and when they acknowledge the affair, they embark on a writing project, writing a martial arts story together in a hotel room. These events occur during a lengthy period of time, however, and Kar-Wai chooses to show the development of their relationship at a slow pace, indicating a desire to depict such matters as subjectively as possible. He does this through the use of slow motion, repetition and the graphic depiction of quotidian acts: the most frequent of these is the ritual of fetching noodles from a street stand, which the two characters perform accompanied by a non-diegetic folk waltz. The end result of this strategy is an almost choreographed movement between the two, a dance in which an effective representation of blossoming love or the withering of alienation can be visualized. All the characters in the film are often framed in doorways, hallways or shot through windows and wineglasses: the frame bisected by an obstruction or physical divide of some sort. This produces the uncanny effect of foregrounding the alienation between characters, and is a visual motif that carries through into *2046*.

Chow and Su Li-zhen start eating out together regularly when they have openly admitted their partners' infidelity, ordering what their partners would eat, performing their partners' roles in a kind of pathetic pastiche. However, they are careful to allay the gossip of their neighbours by never being seen coming home together. It is after one such dinner outing that a change occurs in their relationship. Walking home from the restaurant and accompanied by the same folk waltz, Chow makes a pass at Su – he is rebutted. Something curious then happens. Without warning the scene is replayed in both words and actions, only this time Su responds by being flirtatious, before backing off. It is clear that Su has much more to lose than Chow: She is a woman, and although she has financial independence, she is seen to be cowed by the prurient interest of her gossiping landlady, who rebukes her for going out so much without her husband. Nonetheless, she carries on seeing Chow and together in the hotel room, they rehearse a scene in which she makes her husband confess to his affair, playing out events before they have happened in order to experience what they might feel like. This scene is curious for repetition too: Su asks what appears to be her husband if he is having an affair, and a drawn out series of questions and pauses ensues until we see Chow's face and realize it is a game. When it is repeated, we are privy to the characters' complicity, but it is a curious doubling within the characters' world that mirrors the filmic strategy of Kar-Wai's repetition a few moments before. This curious interplay between diegetic and non-diegetic spaces is perhaps a commentary on character interiority, additionally reflecting the intuitive simultaneity that can occur between interior feeling and the actions of oneself and others. Again in common with Tarkovsky, Kar-Wai is attempting to represent the fragility and the irrepressibility of the experience of cause-and-effect. This scene has further resonance only when the two characters rehearse their parting after Chow announces his decision to leave for Singapore – it is another doubling of experience for which there is no logical causality other than an emotional desire to experience out of time. Perhaps not a synchronicity, this is a representation of something akin to it. He also announces that he has fallen in love with her, asking her to go with him, saying that one can't help it when feelings just creep up on one. It is this statement that makes clear the visualization of interiority through stylistic means (the bisected framing, the repetition).

What follows is a series of ambiguous events, the temporality of which is jumbled and intermittent. Chow does indeed go to Singapore, but not with Su, who stays in Hong Kong and eventually has a son with her husband. During his sojourn in Singapore, however, Chow has a conversation in which he says that he has a secret and recounts a legend. He says that back in the 'old days', if one had a secret they would climb a mountain, find a tree, make a hole in it, whisper the secret into the hole, and then cover it with mud, thereby preserving the secret forever. At the end of the film, in Cambodia 1966, we see Chow performing just such a rite at Angkor Wat. The closing inter-title is a telling statement concerning the film's obsession with memory:

> He remembers those vanished years as though looking through a dusty window-pane. The past is something he could see but not touch. He thinks about the past all the time. If only he could break through the glass and bring it back.

This statement links directly to the events of *2046*, and it is with this closing statement (opening up those concerns in the sequel) that the significance of

In the Mood for Love's plot comes properly into view. The curious title *2046* raises a number of questions, even for an experienced viewer of these films, but most notably, what is 2046 and what is its significance?

There are numerous references to this number in the film: It was the hotel room in which Chow and Su Li-zhen wrote their martial arts novel. It is also a place in Chow's imagination. A series of coincidences prompts him to start writing '2046', a science fiction series set in the year 2046, where a number of characters exist, every bit as alienated as those of the world of *In the Mood for Love*. In fact, the film opens with a depiction of a mysterious future world, accompanied by a voiceover: 'A mysterious train leaves for 2046 every once in a while. Everyone going to 2046 has only one intention: to recapture lost memories . . . Because in 2046, nothing ever changes.' This is a curious series of statements, for it appears that not only is 2046 a place, but it is also the year in which these strange events take place. It is the link to the end of the first film, and Chow is indulging in an imaginative piece of wish-fulfilment: His science fiction characters are able to break through the glass of time and bring back the past, recapture lost memories. There is no explicit acknowledgement that this is a different space to that which follows, except for the fact that this landscape looks very different to that of 1966 Hong Kong. It is only in retrospect that the audience is given full knowledge of this space as the visualization of Chow's imagination. It is a place to somehow return to the past, or at least bring it back in some way: a plenitude, a *jouissance*, or in Jungian terms a *pleroma*: an undifferentiated place without time, where nothing ever changes.

The series of coincidences that prompts Chow to write '2046' is worth noting for Kar-Wai's take on the recapture of memory. Chow bumps into an old flame from his Singapore days called Lulu (Corina Lau). They go drinking and he has to put her to bed drunk. As he leaves the room, he notices the room number – 2046 – that, he states in voiceover, prompts the story. He returns two days later to return her key, but is told that she (or 'Mimi', as she is referred to) has left. He leaves the key with Wang, the landlord (Wang Sum) who closes the door, irritated. A moment later, they are having another conversation, as if this event did not happen. It is not altogether signified as an ellipsis, but some time-lapse may have occurred in some way. Chow wishes to rent room 2046, but ends up with room 2047, later discovering that Lulu/Mimi had been murdered at the hands of a jealous lover in 2046.

The circumstances around Chow's inspiration are significant, as it turns out that '2046' is semi-autobiographical. In the visualization of this imagined place several of the characters are played by actors that portray characters in the world of Hong Kong 1967 – Wang Sum plays both Wang and the train captain. Faye Wong plays Wang's daughter Jing-wen in Hong Kong, as well as the android with delayed reactions in the imagined space of '2046'. Corina Lau appears, as an android we witness getting murdered by a lover, in a cruel replaying of Lulu/Mimi's fate. Although Chow admits that people in his life appear in the novels, Kar-Wai's visualization of this is curious, as if the doubling and repetition theme in *In the Mood for Love* needed to be foregrounded in straightforward visual terms. Far from being clumsy, this strategy opens up new possibilities for him to explore the nature of subjective time, and how feelings effect change in the way that time is recalled. Many of those feelings are, of course, nostalgic and employ a desire to somehow recapture a lost time. In this film, however, thanks in large part to its ambiguous presentation of imagery, this is partially achieved. It is a very similar effect to that found in the Tarkovsky example, where a hesitation between explanations of ambiguous experiences is a condition of the fantastic: This is subjective time disrupting absolute Time, a kind of inverse synchronistic disruption.

Partially achieved through filmic means, the recapturing of lost time is also partially achieved through Chow's own actions. In an intermittent subplot, Jing-wen has fallen in love with a Japanese boy of whom her father disapproves. Feeling sorry for her, he offers to post the letters she sends and to have her boyfriend's letters sent to him. She agrees, and they spark up a friendship. When it becomes apparent that she is a fan of martial arts novels and is a budding author herself, they embark on a writing project, in a repeat of his summer of writing with Su Li-zhen. He claims that this is his happiest summer, but rather inevitably, 'feelings can creep up on you' and he ends up feeling more for Jing-wen than he expected. He imagines himself as a Japanese man in '2046' falling in love with an android (played by Wong), the key motif here being a repetition of the story about the ancient art of keeping secrets as explained earlier. This is Chow's curse and redemption simultaneously: He is fated to have feelings of love creep up on him repeatedly, but compelled to help the objects of his affection in their own stories. In the case of Jing-wen, he persuades her to re-engage the relationship with her Japanese boyfriend. In the case of Bai Ling (Zhang Ziyi), it is giving her the money and transportation she needs to escape Hong Kong and a life of prostitution. The film ends with time fragments and jumps to and fro between Hong Kong in 1969, '2046', and what appears to be Singapore, 1963 in flashback. It seems that Chow cannot bring himself to write a happy ending to '2047' – a parody of '2046' that he wrote for Jing-wen. Perhaps his recapture of lost time is only fleeting, as memories can only exist for the present.

Time capture and synchronicity in the work of Michel Gondry

The recapturing of time seems to be an existential function of film in the most general sense: a human preoccupation that many analysts might encounter quite frequently in clinical work. The 'what if' factor and causal nature of the anthropocentric view of life as it is lived, and time as it is most comfortably known (as linear, causal), are a characteristic of Western thinking. It is also the artistic preoccupation of some non-Western directors, such as Tarkovsky and Kar-Wai. To round off this discussion (and, indeed, this book), I would like to add to this list the French director and video artist Michel Gondry. Gondry now works in mainstream feature production, but has a sensibility that still belongs on the fringes of video art and owes much to his origins as a short filmmaker. Along with contemporaries such as Chris Cunningham and Spike Jonze (to whom, he is most frequently compared) his work feeds off avant-garde techniques and idiosyncratic concerns with repetition and the human mind, and a preoccupation with visual illusion and narrative trickery. The result of these concerns is that his work often comes close to representing synchronistic phenomena such as doubling, acausality and incidence/coincidence, perhaps more than any other director working in popular film today.[4]

Although Gondry is perhaps currently best known for his feature film *Eternal Sunshine of the Spotless Mind* (US, 2004), co-written with Charlie Kaufman, the stylized nature of his films still betrays a background in music video, advertising and short film. I am here choosing to discuss his video work as frequent attempts to represent synchronistic phenomena, or at least phenomena that, thanks to his unique creative imagination, have come to resemble acausal incidents. It is possible that studio productions of feature film will, in the future, become much more open to Gondry's brand of surreal art, and indeed *Eternal Sunshine . . .* is a wonderfully warped vision of memory and loss.

However, it is in his back catalogue of videos that we may discern this in a richer capacity. This is largely due to the use of 'impact aesthetics' in conventions of music video and advertising, whereby narrative in its most conventional sense is less important than promotion of the product. His promo video for Japanese duo Cibo Matto's 'Sugar Water' is an extraordinary feat of imaginative filmic choreography and sophisticated in its use of music, rhythm, tempo and lyrics. It is, in fact, a very simple but elegant narrative device that drives the video, informing the visual action, in which a series of 13 simple events in a day in the life of the two musicians takes place. The presentation of these events is in the form of a split-screen technique: The frame is divided vertically by a single black line down the centre throughout. On the left side, the action runs forward, from start to finish, while simultaneously on the right side, the same footage is shown, except that the action runs from finish to start (in reverse), and the image is mirrored. However, it should be noted that in narrative terms both sides are moving chronologically, and that events are unfolding from past to future in the same fashion.

The left-hand side of the screen begins with Yuka waking up, with Miko waking up at the same time on the right in another apartment. As we hear the vocal say the words 'sugar water', the words appear across both sides of the screen in reverse. As Yuka takes a water shower on the left, Miko takes a 'sugar shower' on the right, and it is clear for the first time that the action is in reverse motion on this side of the screen: The sugar pours upwards and into the box. The third incident, coinciding with the lyric 'the wind is blowing', has Yuka drying her hair, whereas Miko has a fan blowing through hers. The two women then walk out of their respective apartment doors and to the mailboxes in the hallway. As Miko sings 'when a black cat crosses my path', we see a black cat jump into a hole in the wall backwards, and later jump forwards out of a hole in the wall next to Yuka, seemingly from one side of the screen to the other. At about the same time, Miko is seen putting a letter into the mailbox, and a second later Yuka opens hers and takes out what appears to be the same letter. It is as if events on both sides of the divide are inexorably drawn to one another, as a compulsion to erase time and space as it is commonly known and to synthesize a causality that the audience is by now aware, cannot exist between the two sides.

These events are thus charged with significance, with meaning. They are species of synchronicity in that they are phenomena that coincide, and appear to have some semblance of causality through their meaningfulness. Yet as one watches it becomes clear that these two sides are in very different places: They occupy different time-space and are contradictory in the characters' experience. Both characters then leave their buildings and walk out onto the street. Yuka posts the letter in a red pillar-box, and seconds later Miko takes what appears to be the same letter from another pillar box. It seems as if the exchange of letters is a kind of forewarning about something, but this is difficult to discern without retrospect. It remains, in fact, impossible to predict future events in this exchange scenario, as it is unclear as to whether an event on one side begets an event on the other. It is not causal in the clear, unambiguous way that causality is generally perceived to be in everyday life. Something alien is occurring here, something deterministic possibly, and yet acausal.

The 13 coincidences in the video centre on a pivotal moment halfway through, when a car accident occurs. The action swaps sides from here, and the video is revealed as a kind of visual palindrome, where everything happens to both characters in a circular, acausal way. Does the palindromic structure allow for meaningfulness without having to resort to fate? This is a complex question in retrospect, because, having watched the video, the viewer is aware that a trick has been played (without necessarily knowing how that trick was played) and that both characters end up back where they started. They are therefore fated to participate in events that have already been seen by the audience. It is an alienation narrative, where, despite the day's events (a horrific car crash, in which the fate of Miko is seemingly foretold), both Miko and Yuka end up in what appears to be the same emotional state as before. The fatalism depicted in the video is, therefore, the systemic total within which the unfolding of events is already anticipated because they have already been seen from a different perspective, and are thus predetermined. However, because time is here depicted as circular and not linear, we can only predict events in time within that loop. Concepts such as 'future' and 'past' only have limited meaning in the time of 'Sugar Water', and only if each side is taken on its own unfolding independently from past to future. Causality dips in and out of the video, appearing particularly at times when events coincide with lyrics. To paraphrase David Peat, the meaningful co-ordination of events taking place in this video may be a more appropriate description than a simple cause-and-effect model. There seems to be a self-contained, internal meaning in the way events on either side of the screen happen together and their integration with the lyrics, driving the narrative, helps maintain the chain of events as meaningful in the world of the video.

After the accident, the significance of the letter 'exchange' becomes apparent, as Miko lies in the road having been run over by Yuka's car. A zoom-in to her body, simultaneous to both sides of the screen, reveals that she is holding the letter open and it reads across the screen in newspaper cut-up letters the words 'you killed me'. The emphasis on personal narrative is then exchanged, with Miko being followed on the left side of the screen. We see her posting the letter, while on the right, Yuka picks up the letter from the pillar-box. The words 'when a black cat crosses my path' are heard, as well as mouthed by Miko as the cat we have already seen goes into the hole in the wall on the right hand side, emerging on the left side. This goes on – posting the letter/taking the letter, fan/hairdryer, the sugar shower/the backward shower – until at the end of the video, Miko sings the words 'we are drinking sugar water'. At this point, we see the words 'SUGAR WATER' drawn in lipstick on the windows of the two apartments, across the screen, mirroring the opening shots. Both women fall asleep.

In summary, the video releases an enormous sense of resolution, despite the tension that hangs throughout its duration. The tension is reinforced through the physical divide between the two halves of the screen: It is almost as if the circularity that occurs through the unfolding of events during the course of the video is repeatedly both cut and sutured throughout. This sensation is largely due to the mirroring of events from one side to another, and the coincidence of lyrics narrating those moments. It is clear that Gondry is setting up visual effects, not so much interested in using them as special effects in the conventional sense of creating spectacle, but nevertheless there is a discernible effort to present them as magic tricks of some sort. The audience is distracted by an event that happens in the foreground of the field of vision in one part of the screen, while the real 'trick' happens elsewhere. In most cases in this particular video, this happens when coincidences occur holistically, between the two sides of the screen, and in conjunction with the lyrics, which become a narration of events. Spike Jonze, commenting on this in the Gondry documentary *I've been 12 forever*, says of Gondry's work, 'In the shot it doesn't look like there was a trick, but there was a trick.' This simple visual device has its roots in the earliest cinema: The audience is drawn into a fascination or astonishment via the spectacle of having been tricked. This realization is, once again, a largely retrospective phenomenon, becoming fully conscious and realized through the audience's awareness of the trickery. One might argue, in fact, that it does not matter whether the audience knows the secret of the trick or not – it is the perception that they have been 'tricked' that is uncomfortable or pleasurable, and therefore spectacular.

In many ways, it is fitting that this book should close with a discussion of such experimental and kitschy filmmaking as that of Michel Gondry. The perceptibility or imperceptibility of such tricks is found in George Méliès' groundbreaking *trucage* films of the 1890s, where a mix of stagecraft and cinematic effects produced a sense of wonder and astonishment in the earliest audiences. From his use of simple Lego animation in the video for The White Stripes' 'Fell in Love with a Girl', to the visual and narrative sophistication of Kylie Minogue's 'Come into My World', Gondry's *trucage* videos and films point to a creative future in popular film. This is a future that takes trends in blockbuster movies such as spectacle over action, so-called impact aesthetics, and effects-for-effects'-sake and subverts them to engage a meaningful viewing experience for its (mass) audience. Gondry takes contemporary filmmaking back to its origins, stripping off the somewhat unnecessary accoutrements of stardom and commerciality, while simultaneously pushing the medium to its extreme, going beyond what has gone before. His filmmaking and video art point to a future in which subversive humour, carnivalesque attention to detail, and careful visualization of meaningful relations between subjects, objects and the world have a place. When watching his films, we are looking at a vision of the future, and it is a very welcome one.

Notes

Introduction

1 Here, I refer the reader to the recent dossier on the BFI in *Cinema Journal*, Summer 2008. In this dossier, seasoned veterans of film scholarship and education such as Geoffrey Nowell-Smith, Pam Cook, Manuel Alvarado, Charlotte Brunsdon, Toby Miller and Ed Buscombe contribute various histories and commentaries on the alarming short-sightedness of government policy on film culture. There is, of course, the hurried sale of BFI publishing to Palgrave, on which many of the authors express concern. The most worrying facet of this general shift in policy to my mind, however, is the shift of emphasis towards 'production and exhibition rather than on the wider context of moving image culture and education' (Cook, 2008: 143). Certainly, a robust film industry, supported by bodies such as the UK Film Council, is a thing to applaud. However, current policy feeds the myth that films are made purely for entertainment, rather than their capacity to enhance lives.

Chapter 3

1 Although the optical apparatus is not a subject for explicit discussion here, it has often been the subject of film theory. Jean-Louis Baudry's work, for example, discusses certain mimetic correspondences between the eye and cinematic projection in Apparatus Theory. Also, recent interventions from visual science into creative image design have noted the remarkable consistencies between the perennial problems presented to visual artists (of whatever medium) and phenomena occurring in optical perception. See, for example, Singh and Pickard (2007).

2 For a more specialized account of this, see Frederic Jameson's ground-breaking work on postmodernism (1991) and Ernst Mandel's 'monopoly capitalism' (1967).

Chapter 4

1 A term I use in the loosest sense to characterize, rather than formulate, the work of Bordwell, Thompson, Carroll, Staiger, *et al.* as a collective anti-political stance towards the study of film.

Chapter 5

1 See my discussion on Gibbs and Pye (2005) in Chapter 1 of this book.
2 This problematic anthropormorphic position is, phenomenologically speaking, an anachronism. I refer the reader to my lengthy critique on this in the previous chapter.

Chapter 6

1 Perhaps emancipation is a questionable aspiration for any kind of industrial filmmaking anyway, given the abovementioned and commonly assumed place of popular film within consumer culture as 'only entertainment'.

Chapter 7

1 I refer the reader here to Sean Homer's work on fetishism and cinema (2005) and Eileen R. Meehan's article 'Holy Commodity Fetish, Batman!' (2000) on this matter.
2 I refer the reader to Spike Lee's excellent HBO documentary mini-series, *When the Levees Broke: A Requiem in Four Parts.* Had I the space to discuss this, I would fully acknowledge it as a courageous and moving work about the real plight of African America and the nation's poor, both before and after the disaster. Spike Lee's best work to date.
3 I use the term 'mixed-race' with caution throughout. Although the current politically correct term might be 'dual-heritage', this is, epistemologically speaking, a nonsense. Writing from a hybridized racial background, I can state from experience that 'heritage' is a dubious descriptor for this political identity, because of the problems associated with multiculturalism, subculture and cultural inheritance.
4 I refer the reader to Bruce Bettelheim in particular, and his book *The Uses of Enchantment* (1976), a thoroughgoing analysis of folk and fairy tales and their use in the popular imagination.
5 For example, in the *Matrix* franchise, one may consume the following: the cinematic trilogy, the DVD trilogy, the documentary DVD *Matrix Revisited*, the MOG, the *Enter the Matrix* and *Path of Neo* console games, the graphic novels, the online fan-fiction, and the *Animatrix* animated shorts collection. This list is far from exhaustive, but gives one a sense of the cultural impact of this franchise, and of the impact that viewing practices within film culture have on the reception of narrative.
6 See, in particular, Singh (2009).
7 However, it should be noted that Withers then regards this as a contradiction: as helpful 'and trapped – caught additionally in its own ideology and in the person of its creator'. This is perhaps one of the many reasons why classical Jungian thought is often felt to be too dogmatic and theological – it succumbs to the trap of performing religion, rather than acting as an analytical and critical tool. While this is often true of Jung's work, I do not believe it is an accusation that can be made in the context of Jung's consideration of the dogma of the Trinity. In this, he is both thorough and accommodating of several viewpoints, which build a logical analysis.

Chapter 8

1 Without venturing too far into the mechanics of cosmology here, relativity is for Peat and others a key modernist principle of both physics and psyche. For an easily understandable, if somewhat populist, explanation of singularities and the breakdown of causality in space-time, read Jeremy Bernstein's *Cranks, Quarks and the Cosmos*. Bernstein defines the singularity as 'a point in space-time where the physical quantities become literally infinite, as opposed to unimaginably large' (1993: 84). It is the point of infinite density, where time becomes another dimension of space – *undifferentiated* from space according to our laws of measurement and causality, and is therefore no longer representable.

2 I should note here that, although the approach to the films of Tarkovsky (as well as any of the directors discussed in this chapter) may appear auteurist, the expression 'creative practice' and its filmic derivatives are used throughout as a means to engage these films as a creative enterprise holistically. The analyses offered, therefore, should be read with the criticisms laid out in Chapter 2 of this book in mind. It should also be noted that, whereas Tarkovsky was not working within the Hollywood studio system, he was working within a state-sponsored Soviet context, and therefore was subject to restraints specific to that context. I refer the reader to Le Fanu (1987), Green (1993), Turovskaya (1989) and Tarkovsky himself (1989) for more on this issue.

3 There is a third film in Kar-Wai's catalogue, *The Days of Being Wild* (*A Fei zheng chuan*, HK, 1990) that shares many of the cast members of these two films. However, whereas many of the characters share the same names and are played by the same actors featured in the other two films (Su Li-zhen and Chow, for example) they are not the same. There are some narrative cues to suggest that Mimi (Carina Lau) is the same Mimi who appears in *2046*, but this is speculative. Therefore, *The Days of Being Wild* should perhaps be considered a companion piece rather than the first of a trilogy.

4 His most recent film at the time of writing, *Be Kind Rewind* (US, 2008), carries on many of these concerns, despite Jonathan Ross' dismissal of it as 'too quirky' to enjoy in any meaningful way. It was released too recently for a thoroughgoing discussion to be included here, as was Gondry's *The Science of Sleep* (*La Science des rêves*, Fr/It, 2008).

Bibliography

Adorno, T. W. (2002) *The Culture Industry*. London: Routledge Classics.

Alister, I. and C. Hauke (eds) (1998) *Contemporary Jungian Analysis: Post-Jungian Perspectives from the Society of Analytical Psychology*. London: Routledge.

Allen, R. and M. Smith (1999) *Film Theory and Philosophy*. Oxford, UK: Oxford University Press.

Althusser, L. (1971) *Lenin and Philosophy*. New York: Monthly Review Press.

Anderson, B. (1983) *Imagined Communities*. London: Verso.

Arnheim, R. (1957) *Film as Art*. London: University of California Press.

Astruc, A. (1968) 'The Birth of a New Avant-Garde: Le Camera-Stylo' in P. Graham (ed.), *The New Wave*. London: Secker and Warburg.

Balibar, E. (1995) *The Philosophy of Marx*. London: Verso.

Barthes, R. (1977) *Image/Music/Text*, London: Fontana.

—— (1993) *Mythologies* (trans. Annette Lavers). London: Vintage.

—— (2006) 'Myth Today' in J. Storey (ed.), *Cultural Theory and Popular Culture: A Reader* (3rd ed.). Harlow, UK: Pearson.

Baudry, J.-L. (1999) 'The Apparatus: Metapsychological Approaches to the Impression of Reality in Cinema' in L. Braudy and M. Cohen (eds), *Film Theory and Criticism: Introductory Readings* (5th ed.). Oxford, UK: Oxford University Press.

Bazin, A. (1968) 'La politique des auteurs' in P. Graham (ed.), *The New Wave*. London: Secker and Warburg.

Beatty, L. (1996) *The Garden of the Golden Flower: The Journey to Spiritual Fulfilment*. London: Senate.

Beebe, J. (1996) 'Jungian Illumination of Film', *Psychoanalytic Review*, 83: 4, August, 579–587.

Ben-Shaul, N. (2007) *Film: The Key Concepts*. Oxford, UK: Berg.

Bernstein, J. (1993) *Cranks, Quarks and the Cosmos*. Oxford, UK: Oxford University Press.

Berry, P. (2001) 'Image in motion' in C. Hauke and I. Alister (eds), *Jung and Film: Post-Jungian Takes on the Moving Image*. Hove, UK: Brunner-Routledge.

Bettelheim, B. (1976) *The Uses of Enchantment: The Meaning and Importance of Fairy Tales*. New York: Knopf.

Bobo, J. (1995) *Black Women as Cultural Readers*. Chichester, UK: Columbia University Press.

Bogle, D. (2001) *Toms, Coons, Mulattoes, Mammies and Bucks: An Interpretive History of Blacks in American Films*. London: Continuum.

Bordwell, D. and N. Carroll (eds) (1996) *Post-Theory: Reconstructing Film Studies*. London: University of Wisconsin Press.

—— (1996) 'Contemporary Film Studies and the Vicissitudes of Grand Theory' in D. Bordwell and N. Carroll (eds), *Post-Theory: Reconstructing Film Studies*. London: University of Wisconsin Press.

Bordwell, D., J. Staiger and K. Thompson (1980) *The Classical Hollywood Cinema: Film Style and Mode of Production to 1960*. London: Routledge.

Bould, M. (2002) 'The Dreadful Credibility of Absurd Things: A Tendency in Fantasy Theory', *Historical Materialism, 10*: 4, 51–88.

—— (2005) *Film Noir*. London: Wallflower.

Bowie, M. (1991) *Lacan*. London: Harvard University Press.

Bowlby, R. (1985) *Just Looking: Consumer Culture in Dreiser, Gissing and Zola*. London: Methuen.

Braudy, L. and M. Cohen (eds) (1999) *Film Theory and Criticism: Introductory Readings* (5th ed.). Oxford, UK: Oxford University Press.

—— (eds) (2004) *Film Theory and Criticism: Introductory Readings* (6th ed.). Oxford, UK: Oxford University Press.

Brooke, R. (1991) *Jung and Phenomenology*. London: Routledge.

Bruce, D. D. Jr. (1999) 'W. E. B. Du Bois and the Idea of Double Consciousness' in *The Souls of Black Folk* (H. L. Gates Jr and T. H. Oliver (eds)). London: W. W. Norton.

Buscombe, E. (1981) 'Ideas of Authorship' in J. Caughie (ed.), *Theories of Authorship*. London: Routledge.

Cameron, I. (1981) 'Films, Directors and Critics' in J. Caughie (ed.), *Theories of Authorship*. London: Routledge.

Camolli, J.-L. and J. Narboni (1999) 'John Ford's *Young Mr. Lincoln*' in L. Braudy and M. Cohen (eds), *Film Theory and Criticism: Introductory Readings* (5th ed.). Oxford, UK: Oxford University Press. Complete article in *Screen, 13*: 3, 1972, 5–44.

Campbell, J. (1993) *The Hero with a Thousand Faces*. London: Fontana.

Campbell, R. (1992) *Truth and Historicity*. Oxford, UK: Clarendon Press.

Carroll, N. (1988) *Mystifying Movies: Fads and Fallacies in Contemporary Film Theory*. New York: Columbia University Press.

—— (1990) *The Philosophy of Horror: Or, Paradoxes of the Heart*. London: Routledge.

Caughie, J. (1975) 'Teaching through Authorship', *Screen Education, 17*: Autumn, 3–13.

Conger, J. (2005) *Jung and Reich: The Body as Shadow*. Berkeley, CA: North Atlantic Books.

Constable, C. (2005) *Thinking in Images*. London: BFI.

Cook, P. (2008) 'Whatever Happened to BFI Publishing?', *Cinema Journal, 47*: 4, Summer, 140–147.

Cook, P. and C. Johnston (1985) 'The Place of Woman in the Cinema of Raoul Walsh' in B. Nichols (ed.), *Movies and Methods* (vol. 2). London: University of California Press.

Creed, B. (1993) *The Monstrous-Feminine: Film, Feminism, Psychoanalysis*. London: Routledge.

Cubitt, S. (2004) 'Digital Filming and Special Effects' in D. Harries (ed.), *The New Media Book* (2nd ed.). London: BFI.

Davis, A. (1981) *Women, Race and Class*. New York: Random House.

Deleuze, G. (1998) 'Having an Idea in Cinema' in E. Kaufman and K. J. Heller (eds), *Deleuze and Guattari: New Mappings in Politics, Philosophy and Culture*. Minneapolis: University of Minnesota Press.

Diawara, M. (1999) 'Black Spectatorship: Problems of Identification and Resistance' in L. Braudy and M. Cohen (eds), *Film Theory and Criticism: Introductory Readings* (5th ed.). Oxford, UK: Oxford University Press.

Doane, M. A. (1982) 'Film and the Masquerade', *Screen*, *23*: 3/4, September/October, 78–87.

—— (1987) *The Desire to Desire: The Woman's Film of the 1940s*. Bloomington: Indiana University Press.

Doane, M. A. and J. Bergstrom (cds) (1989) *Camera Obscura*, *20/21*, May–September.

Driver, D. (2006) '*Fight Club*: Lashing out against the Commercialisation of Masculinities', conference paper, *Psyche and Imagination*, University of Greenwich/International Association of Jungian Studies, 6–9 July 2006.

DuBois, W. E. B. (1999) *The Souls of Black Folk* (H. Gates Jr and T. H. Oliver (eds)). London: W. W. Norton.

Eagleton, T. (1990) *The Ideology of the Aesthetic*. Oxford, UK: Basil Blackwell.

Easthope, A. (ed.) (1993) *Contemporary Film Theory*. London: Longman.

Easthope, A. and K. McGowan (eds) (2004) *A Critical and Cultural Theory Reader*. Toronto, Canada: University of Toronto Press.

Eisenstein, S. (1999) 'Dramaturgy of Film Form' in L. Braudy and M. Cohen (eds), *Film Theory and Criticism: Introductory Readings* (5th ed.). Oxford, UK: Oxford University Press.

Ellis, J. (1975) 'Made in Ealing', *Screen*, *16*: 1, 78–126.

Fanon, F. (1986) *Black Skin, White Masks*. London: Pluto.

Foucault, M. (1984) 'What is an Author?' in P. Rabinow (ed.), *The Foucault Reader*. New York: Pantheon.

Frampton, D. (2006) *Filmosophy*. London: Wallflower.

Fredericksen, D. (2001) 'Jung/sign/symbol/film' in C. Hauke and I. Alister (eds), *Jung and Film: Post-Jungian Takes on the Moving Image*. Hove, UK: Brunner-Routledge.

—— (2006) Seminar on Jung and film, *Psyche and Imagination*. University of Greenwich/International Association of Jungian Studies, 6–9 July 2006.

Freeland, C. (2000) *The Naked and the Undead: Evil and the Appeal of Horror*. Boulder, CO: Westview Press.

Freud, S. (2003) *Beyond the Pleasure Principle*. London: Penguin Modern Classics.

—— (2004) 'On the Universal Tendency towards Debasement in Love' in A. Easthope and K. McGowan (eds), *A Critical and Cultural Theory Reader*. Toronto, Canada: University of Toronto Press.

Frome, J. (2006) 'Representation, Reality, and Emotions across Media', *Film Studies*, *8*, Summer, 12–25.

Frye, N. (1966) *Anatomy of Criticism: Four Essays*. New York: Antheneum.

Fuery, P. (2000) *New Developments in Film Theory*. Basingstoke, UK: Macmillan.

Galloway, A. R. (2004) 'Playing the Code: Allegories of Control in *Civilization*', *Radical Philosophy*, *128*, Nov./Dec., 33–40.

Gibbs, J. and D. Pye (eds) (2005) *Style and Meaning*. Manchester, UK: Manchester University Press.

Giegrich, W. (1998) 'Jung's Betrayal of His Truth: The Adoption of a Kant-based Empiricism and the Rejection of Hegel's Speculative Thought', *Harvest*, *44*: 1, 46–64.

Gledhill, C. (1988) 'Pleasurable Negotiations' in E. D. Pribam (ed.), *Female Spectators: Looking at Film and Television*. London: Verso.

Gray, F. (2008) *Jung, Irigaray, Individuation*. Hove, UK: Routledge.

Green, P. (1993) *Andrei Tarkovsky: The Winding Quest*. London: Macmillan.

Greenberg, C. (1961) *Art and Culture: Critical Essays*. Boston: Bacon Press.

Grodal, T. (1997) *Moving Pictures: A New Theory of Film Genres, Feelings, and Cognition*. Oxford, UK: Clarendon Press.

Grosz, E. (1990) *Jacques Lacan: A Feminist Introduction*. London: Routledge.

Guerrero, E. (1993) *Framing Blackness: The African American Image in Film*. Philadelphia: Temple University Press.

Gunn, S. (2006) *History and Cultural Theory*. Harlow, UK: Pearson.

Gunning, T. (2004) 'An Aesthetic of Astonishment: Early Film and the (In)Credulous Spectator' in L. Braudy and M. Cohen (eds), *Film Theory and Criticism: Introductory Readings* (6th ed.). Oxford: Oxford University Press.

Hall, S. (ed.) (1997) *Representation*. London: Sage.

Harries, D. (ed.) (2004) *The New Media Book* (2nd ed.). London: BFI.

Haskell, M. (1987) *From Reverence to Rape: The Treatment of Women in the Movies* (2nd ed.). London: University of Chicago Press.

Hauke, C. (2000) *Jung and the Postmodern: The Interpretation of Realities*. London: Routledge.

Hauke, C. and I. Alister (eds) (2001) *Jung and Film: Post-Jungian Takes on the Moving Image*. Hove, UK: Brunner-Routledge.

Hayward, S. (1999) *Key Concepts in Cinema Studies*. London: Routledge.

Heath, S. (1973) 'Comment on "Ideas of Authorship"', *Screen*, *14*: 3, Autumn, 66–91.

—— (1975/1976) 'Anato Mo', *Screen*, *16*: 4, Winter, 49–66.

—— (1981) *Questions of Cinema*. Bloomington: Indiana University Press.

—— (1999) 'Cinema and Psychoanalysis: Parallel Histories' in J. Bergstrom (ed.), *Endless Night: Cinema and Psychoanalysis, Parallel Histories*. London: University of California Press.

Henderson, B. (1980) *A Critique of Film Theory*. New York: E. P. Dutton.

—— (1981) 'Critique of Cine-Structuralism' in J. Coughie (ed.), *Theories of Authorship*. London: Routledge.

Hillier, J. (1985) *Cahiers du Cinema: The 1950s; Neo Realism; Hollywood; The New Wave*. London: BFI.

Hillman, J. (1983) *Healing Fiction*. Woodstock, CT: Spring.

Hills, M. (2005) *The Pleasures of Horror*. London: Continuum.

Hirst, P. (1979) *On Law and Ideology*. London: Macmillan.

Hockley, L. (2001) *Cinematic Projections: The Analytical Psychology of C. G. Jung and Film Theory*. Luton, UK: University of Luton Press.

Hollows, J. and M. Jancovich (eds) (1995) *Approaches to Popular Film*. Manchester, UK: Manchester University Press.

Hollwitz, J. (2001) 'The Grail Quest and *Field of Dreams*' in C. Hauke and I. Alister (eds), *Jung and Film: Post-Jungian Takes on the Moving Image*. Hove, UK: Brunner-Routledge.

Homer, S. (2005) 'Cinema and Fetishism: The Disavowal of a Concept', *Historical Materialism*, *13*: 1, 85–116.

hooks, b. (1992) *Black Looks*. Cambridge, MA: South End Press.

Huskinson, L. (2004) *Nietzsche and Jung: The Whole Self in the Union of Opposites*. Hove, UK: Brunner-Routledge.

Irigaray, L. (1991) *The Irigaray Reader*. Oxford, UK: Blackwell.

Izod, J. (2001) *Myth, Mind and the Screen: Understanding the Heroes of our Time*. Cambridge, UK: Cambridge University Press.

—— (2006) *Screen, Culture, Psyche: A Post-Jungian Approach to Working with the Audience*. Hove, UK: Routledge.

Jaffé, A. (1964) 'Symbolism in the Visual Arts' in C. G. Jung (ed.), *Man and His Symbols*. London: Aldus.

Jameson, F. (1991) *Postmodernism, or, The Cultural Logic of Late Capitalism*. London: Verso.

—— (1996) *The Political Unconscious: Narrative as a Socially Symbolic Act*. London: Routledge.

Jancovic, M. (1995) 'Screen Theory' in J. Hollows and M. Jancovic (eds), *Approaches to Popular Film*. Manchester, UK: Manchester University Press.

Jones, R. A. (2007) *Jung, Psychology, Postmodernity*. Hove, UK: Routledge.

Johnston, C. (1985) 'Towards a Feminist Film Practice' in B. Nichols (ed.), *Movies and Methods* (vol. 2). London: University of California Press.

Jung, C. G. (1936) *The Collected Works of C. G. Jung* (2nd ed., vol. 9, part 1), H. Read, M. Fordham and G. Adler (eds), R. F. C. Hull (trans.). London: Routledge.

—— (ed.) (1964) *Man and His Symbols*. London: Aldus.

—— (1966) 'The Relations between the Ego and the Unconscious' in H. Read, M. Fordham and G. Adler (eds), R. F. C. Hull (trans.), *The Collected Works of C. G. Jung* (2nd ed., vol. 7). London: Routledge.

—— (1970) *The Collected Works of C. G. Jung* (2nd ed., vol. 14), H. Read, M. Fordham and G. Adler (eds), R. F. C. Hull (trans.). London: Routledge.

—— (1988) *Psychology and Western Religion*. London: Ark.

—— (1998) *The Essential Jung: Selected Writings*. London: Fontana.

—— (1999) *Synchronicity: An Acausal Connecting Principle*. London: Routledge.

Kant, I. (1974) *Critique of Pure Reason* (trans. J. M. D. Meiklejohn). London: Dent.

Kermode, F. (2000) *The Sense of an Ending*. Oxford, UK: Oxford University Press.

Kojima, H. (2000) *Monad and Thou: Phenomenological Ontology of Human Being*. Athens: Ohio University Press.

Kracauer, S. (1968) *Theory of Film: The Redemption of Physical Reality*. Oxford, UK: Oxford University Press.

—— (1999) 'From *Theory of Film*' in L. Braudy and M. Cohen (eds), *Film Theory and Criticism: Introductory Readings* (5th ed.). Oxford, UK: Oxford University Press.

Krzywinska, T. (2006) *Sex and the Cinema*. London: Wallflower.

Kuhn, A. (1985) *The Power of the Image: Essays on Representation and Sexuality*. London: Routledge.

Kuhn, T. S. (1996) *The Structure of Scientific Revolutions*. London: University of Chicago Press.

Lacan, J. (2004) 'Excerpt from *Écrits*' in A. Easthope and K. McGowan (eds), *A Critical and Cultural Theory Reader*. Toronto, Canada: University of Toronto Press.

Lapsley, R. and M. Westlake (1988) *Film Theory: An Introduction*. Manchester, UK: Manchester University Press.

Le Fanu, M. (1987) *The Cinema of Andrei Tarkovsky*. London: BFI.

Littau, K. (2008) 'The Physiology of Momentary Angels: Towards Reception Aesthetics of Media'. Conference keynote paper, *Philosophy and Film/Film and Philosophy*, University of the West of England, Bristol, UK, 4–6 July 2008.

Lunenfeld, P. (2004) 'The Myths of Interactive Cinema' in D. Harries (ed.), *The New Media Book* (2nd ed.). London: BFI.

McCabe, C. (1974) 'Realism and the Cinema: Some Brechtian Theses', *Screen*, *15*: 2, 7–24.

Mandel, E. (1967) 'The Labor Theory of Value and *Monopoly Capitalism*', *International Socialist Review*, *28*: 4, July–August, 29–42.

Marx, K. (1961) *Capital: A Critique of Political Economy* (vol. 1) (trans. B. Fowkes). London: Penguin.

Meehan, E. R. (2000) ' "Holy Commodity Fetish, Batman!": The Political Economy of a Commercial Intertext' in J. Hollows, P. Hutchings and M. Jancovich (eds), *The Film Studies Reader*. London: Arnold.

Merleau-Ponty, M. (2005) 'The Experience of the Body in Classical Psychology' in M. Fraser and M. Greco (eds), *The Body: A Reader*. London: Routledge.

Metz, C. (1975) 'The Imaginary Signifier', *Screen*, *16*: 2, Summer, 14–76.

—— '*Trucage* and the Film', *Critical Inquiry*, *3*, Summer, 657–675.

Miller, M. A. (1998) 'The Mists of Lake Wobegon: The Archetypal Foundation of an American Storyteller' in M. L. Kittleson (ed.), *The Soul of Popular Culture: Looking at Contemporary Heroes, Myths and Monsters*. Chicago: Carus Publishing.

Miller, T. (ed.) (2008) 'In Focus: The British Film Institute', *Cinema Journal*, *47*: 4, Summer, 121–163.

Mulvey, L. (1989) *Visual and Other Pleasures*. London: Macmillan.

—— (1996) *Fetishism and Curiosity*. London: BFI.

—— (1999) 'Visual Pleasure and Narrative Cinema' in L. Braudy and M. Cohen (eds), *Film Theory and Criticism: Introductory Readings* (5th ed.). Oxford, UK: Oxford University Press.

Münsterberg, H. (1999) 'The Means of the Photoplay' in L. Braudy and M. Cohen (eds), *Film Theory and Criticism: Introductory Readings* (5th ed.). Oxford, UK: Oxford University Press.

Nagy, M. (1991) *Philosophical Issues in the Psychology of C. G. Jung*. Ithaca, NY: State University of New York Press.

Nichols, B. (ed.) (1976) *Movies and Methods* (vol. 1). London: University of California Press.

Nichols, B. (ed.) (1985) *Movies and Methods* (vol. 2). London: University of California Press.

O'Toole, L. (1998) *Pornucopia: Porn, Sex, Technology and Desire*. London: Serpent's Tail.

Palmer, M. (1997) *Freud and Jung on Religion*. London: Routledge.

Peat, F. D. (1987) *Synchronicity: The Bridge Between Matter and Mind*. London: Bantam.

Perkins, V. F. (1990) 'Must we say what they mean? Film Criticism and Interpretation', *Movie, 34*, October, 1–6.

—— (1991) *Film As Film: Understanding and Judging Movies*. London: Penguin.

Phillips, P. (1996) 'The Film Spectator' in J. Nelmes (ed.), *An Introduction to Film Studies*. London: Routledge.

Pierson, M. (1999a) 'No Longer State-of-the-Art: Crafting a Future for CGI', *Wide Angle, 21*: 1, January, 29–47.

—— (1999b) 'CGI Effects in Hollywood Science-fiction Cinema 1989–95: The Wonder Years', *Screen, 40*: 2, Summer, 158–176.

—— (2002) *Still in Search of Wonder*. New York: Columbia University Press.

Popper, K. (1986) *The Poverty of Historicism*. London: Ark.

Propp, V. (2000) *Morphology of the Folktale*. Austin: Univeristy of Texas Press.

Pudovkin, V. (1958) *Film Technique and Film Acting*. London: Mayflower.

Reisman, D. (1965) *The Lonely Crowd*. London: Yale University Press.

Ricoeur, P. (1984) *Time and Narrative* (vol. 1) (trans. K. McLaughlin and D. Pellauer). London: University of Chicago Press.

Riviere, J. (1929) 'Womanliness as a Masquerade', *International Journal of Psychoanalysis, 10*, 303–313.

Rosen, M. (1973) *Popcorn Venus: Women, Movies and the American Dream*. New York: Avon.

Ross, F. (1998) 'Pattern' in I. Alister and C. Hauke (eds), *Contemporary Jungian Analysis: Post-Jungian Perspectives from the Society of Analytical Psychology*. London: Routledge.

Rowland, S. (1999) *C. G. Jung and Literary Theory: The Challenge from Fiction*. London: Macmillan.

Ryan, M. (1988) 'The Politics of Film: Discourse, Psychoanalysis, Ideology' in C. Nelson and L. Grossberg (eds), *Marxism and the Interpretation of Culture*. Urbana: University of Illinois Press.

Samuels, A. (2001) *Politics on the Couch: Citizenship and the Internal Life*. London: Profile Books.

Sarris, A. (1999) 'Notes on the Auteur Theory in 1962' in L. Braudy and M. Cohen (eds), *Film Theory and Criticism: Introductory Readings* (5th ed.). Oxford, UK: Oxford University Press.

Scarry, E. (1994) 'The Merging Bodies and Artefacts in the Social Contract' in G. Bender and T. Druckery (eds), *Culture on the Brink: Ideologies of Technology*. Seattle, WA: Bay Press.

Schwartz, C. (1998) 'Marie Louise von Franz', *Harvest, 44*: 1, 105–107.

Shinkle, E. (2006) 'Sensory Engagement and Affective Response in Digital Game Environments', conference paper, *Synthetic Sensations: The Five Senses and New Technology*, Kingston University, 30 June 2006.

Singh, Greg (2007) 'CGI: A Future History of Assimilation in Mainstream Science Fiction Film', *Extrapolation, 48*: 3, Winter, 543–557.

—— (2009) 'The Kitsch Affect; or, Simulation, Nostalgia and the Materiality of the

Contemporary CGI Film' in J. Sperb and S. Balcerzac (eds), *Cinephilia in the Age of Digital Reproduction: Film, Pleasure, and Digital Culture* (vol. 2). London: Wallflower.

Singh, Gurpreet and M. Pickard (2007) 'Using Knowledge of Vision Science to Inform Creative Image Design', Conference paper, MeCCSA-PGN Conference, University of the West of England, 13 July.

Smith, G. M. (2003) *Film Structure and the Emotion System*. Cambridge, UK: Cambridge University Press.

Smith, M. (1995) *Engaging Characters: Fiction, Emotion and the Cinema*. Oxford, UK: Clarendon Press.

Sobchack, V. (1992) *The Address of the Eye: A Phenomenology of Film Experience*. Princeton, NJ: Princeton University Press.

—— (2004) *Carnal Thoughts: Embodiment and Moving Image Culture*. London: University of California Press.

Stacey, J. (1994) *Star Gazing: Hollywood Cinema and Female Spectatorship*. London: Routledge.

Stoddart, H. (1995) 'Auteurism and Film Authorship' in J. Hollows and M. Jancovich (eds), *Approaches to Popular Film*. Manchester, UK: Manchester University Press.

Storey, J. (ed.) (2006) *Cultural Theory and Popular Culture: A Reader* (3rd ed.). Harlow, UK: Pearson.

Storr, A. (1998) 'Introduction'. In C. G. Jung, *The Essential Jung: Selected Writings*. London: Fontana.

Studlar, G. (1988) *In the Realm of Pleasure: Von Sternberg, Dietrich and the Masochistic Aesthetic*. Urbana: University of Illinois Press.

Taborsky, E. (1998) *The Architectonics of Semiosis*. London: Macmillan.

Tacey, D. (2006) *How to Read Jung*. London: Granta Books.

Tan, E. S. (1995) 'Film induced affect as a witness emotion', *Poetics*, 23, 7–32.

—— (1996) *Emotion and the Structure of Narrative Film: Film as an Emotion Machine*. Mahwah, NJ: Lawrence Erlbaum Associates.

Tarkovsky, A. (1989) *Sculpting in Time*. London: Faber & Faber.

Taylor, C. (1989) *Sources of the Self*. Cambridge, UK: Cambridge University Press.

Todorov, T. (1975) *The Fantastic: A Structural Approach to a Literary Genre*. Ithaca, NY: Cornell University Press.

Tredell, N. (2002) *Cinemas of the Mind: A Critical History of Film Theory*, Cambridge, UK: Icon Books.

Truffaut, F. (1976) 'A Certain Tendency of the French Cinema', first published in *Cahiers du cinema*, 31 January 1954, as 'Une Certaine Tendance du Cinéma Français'. Reprinted in English translation in B. Nichols (ed.) (1976) *Movies and Methods* (vol. 1). London: University of California Press.

Turovskaya, M. (1989) *Tarkovsky: Cinema as Poetry*. London: Faber & Faber.

Vogler, C. (2007) *The Writer's Journey: Mythic Structure for Writers* (3rd ed.). Studio City: Michael Wiese Productions.

Von Franz, M.-L. (1964) 'The Process of Individuation' in C. G. Jung (ed.), *Man and His Symbols*. London: Aldus.

Wasko, J. (1994) *Hollywood in the Information Age*. Cambridge, UK: Polity Press.

Weber, M. (1996) *The Protestant Ethic and the Spirit of Capitalism* (trans. T. Parsons). London: Routledge.

Wheeley, S. (1997) 'Fluid Thoughts – Tablets of Stone: Self, Relationship, and the Emergence of Ideas', *Harvest*, *43*: 1, 55–80.

Wheelwright, P. (1955) 'The semantic approach to myth' in T. A. Sebeok (ed.), *Myth: A Symposium*. Bloomington: Indiana University Press.

Williams, L. (1991) *Hard Core: Power, Pleasure, and the 'Frenzy of the Visible'*. Berkeley: University of California Press.

Withers, M. (2003) 'Religion and the Terrified' in R. Withers (ed.), *Controversies in Analytical Psychology*. Hove, UK: Brunner-Routledge.

Wollen, P. (1999) 'The Auteur Theory' in L. Braudy and M. Cohen (eds), *Film Theory and Criticism: Introductory Readings* (5th ed.). Oxford, UK: Oxford University Press.

Wright, E. (1998) *Psychoanalytic Criticism: A Reappraisal*. Oxford, UK: Polity Press.

Index